Beyond Principles of

PERSONNEL ECONOMICS

Incentives and Information in the Workplace

William S. Neilson

Texas A&M University

PEARSON

Prentice Hall

Upper Saddle River, NJ 07458

Library of Congress Cataloging-in-Publication Data

Neilson, William S.,
  Personnel economics : incentives and information in the workplace /
William S. Neilson.
    p. cm.
  Includes bibliographical references and index.
  ISBN 0-13-148856-2 (alk. paper)
  1. Personnel management. 2. Labor economics. I. Title.
  HF5549.N36 2007
  658.3—dc22

                                        2005034620

Acquisitions Editor: Jon Axelrod
VP/Editorial Director: Jeff Shelstad
Manager Product Development: Pam Hersperger
Project Manager: Francesca Calogero
Editorial Assistant: Michael Dittamo
Marketing Manager: Sharon Koch
Marketing Assistant: Tina Panagiotou
Senior Managing Editor (Production): Cynthia Regan
Production Editor: Carol Samet
Permissions Supervisor: Charles Morris
Manufacturing Buyer: Michelle Klein
Design and Formatting Manager: Christy Mahon
Cover Design: Kiwi Design
Cover Photo: Getty Images, Inc.
Composition: Laserwords
Full-Service Project Management: Elaine Lattanzi, Bookmasters, Inc.
Printer/Binder: Courier Stoughton
Typeface: 10/12 Times Ten

Credits and acknowledgments borrowed from other sources and reproduced, with permission, in this textbook appear on appropriate page within text.

Pearson Education LTD.   Pearson Education Australia PTY, Limited
Pearson Education Singapore, Pte. Ltd   Pearson Education North Asia Ltd
Pearson Education, Canada, Ltd   Pearson Educación de Mexico, S.A. de C.V.
Pearson Education–Japan   Pearson Education Malaysia, Pte. Ltd

10 9 8 7 6 5 4 3 2 1
ISBN 0-13-148856-2

To my parents

Contents

Preface

INTENDED AUDIENCE

This textbook is designed for students who have already completed a course in intermediate microeconomics. It is intended for an upper-division undergraduate economics class, but may be suitable for master's students in economics or an analytical course in an MBA program.

Two of the chapters (Chapter 3 on traditional labor markets and Chapter 20 on benefits) use indifference curve–budget line analysis. Many of the chapters use game theory, but because some intermediate micro courses cover game theory in more depth than others, the text includes a chapter on the game theory techniques that are actually used to study personnel economics.

The topics in this course either do not appear or receive only limited coverage elsewhere in the undergraduate curriculum. In particular, labor economics texts typically have only one chapter on how compensation affects productivity, while half of this book is devoted to covering that topic in depth. Intermediate microeconomics courses cover game theory and adverse selection, but this text covers adverse selection more thoroughly than a typical intermediate micro book.

PERSONNEL ECONOMICS

Personnel Economics is, at its core, a book about the economics of incentives and information, but with all of its motivation, examples, and applications taken from the employment relationship. In the language prevalent in the economics research literature, it covers such topics as principal-agent theory, moral hazard in terms of both imperfectly observed actions and privately-known types, adverse selection and signaling, and repeated games. In the more compelling (to students) language of the employment relationship, these topics translate respectively into using compensation schemes to motivate employees, motivating workers when their actions are only imperfectly monitored by supervisors, motivating workers when different workers have different productivity levels that are unknown to the supervisor, trying to hire high-productivity workers while avoiding low-productivity ones, and using efficiency wages as a motivational tool.

The language of the employment relationship is an appropriate channel for introducing students to these important topics from economics, primarily because undergraduate students find the employment relationship both relevant and inherently interesting. After all, most of them will be entering the workforce in the near future, and many of them have worked somewhere and will be able to relate to the material in the course. The topics covered are of interest from both the employer's and the employee's side of the market. More specifically, students will learn how their employers attempt to motivate them and also about many issues related to the job search, including models of optimal search and bargaining. The book is written so that all problems are motivated by the employment relationship, not the theoretical topic to be discussed.

Each chapter contains:

- Motivating examples
- A thorough economic analysis of the problem
- A summary of the general lessons to be learned
- Homework problems (except Chapter 1)

OUTLINE OF THE BOOK

The book is loosely organized around the two major topics of paying and hiring employees. The compensation section can be subdivided into a section on piece rate pay and a section on other, more strategic methods of compensation. The hiring section can be subdivided into one on adverse selection, one on finding a job and negotiating a contract, and one on other, less information-based topics. The text contains two tools chapters, one on optimization, but without calculus, and one on game theory.

The text begins with a chapter reviewing optimization without calculus (Chapter 2). This will be a review chapter for every student who has ever taken an economics course, but I have found it best to reacquaint students with the concepts of marginal analysis and cost-benefit analysis because these are the primary tools used in the analysis of incentive schemes. A chapter on traditional labor market analysis follows. It shows how time and output are treated as being the same thing in the traditional supply and demand model, and it therefore serves as a point of departure for a discussion of how workers must be paid to work; otherwise they will not produce anything. The next chapter takes a simple setting and shows that if the worker is paid on the basis of time he will produce as little as possible, but that there are a number of ways to base pay on output that can get the worker to produce the Pareto efficient level of output.

The text then moves on to specific compensation schemes, beginning with piece rate schemes in Chapter 5. These are the familiar linear incentive contracts from principal-agent theory, and all of the major results from principal-agent theory make their way into the book, but of course with the firm taking the role of the principal and the worker taking the role of the agent. The terms "principal" and "agent" do not appear in the book. Chapter 5 establishes the importance of aligning incentives with the worker's effort costs if the firm is to obtain the efficient level of output, Chapter 6 shows that compensation must be equated across tasks and that incentives should be reduced in the presence of imperfect monitoring, and Chapter 7 shows that when linear incentive schemes are used with high- and low-effort-cost agents, incentives are reduced for the high-cost agents and the low-cost agents earn information rents.

Chapter 8 is a game theory chapter, covering the basics of simultaneous and sequential games that are needed for later chapters. The chapter is not intended to be comprehensive, or even remotely so; instead it is designed to provide students with only the game theory tools they will need for the remainder of the book. Game theory is used in the analysis of tournaments, efficiency wages, team incentives, and bargaining.

The tournament chapter is constructed using a model that is roughly analogous to the Cournot duopoly model. Specifically, the workers' marginal conditions are used to derive best-response functions, which can then be used to identify the equilibrium. It is shown how workers respond to increases in their opponent's effort level and how an increase in the size of the prize leads contestants to exert more effort. Efficiency wages are also presented as a way to motivate employees, and this analysis is based on Benoit-Krishna-style finitely-repeated games. An efficiency wage scheme is defined as the event in which the firm pays an above-market wage and the worker exerts extraordinary effort. The focus is on the aspects of the game needed to obtain an efficiency wage scheme. Chapter 10 discusses team incentives using the approaches of game theory, marginal analysis, and the idea of team effort as a public good.

Chapter 12 reviews and compares the four basic compensation methods (piece rates, tournaments, efficiency wages, and team incentives). Chapter 13 uses knowledge of these methods to discuss executive compensation, and Chapter 14 concludes the compensation portion of the book with a discussion of performance evaluation.

The focus turns to the hiring of workers in Chapter 15, which is about adverse selection. It introduces the basic problem of a firm trying to hire workers who have private information about their own productivity levels. Two solutions to the adverse selection problem are proposed. A third solution, signaling, is introduced in Chapter 16. Chapter 17 uses marginal analysis to examine the search process and Chapter 18 moves on to the issue of bargaining, covering both alternating-offers bargaining and the Nash bargaining solution. Many firms offer their workers benefit packages, and Chapter 19 explores employee training and its effect on the bargaining position of the worker. The final chapter discusses benefits.

NOTE REGARDING USE OF TERMS

You might notice that persons in the text are referred to as he/she, instead of they/them. This was done intentionally, following industry standards.

FOR INSTRUCTORS

The following supplements are available to adopting instructors. For detailed descriptions, please visit www.prenhall.com/neilson:

- **Instructor Solutions Manual (online):** Log in at www.prenhall.com/irc

Instructor's Resource Center: Register. Redeem. Log in.

www.prenhall.com/irc is where instructors can access a variety of print, media, and presentation resources available with this text in downloadable, digital format. For most texts, resources are also available for course management platforms such as Blackboard, WebCT, and Course Compass.

It gets better.

Once you register, you will not have additional forms to fill out, or multiple usernames and passwords to remember to access new titles and/or editions. As a registered faculty member, you can log in directly to download resource files and receive immediate access and instructions for installing Course Management content to your campus server.

Need help?

Our dedicated Technical Support team is ready to assist instructors with questions about the media supplements that accompany this text. Visit www.247.prenhall.com/ for answers to frequently asked questions and toll-free user support phone numbers.

FEEDBACK

The author and product team would appreciate hearing from you! Let us know what you think about this textbook by writing to mailto:college_economics@prenhall.com. Please include "Feedback about Neilson Personnel Economics" in the subject line.

If you have questions related to this product, please contact our customer service department online at www.247.prenhall.com.

1

INTRODUCTION

Taking a job in exchange for pay is the single largest transaction most people make in their lives. Although people buy things almost every day, the labor market is one of the few markets in which they are the sellers. The supply side of the market is fundamentally different from the demand side, especially when the sellers have private information about the product they are selling that they can conceal from the buyers.

Personnel economics is the study of the employment relationship, paying particular attention to the information problems inherent therein. It also covers topics from all aspects of a worker's career. The employer must pay workers enough to attract them to the job and do so in a way that induces them to actually produce something and not just collect a paycheck. On the one hand, bad workers might pretend that they are good workers so that they can get a job. On the other hand, once they are hired, good workers might pretend that they are bad workers so that less will be expected of them and they will not have to work as hard for their money. Employers have to search for employees; workers have to search for a job. Once a match is made, the employer and employee must negotiate a contract. These new workers must be trained. Finally, compensation includes not only pay but also benefits. All of these issues lend themselves to economic analysis.

This book concerns all of these aspects of the employment relationship. As such, it is essentially a book about personnel issues. It is more than that, however. It is also a book about incentives because the employer must give workers an incentive to actually produce something. Economists have studied incentives in a number of different settings, not just the employment relationship. Accordingly, this book can be thought of as one about the economics of incentives, with all of the motivation and examples taken from the employment relationship.

Incentives are not the only issue. Workers often know things about themselves that firms do not. For example, workers know more about their abilities than the firm does before they are hired, and they know more about how hard they are working than the firm does after they are hired. If the firm is not vigilant, workers can take advantage of this information. Economists have long been concerned with how agents deal with situations in which one has information that the other does not. A third way to think about this book, then, is that it is about the economics of information, with all of the motivation and examples taken from the employment relationship.

THE ECONOMICS OF THE EMPLOYMENT RELATIONSHIP

The employment relationship has two basic components: the hiring process and the compensation process. The hiring process begins when the firm decides what qualifications to require of its applicants. Why do some jobs require a bachelor's degree, even in an unrelated field, while other jobs do not? After posting their requirements, the firm searches for a worker, but how does the firm know when to hire a particular worker or to hold out for someone better? On the other side of the market, when does a worker accept a job or wait for a better offer? After the firm decides on a worker with whom to proceed, the two parties must negotiate a contract, and the bargaining process is of interest to economists. The hiring process does not end with the successful agreement. Some firms train their workers, and some firms start their workers with probationary periods during which they receive low pay and can be fired immediately if their performance is unacceptable. The rationale for these decisions is of interest.

Compensation must achieve two goals. First, it must be sufficiently high to attract workers to the job and keep them there. Second, it must provide workers with an incentive to produce output because workers who do not produce do not generate any revenue (or profit) for the firm. Firms use many methods to motivate workers. Some methods pay the worker directly for output, such as when a salesperson is paid on commission. Other methods are less direct, such as when a firm awards periodic bonuses to top performers or promotes top performers to higher-paying positions. Some firms even pay workers for other people's hard work, such as when they pay workers as part of a team or when they use a profit sharing plan. Finally, some firms motivate workers by threatening to fire them if they do not perform.

Workers decide how hard to work in response to the firm's compensation plan. Firms must design compensation plans that induce workers to put forth a level of effort that maximizes the firms' profit. Some compensation plans work better in some situations than in others. All of them are complicated by the fact that a worker's supervisor cannot always observe perfectly how hard the worker works. The tools of economics, especially marginal analysis and game theory, enable us to analyze when and how well these compensation schemes work.

Before too long most of you will be entering the labor force. Some of you will have employees to hire and supervise. The material in this course will provide you with information that will allow you to do a better job in these tasks. Whether or not you become supervisors, all of you will go through the hiring process and be compensated. The material in this course will help you understand how the firm goes about hiring and will illuminate some of the practices that employers follow.

THE ECONOMICS OF INCENTIVES AND INFORMATION

One of the central tenets of economics is that people and firms respond to incentives. In fact, most people share this belief. For example, it is widely assumed that if the police begin enforcing speed limits more strenuously, drivers will slow down. The incentive for driving slower is being able to avoid paying a fine (and higher insurance premiums), and drivers respond to this incentive. A child whose parents pay him a fixed amount for every book read will read more books. The incentive is the payment, and the child responds to the incentive. When the market price of a good rises, firms produce more of that product. The incentive for increasing production is the increased revenue from each unit sold. A lack of incentives is also important. If speed limits are not enforced, drivers will not obey them. If it is difficult for people to vote, they will not do so. If people are unwilling to pay for a product, no firm will produce it.

The economic analysis of incentives concerns the design of systems that provide the incentives for an agent to achieve a desired outcome. In the language of the employment relationship, if the firm wants the worker to produce a certain amount of output, it must design a compensation scheme that will induce the worker to produce exactly that amount of output. This problem is complicated by the fact that the firm cares about how hard the worker works but cannot compensate the worker for effort. Instead, it must compensate the worker for something tangible, such as output or time spent at the job. Sometimes, however, the worker exerts considerable effort but has no output to show for it, such as when a salesperson works every day but does not manage to close any deals in a month. The firm must find a way to deal with the fact that pay is not perfectly correlated with effort.

This same problem occurs in the classroom. Some students work really hard but do poorly on exams, while other students do not study at all and still perform well. The instructor may even know which students are working and which ones are not but must still assign grades based on tangible outcomes, in this case test scores. In many cases professors make grades depend on more than just test scores so that those students who work hard but test poorly can get better grades. The construction of course requirements is the design of a compensation policy.

Someday many of you will hire someone to build a house for you. You would like the builder to do a good job and do it on time, but many things are outside the builder's control, such as the weather and the availability of subcontractors. How do you design a contract that gets the builder to make the right tradeoff between speed and quality? This is a problem in the economics of incentives.

Information causes problems for the design of incentive schemes in two ways. First, as already discussed, the firm cannot reward the worker based on effort but must reward the worker based on something tangible, such as output or time spent working. Second, the worker sometimes possesses information that would be valuable to the firm, but it is not in his best interest to reveal it. For example, the firm may want to pay highly skilled workers differently than less-skilled workers, but it cannot tell which workers are which. The workers know to which group they belong, but they might find it worthwhile to behave as if they are in the other group. The firm must design an incentive scheme that compels workers to reveal this information.

This problem obviously arises in the hiring process. A firm might want to hire a highly skilled worker but not a less-skilled one. Put differently, it might want to *pay* a highly skilled worker but not a less-skilled one. Often, however, the two types of workers look the same on paper, so the firm has no basis for determining which workers are in which group. The firm must design a compensation scheme that enables it to hire only highly skilled workers and not less-skilled ones.

The economics of incentives and information is a major research topic among academic economists. This course provides you with an introduction to the topic.

CHAPTER

2 | OPTIMIZATION

The primary fundamental principle used throughout this book is optimization. Workers act in their own best interest and make themselves as well off as possible. Firms act in their own best interest and maximize profits. None of this should come as a surprise to economists, and the techniques discussed in this chapter are also discussed in introductory classes.

Why, then, discuss optimization here? There are three good reasons. First, it refreshes your memory. Second, it helps you to think about optimization in the way that it will be used in the book. Third, in principles classes optimization is almost hidden in the sections on consumer and producer behavior. Here optimization is treated as a general principle, reinforcing and extending what you learned in your introductory class.

"HOW MUCH" DECISIONS AND MARGINAL ANALYSIS

Many of the important questions in economics involve "how much" decisions. How much of a product does a consumer buy? How much should a firm produce? How much labor should a firm employ? How many hours should a worker work? All of these questions involve choosing the amount of an activity to perform.

The answer to all of these questions involves marginal analysis. **Marginal benefit** is the additional benefit from engaging in one more (small) unit of the activity. **Marginal cost** is the additional cost of engaging in one more unit of the activity. If marginal benefit is greater than marginal cost, the individual should engage in more of the activity, and if marginal cost is greater than marginal benefit, the individual should decrease the activity.

Marginal benefit typically either decreases or is constant as more of the activity is undertaken. For example, when a person consumes pizza, the first slice provides more benefit than the second, which provides more benefit than the third, and so on. The marginal benefit of a slice of pizza decreases as the number of pieces consumed rises. An example of constant marginal benefit comes from a firm in a perfectly competitive industry. The benefit a competitive firm receives from

5

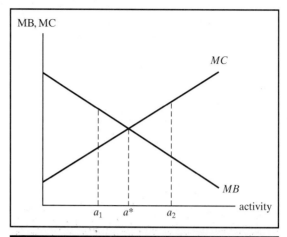

FIGURE 2.1 Marginal Benefit and Marginal Cost Curves

Marginal benefit curves typically slope downward, and marginal cost curves typically slope upward. At activity level a_1 the marginal benefit of the activity exceeds the marginal cost, so the individual should increase the activity. At level a_2, $MB < MC$, so the individual should decrease the activity. At a^*, MB and MC are equal, and the individual should neither increase nor decrease the activity.

selling an additional unit of output is the price of that output, and when the firm is competitive, that price is constant no matter how much the firm sells (perfect competition is reviewed later in this chapter). The line labeled *MB* in Figure 2.1 shows a declining marginal benefit curve.

Marginal costs typically either increase or are constant as more of the activity is undertaken. For example, removing the first 10 percent of pollutants from automobile exhaust costs a lot less than removing the last 10 percent of pollutants. For an example of constant marginal cost, the price for a gallon of milk at the grocery store is the same no matter how many gallons a person buys. The line labeled *MC* in Figure 2.1 shows an increasing marginal cost curve.

When the activity level is a_1 in Figure 2.1, the marginal benefit curve is higher than the marginal cost curve. This means that the extra benefits generated by a small increase in the level of the activity outweigh the extra costs, so the level of the activity should increase. More specifically, increasing the activity by one unit increases benefit by *MB* and increases cost by *MC*, so **net benefit**, defined as benefit minus cost, increases by $MB - MC$, which is greater than zero. This is true for every activity level where the marginal benefit curve lies above the marginal cost curve.

When the activity level is a_2, the marginal cost curve is higher than the marginal benefit curve. This time a decrease in the level of the activity leads to a cost saving that outweighs the loss in benefits. Decreasing the activity by one unit reduces costs by *MC* and benefits by *MB*. Because $MC > MB$, decreasing the activity by one unit leads to an increase in net benefit of $MC - MB$, which is greater than zero. This is true for every activity level where the marginal cost curve lies above the marginal benefit curve.

When marginal benefit and marginal cost are equal, there is no reason either to increase or decrease the activity by a small amount. In the figure we have been discussing, this is activity level $a*$, where the marginal benefit and marginal cost curves intersect. This is a **local optimum**, with the term *local* meaning that no nearby activity level generates higher net benefit. So at a local optimum, neither a small increase nor a small decrease in the activity level leads to an increase in net benefit.

GLOBAL OPTIMIZATION

Marginal analysis is an important part of answering "how much" questions, but it is not the only part. Marginal analysis finds a local optimum, but the answer to the how much question is a **global optimum**, that is, a level of activity such that no other level of activity generates strictly higher net benefit. If an activity level is a global optimum, it must also be a local optimum, because if it is true that no other level of activity anywhere generates higher net benefit, then it must also be true that no nearby activity level generates higher net benefit. A local optimum, however, may not be a global optimum.

Figure 2.2 shows a case where the local optimum found by marginal analysis is also a global optimum. We can see this by looking at the cost and benefit curves. The global optimum is the point where the benefit curve is the farthest above the cost curve. In the figure, the benefit curve rises at a decreasing rate, which is consistent with a downward-sloping marginal benefit curve (recall that one finds a marginal curve by graphing the slope of the original curve), and the cost curve rises at an increasing rate, which is consistent with an upward-sloping marginal cost curve, exactly as in Figure 2.1. The local optimum $a*$ is found where $MB = MC$. Because marginal benefit is the slope of the benefit curve and marginal cost is the slope of the cost curve, the local optimum is where the two curves in Figure 2.2 have the same slope. As one can see in the figure, there is no other point where the benefit curve is farther above the cost curve, and $a*$ is indeed a global optimum.

Figure 2.3 shows a case where the local optimum found by marginal analysis is *not* a global optimum. The cost curve has the same shape as before, but the benefit curve is different. This time the benefit curve is

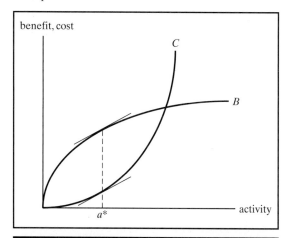

benefit, cost

C

B

activity

$a*$

FIGURE 2.2 Benefit and Cost Curves

To find the global optimum, look at the benefit and cost curves. The global optimum is where the benefit curve is farthest above the cost curve. The local optimum is where $MB = MC$, which is where the benefit and cost curves have the same slope, as at point $a*$. In this figure, the local optimum is also a global optimum, because there is no other point where the benefit curve is farther above the cost curve.

horizontal when the activity level is between zero and a_0, and it becomes an upward-sloping line when the activity level is above a_0. Marginal analysis identifies the local optimum $a*$ where the two curves have the same slope. However, the vertical distance between the two curves is greater when the activity level is zero than when the activity level is $a*$. So the global optimum is zero, and it is labeled $a**$ in the figure.

The benefit curve in Figure 2.3 can occur in the following scenario. Suppose that a salesperson receives a salary of B_0 and gets no additional pay until reaching a quota of a_0 units. After selling a_0 units, the salesperson receives a commission of b for every additional unit sold, where b is the slope of the benefit curve above a_0. Selling is costly to the salesperson because it requires time and effort. According to the figure, the salesperson is best off taking the salary and selling nothing because that is where the benefit curve is the farthest above the cost curve.

Figure 2.4 shows the marginal curves that correspond to the curves in Figure 2.3. When the activity level is below a_0, small increases in activity generate no additional benefit, so the marginal benefit is zero. When the activity level is above a_0, increasing the activity level by one unit increases the benefit by b, and so the marginal benefit curve is horizontal at b. Because the cost curve in Figure 2.3

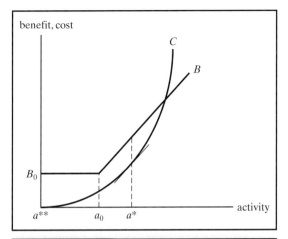

benefit, cost

FIGURE 2.3 Benefit and Cost Curves When Marginal Analysis Does Not Yield a Global Optimum

The marginal benefit curve is horizontal from zero to a_0, and then it is an upward-sloping line. The local optimum is a^*, where the benefit curve and the cost curve have the same slope. However, the vertical distance between the two curves is greater when the activity level is zero than when it is a^*, and so a^* is not a global optimum. The global optimum is zero, and is denoted a^{**}.

becomes steeper as the activity level increases, the marginal cost curve is upward sloping. The local optimum is found where the marginal benefit and marginal cost curves intersect. But, as shown in Figure 2.3, this is not the global optimum.

We now have two examples, one in which marginal analysis correctly identifies the global optimum (Figures 2.1 and 2.2) and one in which it does not (Figures 2.3 and 2.4). Determining this took two graphs for each example. It would be more efficient if there were a way to tell from the marginal graph whether the second graph is needed. There is, in fact, a way to tell. Compare the marginal curves in Figure 2.1, where marginal analysis identified the global optimum, and in Figure 2.4, where it did not. In Figure 2.1, the marginal benefit curve crosses the marginal cost curve only once, and from above, whereas in Figure 2.4 the marginal benefit curve crosses the marginal cost curve twice, the first time from below. This represents a general rule: If the marginal benefit curve crosses the marginal cost curve only once, and from above, then marginal analysis identifies the global optimum. If the marginal benefit curve ever crosses the marginal cost curve from below, it is necessary to look at the benefit and cost curves to find the global optimum.

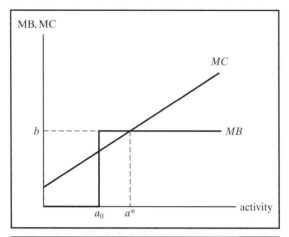

FIGURE 2.4   Marginal Curves Corresponding to Figure 2.3

The marginal benefit curve shown here is derived from the benefit curve in Figure 2.3. Marginal benefit is zero for activity levels below a_0, and it is b for activity levels above a_0. The local optimum, found where $MB = MC$, is at activity level a^*. This is not a global optimum, however, as shown in Figure 2.3. Marginal analysis is not always enough.

GENERAL LESSONS

We can now identify some general rules for optimization.

1. *If the question begins with the words* how much, *the answer involves marginal analysis.* How much questions are central in economics, and one of the things that makes economics different from the other social sciences is our reliance on marginal analysis to answer questions.

2. *Marginal analysis identifies the local optimum.* If marginal benefit is greater than marginal cost, the individual should increase the activity by a small amount. If marginal benefit is smaller than marginal cost, the individual should decrease the activity by a small amount. When the two are equal, neither small change increases net benefit, which is the definition of a local optimum.

3. *If marginal benefit crosses marginal cost only once and from above, then marginal analysis also identifies a global optimum.* If marginal benefit crosses marginal cost only once and from above, there is no need to check the benefit/cost graph to find the global optimum. Marginal analysis is sufficient.

4. *If marginal benefit ever crosses marginal cost from below, then marginal analysis may or may not identify the global optimum.* If

marginal benefit crosses marginal cost from below, it becomes necessary to draw the benefit/cost graph to find the global optimum. The global optimum is the activity level at which the benefit curve is the farthest above the cost curve.

Occasionally in this text we will want to derive a marginal benefit function from a total benefit function or to derive a marginal cost function from a total cost function. The rules for doing so are simple. Suppose that the original function is linear with the form $F(x) = a + bx$. Then the marginal function is $MF(x) = b$. Graphically, the function $F(x)$ is a straight line with slope b and vertical intercept a. The marginal function should be the same as the slope, and it is. Now suppose that the original function is quadratic with the form $G(x) = a + bx + cx^2$. In this case the marginal function is $MG(x) = b + 2cx$. Linear benefit and cost functions yield constant marginal functions, but quadratic benefit and cost functions yield marginal functions that can be either increasing or decreasing. Because we often will want increasing marginal cost functions and decreasing marginal benefit functions, the rule for deriving marginal functions from quadratic functions is extremely useful.

A CLASSIC EXAMPLE: THE SHORT-RUN COMPETITIVE FIRM

The most common textbook example of a case in which marginal analysis fails to generate a global optimum is the profit-maximization problem faced by a competitive firm in the short run. A competitive firm is one that is small enough relative to the market that its actions have no effect on the market price, so that it can sell as much or as little as it wants without causing the price of the good to rise or fall. The short run is a period of time long enough for the firm to change the amounts of some of its inputs but not all of them. In the short run, some inputs are fixed and some are variable, leading to fixed and variable costs.

Figure 2.5 should be familiar because it is found in virtually every introductory economics text. The firm's average total and average variable costs are shown by the curves *ATC* and *AVC*, respectively, and *MC* denotes marginal cost. Because the firm can sell as much as it wants at price p, its marginal revenue is equal to p no matter how much output it sells.

Marginal analysis identifies a local optimum where the marginal revenue curve crosses the marginal cost curve at point q^*. The only issue is whether this is also a global optimum. Notice that in the drawing the marginal revenue curve crosses the marginal cost curve twice, first from below and then from above. As we saw in previous sections, this means that the local optimum might not be a global optimum, and we should graph the benefit and cost curves to decide.

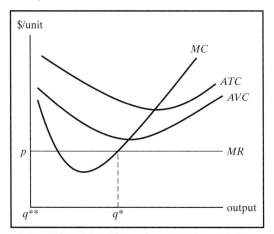

FIGURE 2.5   Marginal Analysis for a Short-Run Competitive Firm

In the case of a short-run competitive firm, marginal analysis identifies the local optimum q^* where MR crosses MC. But, since MR crosses MC twice, the first time from below, the local optimum may not be a global optimum.

Because at q^* the firm does not cover its variable costs, the firm should produce nothing. The local optimum is not a global optimum.

Actually, Figure 2.5 contains enough information to determine whether the local optimum q^* is also a global optimum. The firm must pay its fixed costs no matter how much it produces, so those costs are irrelevant to the analysis. The firm covers its variable costs if the price is above average variable costs; otherwise it loses additional money on every unit it sells. If the price is strictly above average variable cost, every unit sold contributes to profit. Thus, the firm should produce q^* if the price is above average variable cost at q^*, and it should produce nothing at all if the price is below average variable cost at q^*. In Figure 2.5, the price is below average variable cost, so the firm should produce nothing.

It is informative to look at the corresponding benefit/cost diagram. Figure 2.6 has two cost curves, a variable cost curve labeled TVC and a total cost curve labeled TC. The TC curve is obtained from the TVC curve by shifting the TVC curve upward by the amount of fixed costs. The total revenue curve is labeled TR, and it is linear with slope p because the firm's revenue is $p \cdot q$, where p is the price and q is the amount sold. As stated above, the firm should produce if it covers its variable costs, and it should shut down otherwise. In Figure 2.6 the total revenue curve is always below the total variable cost curve, so the firm should not produce any output at all.

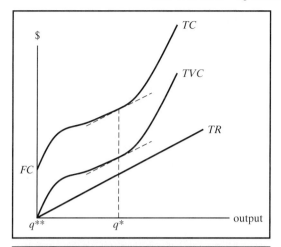

FIGURE 2.6 Total Cost and Revenue Curves for a Short-Run Competitive Firm

The local optimum identified by marginal analysis is q^*, where the *TC, TVC,* and *TR* curves all have the same slope. However, because total revenue is not enough to cover total variable costs, the firm loses money on every unit it sells and would be better off producing zero, which is the global optimum q^{**}.

Homework Problems

1. Explain the difference between a local optimum and a global optimum.

2. Consider a firm that negotiates a lower price for a critical input. Assuming that no other prices change, use a marginal benefit/marginal cost diagram to determine whether the firm will produce more or less output.

3. The benefit function is given by $B(x) = 4 + 12x - 2x^2$, with marginal benefit function $MB(x) = 12 - 4x$. The cost function is given by $x^2 + 6x + 2$, with marginal cost function $MC(x) = 2x + 6$. Find the optimal value of x.

4. Explain how one can tell by looking at a marginal benefit/marginal cost diagram whether a local optimum might not be a global optimum.

5. A hairdresser faces two types of costs: She must pay $400 per month to rent a chair at a local salon, and she must bear the cost of her own effort from cutting hair. Her marginal effort cost increases with the number of haircuts. Once she pays to rent the chair, she gets to keep the $40 per haircut she charges her customers. Draw benefit and cost curves corresponding to the case in which it is worthwhile to pay to rent the chair, and show the optimal number of haircuts per month.

6. The cost function is $C(x) = x^2 + 2$, with marginal cost function $MC(x) = 2x$. The benefit function is given by

$$B(x) = \begin{cases} 60 & 0 \le x \le 5 \\ & \text{if} \\ 12x & x \ge 5 \end{cases}$$

which has marginal benefit given by $MB(x) = 0$ if $0 \le x \le 5$ and $MB(x) = 12$ if $x \ge 5$.

(a) Find the value of x where the marginal condition holds.

(b) Find the global optimum.

CHAPTER 3

TRADITIONAL LABOR MARKET ANALYSIS

Personnel economics is about the employment relationship. So is labor economics. The two fields of economics concern different aspects of the employment relationship and approach the relationship in different ways. Labor economics is the older of the two fields and uses more traditional tools. This chapter briefly outlines some of the results from traditional labor market analysis, which can then be used as a point of departure when we delve into personnel economics in the next chapter.

THE FIRM'S PROBLEM

The first step in analyzing the firm's problem is to determine exactly what the firm is doing. More specifically, the firm makes a choice, and we must ascertain what the firm chooses and also its objective. The answer is familiar: Firms choose the amounts of inputs to use in order to maximize profit. Typically in economics we look at two inputs, capital and labor.

If the firm uses L units of labor, typically measured in hours, and K units of capital, it produces output $Q = F(L,K)$, where F is the production function. The firm also faces a demand curve, and $P(Q)$ is the market-clearing price when the firm tries to sell Q units. Labor costs w per unit, where w is the hourly wage, and finally, the rental price of capital is r per unit.

This gives us enough information to write the firm's profit function. If the firm uses L units of labor and K units of capital, it produces $F(L,K)$ units of output and sells them at the market-clearing price. The firm's total revenue is $R(Q)$, and because $Q = F(L,K)$, total revenue can be written $R(F(L,K))$. The firm's labor cost is wL, which is the hourly wage times the number of hours of labor employed, and its capital cost is rK, the rental price per unit of capital times the number of units of capital. Profit, then, is given by

$$\pi = R\,(F(L,K)) - wL - rK$$

The firm chooses the amounts of capital and labor to maximize profit.

Because this chapter is concerned with labor markets, we will restrict attention to how much labor the firm employs. This is a "how much" problem, so the answer involves marginal analysis, equating marginal benefit and marginal cost. Begin by looking at marginal benefit. Using labor benefits the firm by increasing revenue, and an additional unit of output increases revenue by MR, marginal revenue. An additional hour of labor increases output by MP_L, the marginal product of labor. Thus, an additional hour of labor increases revenue by $MR \cdot MP_L$, or MP_L units of output that each generate MR dollars of additional revenue.

Using labor also carries a cost because workers must be compensated, and each additional hour of labor requires the firm to pay the wage w. The firm's marginal condition equates the marginal benefit of labor with the marginal cost, or

$$MR \cdot MP_L = w$$

The left-hand side of the equation represents the additional revenue generated by a one-hour increase in labor, and the right-hand side represents the additional cost. The firm employs labor until the extra revenue generated by an additional unit of labor equals the extra cost of that labor, which is the hourly wage. The left-hand side is often called the **marginal revenue product of labor**. The marginal condition states that the firm employs labor until the marginal revenue product of labor equals the wage rate.

Figure 3.1 graphs the marginal condition. The horizontal axis measures hours of labor, and the unit for the vertical axis is dollars per hour of labor, which is the appropriate unit for both the wage rate (workers are paid a certain number of dollars per hour) and the marginal revenue product of labor (an additional hour of labor generates a certain number of dollars in revenue). The marginal revenue product curve is downward sloping for two reasons. Each additional unit of output generates less additional revenue than the unit before it, so that marginal revenue is declining in output. Also, each additional unit of labor generates less additional output than the unit before it, holding capital fixed, so the marginal product of labor is also declining. Both components of marginal revenue product are decreasing functions, so marginal revenue product is also a decreasing function. The wage curve is a horizontal line at the market wage. The firm employs the amount of labor where the two curves cross, marked L^* in the figure. Because the marginal benefit curve (MRP_L) crosses the marginal cost curve (w) only once and from above, L^* is a global optimum as well as a local optimum.

The marginal revenue product curve is the firm's labor demand curve. It shows how much labor the firm chooses to employ for every given wage rate. Using the components of marginal revenue product,

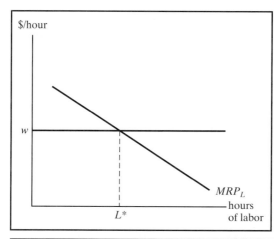

FIGURE 3.1   The Firm's Marginal Condition

The firm's marginal condition states that it employs labor until the marginal revenue product of labor equals the wage rate, or $MR \cdot MP_L = w$. The downward-sloping curve is the marginal revenue product of labor, and it is also the firm's labor demand curve. The horizontal line represents the wage. The firm maximizes profit by employing L^* hours of labor, which is where the two curves cross.

it is straightforward to find the factors that cause the firm's labor demand curve to shift. An increase in the demand for the firm's output causes prices to rise, which causes marginal revenue to rise, which in turn shifts the labor demand curve outward. An increase in worker productivity causes the marginal product of labor to rise, also shifting the labor demand curve outward.

THE WORKER'S PROBLEM

We now turn to the choices made by workers. Once again we address the problem by first determining what workers choose and what their objective is. Workers maximize their utility, which is the way economists usually discuss the behavior of individual people. What workers choose is a more subtle issue. Because this chapter is about labor markets, we want labor to enter the analysis somehow. But how?

Some people really like their jobs and get utility from working. More people, however, only work because it is a source of income, and income allows them to buy things that give them utility. Labor should not be an entry in the worker's utility function, because work does not provide any utility, but the income generated by work can be an entry in the utility function. We need a second argument, however. If income is the only argument, the worker should work as much as possible to maximize income. But this is not what people do. They work for part of the day and then enjoy leisure time the rest of the day. We can make leisure be the other argument of the utility function. There are 168 hours in a week. If workers choose to work L hours in a week, then they are also choosing to devote $168 - L$ hours to leisure activities. Leisure time generates utility, so the second argument of the utility function should be leisure time.

Workers choose the amount of time to spend working to maximize their utility. A worker's utility function can be written $U(Z,I)$, where Z denotes leisure and I denotes income. Working provides a benefit in the form of increased income, but it also imposes a cost in the form of lost leisure time. Working for one additional hour generates an additional hour's pay, w, and each additional dollar of income increases utility by MU_I, the marginal utility of income. Therefore, the worker's marginal benefit of labor is $w \cdot MU_I$, the additional utility from the income generated by working for another hour. Working for another hour reduces leisure time by one hour, and that causes utility to fall by MU_Z, the marginal utility of leisure. The worker's marginal cost of labor, then, is MU_Z. The marginal condition can be written

$$w \cdot MU_I = MU_Z$$

The marginal condition states that the worker spends time at work until the marginal benefit in terms of increased income is equal to the marginal cost in terms of decreased leisure time. Put another way, workers spend time at work until they are indifferent between spending one more hour at work to earn additional income and spending one more hour of leisure time.

It is customary to rearrange the above expression by dividing both sides by MU_I:

$$w = \frac{MU_Z}{MU_I}. \tag{3.1}$$

The right-hand side of the expression is the marginal rate of substitution of income for leisure. To interpret it, think about the units in which the two terms are measured. MU_Z is utility per hour of leisure, and MU_I is utility per dollar of income. Consequently, MU_Z/MU_I is (utility/hour of leisure)/(utility/dollar), which reduces to dollars per hour of leisure. Consequently, the right-hand side of expression (3.1) is the number of dollars the worker is just willing to give up to get one more hour of leisure. The left-hand side is the wage, which is the number of dollars the worker *has to* give up to get one more hour of leisure. The marginal condition states that the amount of money the

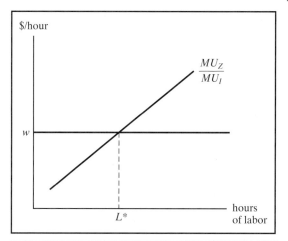

FIGURE 3.2 The Worker's Marginal Condition

The worker's marginal condition states that he works until the marginal rate of substitution of income for labor equals the wage rate, or $MU_Z/MU_I = w$. The upward-sloping curve is the marginal rate of substitution curve, and it is also the worker's labor supply curve. The horizontal line represents the wage. The worker maximizes utility by working for L^* hours, which is where the two lines cross.

worker is just willing to forego for an hour of leisure is equal to the amount he *must* forego to get it.

Figure 3.2 graphs the marginal condition $w = MU_Z/MU_I$. As workers work more, they earn more income, which makes the marginal utility of income fall, and they have less leisure time, which makes the marginal utility of leisure rise. Accordingly, as they work more, MU_Z/MU_I rises, because the numerator gets larger and the denominator gets smaller. The curve is upward sloping in the figure. The marginal condition is satisfied where the marginal rate of substitution curve crosses the horizontal line through the wage w, and the worker chooses to work for L^* hours. Because the marginal benefit curve (w) crosses the marginal cost curve (MU_Z/MU_I) only once and from above, L^* is also a global optimum.

The upward-sloping curve in Figure 3.2 is also the worker's labor supply curve. Because it is a supply curve, we are interested in the factors that cause it to shift. Constructing the supply curve from the worker's utility maximization problem makes this straightforward. Anything that causes the worker to desire income more causes MU_I to rise, which in turn shifts the upward-sloping curve in Figure 3.2 downward. This downward shift is also a rightward shift (draw it to see this), so anything that causes the worker to desire income more causes the labor supply curve to shift to the right. Examples of things that might cause the worker to desire income more would be having to pay for some large expense, such as college or braces or a new vehicle. Anything that causes the worker to desire leisure more causes MU_Z to rise, which in turn shifts the curve in Figure 3.2 upward, which is also a shift to the left. So, for example, as workers become older they value their leisure time more, and this causes their labor supply curve to shift to the left.

An Alternative Approach

Most intermediate microeconomics courses take an alternative approach to analyzing the worker's labor-supply decision. The alternative approach uses indifference curves. It yields some additional insight into the problem and also gives the labor supply curve a more complicated shape.

Figure 3.3 shows a budget line/indifference curve diagram. The axes measure the two variables that generate utility for the worker, leisure and income, with leisure on the horizontal axis and income on the vertical axis. There are 168 hours in a week, so the most leisure the worker can consume in a week is 168 hours. The most income the worker can earn comes from working for a full 168 hours, which is $168w$. The budget

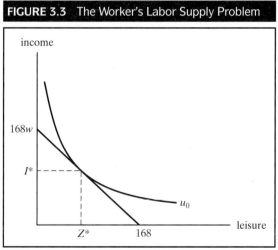

FIGURE 3.3 The Worker's Labor Supply Problem

The worker's budget line is downward sloping. The worker can get a maximum of 168 hours of leisure not working at all, or maximum of $168w$ in income if he works every hour of the week. The worker's indifference curve is downward-sloping, reflecting the tradeoff between income and leisure.

The worker maximizes utility by choosing the point on the budget line that is on the highest indifference curve.

line connects the two points (168,0) and (0,168w). The slope of the budget line is –w, the negative of the wage rate.

An indifference curve is the set of points that all generate the same amount of utility. The worker can get additional utility from either more income or more leisure. To keep the level of utility fixed, then, if workers consume more leisure they must also consume less income. Similarly, if they consume more income, to stay indifferent they must consume less leisure. This makes the indifference curves downward-sloping. Higher indifference curves have higher levels of both income and leisure, which means that higher indifference curves correspond to higher levels of utility. The slope of the indifference curve is the negative of the marginal rate of substitution, $-MU_Z/MU_I$.

The worker maximizes utility by finding the point on the budget line that is on the highest indifference curve; this is the point where the indifference curve is just tangent to the budget line, as shown in the figure. The tangency condition is that the budget line and the indifference curve have the same slope. Because the slope of the budget line is –w and the slope of the indifference curve is $-MU_Z/MU_I$, the tangency condition is

$$w = \frac{MU_Z}{MU_I},$$

which is exactly the condition we found using marginal analysis in expression (3.1).

Figure 3.4 repeats this procedure for many different wage rates, allowing us to see how the worker's choice of how much leisure to consume depends on the wage rate. When the wage rate starts low, the worker chooses to consume less leisure as the wage rises. This makes sense because the wage is the price of leisure, and as the price goes up people consume less. As the wage rate continues to rise, however, something different happens. For high wage rates, increases in the wage lead to increases in the amount of leisure consumed.

Because $L = 168 - Z$, a one-hour increase in leisure corresponds to a one-hour decrease in labor and vice versa. Consequently, when the wage rate is low, increases in the wage lead to increases in the amount of labor supplied, but when the wage rate is high, further increases in the wage lead to decreases in the amount of labor supplied. The corresponding labor supply curve is shown in Figure 3.5. It is upward sloping for low wage rates but downward sloping (or backward bending) for high wage rates.

Figure 3.2 and Figure 3.5 do not match. Why not? Figure 3.2 draws the labor supply curve assuming that MU_Z/MU_I increases as the wage increases. This is a sensible first approximation because when the wage increases the worker's income increases, causing the marginal utility of income to fall. Because Figure 3.5 does not match Figure 3.2, however, something must be wrong with this first approximation. The

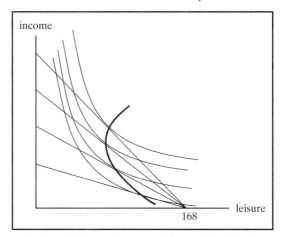

income

168

leisure

FIGURE 3.4   Labor Supply at Several Different Wage Rates

As the wage rate rises, the budget lines become steeper. When the wage rate is low and the budget line is flat, the worker chooses to consume a large amount of leisure. As the wage rate rises the worker works more and consumes less leisure up to a certain point. Eventually the wage rate becomes high enough that the worker responds to further increases by consuming more leisure.

problem is that an increase in income also makes leisure more valuable because increased income expands the possible uses of leisure time. A worker with more income can travel more, see more movies, watch TV using a better video system, or enjoy other activities. The impact of increased income on the value of leisure can make the marginal utility of income rise, which means that the curve MU_Z/MU_I can bend backward, just as in Figure 3.5.

LABOR MARKETS

The primary purpose of the preceding two sections was to construct supply and demand curves for labor in ways that allow us to determine what causes the curves to shift. The most important use of supply and demand curves is to determine the effects of changes in either the workers' or the firms' circumstances on the amount of labor employed and the equilibrium wage. Figure 3.6 shows a supply/demand graph, assuming for the sake of simplicity that the supply curve is upward sloping. The two curves cross where the quantity of labor demanded by firms and the quantity of labor supplied by workers are the same at L^*, and the corresponding wage is w^*.

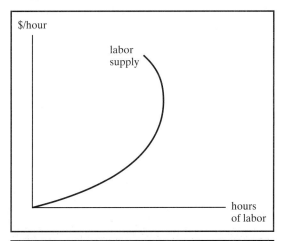

FIGURE 3.5 Backward-Bending Labor Supply Curve

Figure 3.4 shows that as the wage rate rises, the worker first decreases leisure consumption and then increases it. Because a decrease in leisure is an increase in labor, as the wage rate rises the worker first supplies more labor and then supplies less, and the labor supply curve is upward-sloping for low wages and backward-bending for high wages.

Suppose that the property tax on homes increases. What happens to the amount of labor and the equilibrium wage? Workers who own their own homes will find income more valuable than before because they must now pay additional property taxes. When income becomes more valuable the marginal utility of income increases, which in turn shifts the labor supply curve to the right from curve S to S'. The amount of labor employed rises from L^* to L', which makes sense because workers want to work more so they will be able to pay the extra taxes, and the equilibrium wage falls from w^* to w', which makes sense because firms employ more labor only if the wage falls.

Now consider a different example. A wireless phone service provider is the worst in the industry, with terrible customer satisfaction, and the only customers it manages to hold onto are the ones who find it too costly to change their phone numbers when they switch carriers. As a result of a new law that allows customers to keep their phone numbers when they switch wireless providers, the wireless phone company suffers a large drop in the demand for its output. This reduces the firm's marginal revenue, which in turn shifts the labor demand curve to the left. Figure 3.7 shows the resulting equilibrium in which the firm employs less labor and the wage falls.

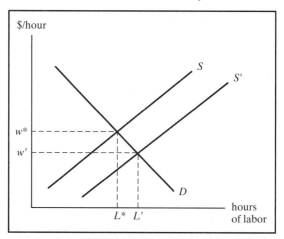

FIGURE 3.6   Labor Market Response to
an Increase in Property Taxes

When workers must pay higher property taxes, the
marginal utility of income rises and the labor supply
curve shifts to the right from S to S'. In the ensuing
equilibrium the amount of labor employed rises from L^*
to L' and the equilibrium wage rate falls from w^* to w'.

FIGURE 3.7   Labor Market Response to a Change
in Demand for the
Firm's Product

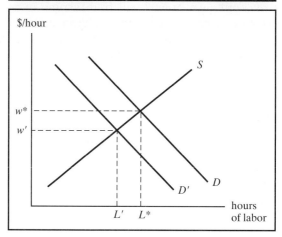

When demand for the firm's product falls, its marginal
revenue also falls and it demands less labor. The labor
demand curve shifts leftward from D to D'. The amount
of labor employed falls from L^* to L' and the
equilibrium wage falls from w^* to w'.

LABOR MARKET ANALYSIS
AND PERSONNEL ECONOMICS

Traditional labor market analysis is quite useful for determining how changes in the circumstances of workers or firms affect the equilibrium wage and the amount of labor employed. It leaves two important issues unaddressed, however.

In the traditional labor market model, a worker chooses to go to work for a certain amount of time, and the firm pays the worker for the amount of time spent at work. Somehow during that time the worker produces some output. Why? More to the point, how does the firm motivate the worker to actually do something while at work? It is certainly possible to spend time at work without doing anything productive. The traditional labor market model makes no distinction between time at work and effort at work.

Personnel economics is concerned with how the firm motivates workers to produce output. Time and effort are not treated as interchangeable, and the firm must design its compensation scheme in a way that induces workers to exert effort. The next several chapters will explore how the firm designs compensation schemes to induce workers to work.

In the traditional labor market model, all workers are the same, and a unit of labor is a unit of labor no matter who provides it. In real life, however, some workers are more productive than others, and workers often know more about what makes them different than firms do. The firm would like to use this information to hire the right workers, but unless it can get prospective employees to truthfully reveal information about themselves, it cannot use the information. This can cause problems both for hiring workers and for motivating them. Personnel economics is also concerned with how firms respond to this information that workers possess but do not necessarily share with prospective employers.

Homework Problems

1. What do firms choose and what do they maximize in the traditional labor market model? What do workers choose and what do they maximize in the traditional labor market model?
2. Explain why the wage is the firm's marginal cost of labor but not the worker's marginal benefit from labor.
3. Using a graph like the one in Figure 3.1, show the effect on hours of labor demanded when consumers boycott the firm's output.
4. Using a graph like those in Figures 3.3 and 3.4, show the effect on hours worked of an increase in the income tax.
5. A firm's labor demand function is given by its marginal revenue product of labor. Explain how the formula changes and how the

demand curve shifts when the firm expands its market by exporting its product to another country.

6. A worker chooses the amount of labor that makes $MU_Z/MU_I = w$. Explain how this expression changes when a person marries a spouse with a high income. What happens to that person's labor supply curve after the marriage?

CHAPTER

4 COMPENSATION AND MOTIVATION

etting paid is great. It provides workers with money to spend on things that they like. However, getting paid also requires work, and work is often not so great. Although some people are self-motivated or really like their jobs, it is uncommon for workers to enjoy every aspect of their jobs. Those unenjoyable tasks only get done because the worker is paid to do them.

Firms must pay workers to perform tasks that they would not otherwise perform. This is not as straightforward as it seems. We can readily observe a wide variety of compensation schemes that firms use to induce their workers to perform. Some pay a fixed amount per unit of time, such as a monthly salary or an hourly wage, whereas others pay a salary plus a bonus or some amount per unit of output or some amount per dollar of revenue produced, such as a commission. Some firms only pay workers if they reach some predetermined quota or other output standard.

In this and the next several chapters, we will explore how the firm's compensation scheme motivates workers to perform tasks they do not enjoy. In this chapter we consider a very simple employment relationship and evaluate the effectiveness of different compensation schemes.

WORKER EFFORT AND EFFICIENCY

In this chapter we restrict attention to an extremely simplified work relationship. The employee has only one task and must decide how much effort to devote to that task. The task results in output for the firm, which it can then sell at the going market price. The worker finds exerting effort on the task to be unpleasant, which we interpret as being costly. This section illustrates how effort affects the worker and the firm and how to determine the optimal level of effort.

The worker's cost of effort is given in Table 4.1. The worker can exert up to ten units of effort. Effort is unpleasant, reducing the worker's utility, and the cost of effort can be interpreted as the dollar

TABLE 4.1 Worker's Cost of Effort	
Units of Effort	**Cost**
0	$ 0
1	20
2	80
3	180
4	320
5	500
6	720
7	980
8	1,280
9	1,620
10	2,000

loss that gives the worker the same utility loss. So, for example, the utility loss from exerting four units of effort equals the utility loss from foregoing $320 in income. Exerting seven units of effort leads to the same utility loss as foregoing $980.

Each unit of effort produces one unit of output for the firm. The firm sells each unit of output for $800. However, the firm has additional costs besides labor costs. Each unit of output also requires $560 worth of materials, so each unit of output generates $240 **net revenue** for the firm, where the term *net revenue* will always mean *revenue minus all non-labor costs* in this book.

Is there a "best" or "right" level of effort in this context? Exerting effort helps the firm but is costly to the worker. Exerting more effort helps the firm even more but is even more costly to the worker. How do we know how much effort the worker should exert in this situation, and how do we know how much effort is too little or too much? Economists use the concept of Pareto efficiency in situations like this. An **allocation is Pareto efficient** if there is no other allocation that makes one party better off without making the other party worse off. If workers exert effort, they are obviously worse off than if they do not exert any effort at all. But, if they exert effort, they produce output that the firm can sell. The proceeds from the sale can be used to compensate the workers.

For example, if the worker exerts one unit of effort, then that worker incurs a $20 effort cost. One unit of output is produced, which the firm sells for $800. After paying the $560 in materials costs, the firm has $240 left over. Because the increase in net revenue outweighs the cost increase, there is a gain to be shared. The firm could pay the worker $30, for example, and both the firm and the worker would be better off than they would be if the worker exerted no effort. Thus, we can determine that zero units of effort do not lead to a Pareto efficient allocation because it is possible to make both parties better off.

It is also not Pareto efficient for the worker to exert 10 units of effort. With 10 units of effort, the worker's cost is $2,000, and the firm sells the 10 units of output for a total of $2,400 in net revenue ($240 net revenue per unit of output). The firm could pay the worker, say, $2,010 to compensate for the effort and still have $230 in profit, so both parties can be better off with 10 units of effort than with zero. This is not the only comparison, however, and it is not the right one. Suppose that the worker exerted 9 units of effort instead. The worker's effort cost would fall by $2,000 - $1,620 = $380, and the firm's net revenue would fall by $240. The cost saving outweighs the net revenue loss, resulting in a gain to be shared. So, both parties could benefit if the worker reduced his effort level.

The first example showed that an effort level could not lead to a Pareto efficient allocation if the net revenue gain from increasing effort outweighed the increase in costs. The second example showed that an effort level could not lead to a Pareto efficient allocation if the reduction in costs from decreasing effort outweighed the loss in net revenue. We say that an **effort level is Pareto efficient** if it can lead to a Pareto efficient allocation. We also sometimes call this the **socially efficient effort** or simply the **efficient effort level**. For an effort level to be Pareto efficient, then, the net revenue gains from increasing effort must not outweigh the costs, and the cost reductions from decreasing effort must not outweigh the losses in net revenue. In economic terms, this translates into a comparison of the marginal net revenue to the firm and the marginal cost of effort to the worker. Here the firm's marginal net revenue is the same for every level of output because the firm receives $240 in additional net revenue for each additional unit of output. The worker's marginal cost of effort must be calculated as found in Table 4.2. We compute marginal cost as the cost of the last unit of effort, so that the marginal cost of the nth unit of effort is simply the

TABLE 4.2 Marginal Cost of Effort and the Pareto Efficient Effort Level

Units of Effort	Effort Cost	Marginal Effort Cost
0	$ 0	—
1	20	20
2	80	60
3	180	100
4	320	140
5	500	180
6	720	220
7	980	260
8	1,280	300
9	1,620	340
10	2,000	380

total cost of the nth unit minus the total cost of the $(n-1)^{st}$ unit. This formula does not yield a value for zero units of effort because the formula requires subtracting the cost of unit -1 from the cost of unit 0, and there is no unit -1. Consequently we place a dash in the table for unit zero.

Using Table 4.2, the Pareto efficient level of effort is six units. The marginal cost of the sixth unit of effort is $220, and the marginal net revenue is $240. Because marginal net revenue exceeds marginal cost, the sixth unit of effort should be exerted. The marginal cost of exerting the seventh unit of effort, however, is $260, which exceeds the $240 net revenue it generates. There is no way to make both parties (strictly) better off by increasing the effort level beyond six; consequently, six units is the Pareto efficient effort level.

The same effort level would be chosen if the worker owned the firm. In that case, all of the net revenue would go to the worker, so the worker would choose the Pareto efficient effort level automatically. As the owner of the firm, the worker would choose to maximize profit, which would be net revenue minus effort cost. As discussed in Chapter 2, the solution to this problem is to exert effort as long as the marginal net revenue exceeds the marginal effort cost, which is what was done in Table 4.2 in choosing six units of effort.

Net revenue minus effort cost can also be considered a measure of social welfare. Net revenue is a gain to the firm, while effort cost is a loss to the worker. Combining the two yields net revenue minus effort cost, a quantity we call **total surplus**. In general, total surplus is the sum of all benefits minus the sum of all costs for all parties involved in the transaction, which in this case includes the worker and the firm but not consumers. According to standard marginal analysis, the effort level that maximizes total surplus is the one at which marginal net revenue equals marginal effort cost.

We now have three interpretations of the Pareto efficient effort level. The first is the effort level that can lead to a Pareto efficient allocation. The second is the effort level workers would choose if they owned the firm. The third is the effort level that maximizes total surplus, a measure of social welfare. The first is the definition we began with, while the second works because it makes the same individual act as both the worker and the firm, so that the worker will exploit all gains. The third works because maximizing total surplus gives the same marginal condition as with the worker-owned firm.

COMPENSATION SCHEMES AND EFFORT CHOICES

We have now found the level of effort that is best in the sense of both Pareto efficiency and maximizing total surplus. If the firm wants workers to exert that level of effort, however, it must pay them to do so. Workers are selfish and will behave in their own best interest, not necessarily in the best interest of the firm or social welfare. The purpose of this section is to explore some common compensation schemes and see if they are able to entice the worker to exert the Pareto efficient level of effort.

Each compensation scheme presents two issues to explore. First, what level of effort will the worker choose? Workers choose the effort level that maximizes their compensation from the firm minus their effort cost. Second, does the firm gain or lose from the compensation scheme? The firm will not use a compensation scheme that leads to negative profit.

The compensation schemes considered here are commonly found in the real world. They include paying workers per unit of output, commonly called a piece rate; paying workers a straight salary; paying workers after they meet a production quota; and paying workers a percentage of the revenue they generate, commonly called a commission.

Piece Rates

In a **piece rate compensation system**, the firm pays the worker a fixed amount for each unit of output produced. The **piece rate** is the amount paid per unit of output. For example, migrant farm workers are often paid by the amount of fruit picked rather than the time spent picking. Some automobile windshield replacement companies pay installers by the number of installations they make instead of by the hour.

To analyze such a compensation system, we must choose a piece rate to analyze. Start with a piece rate of $120. Workers receive $120 for each additional unit of effort, so their marginal benefit of effort is $120. Their marginal cost is given in Table 4.2. The marginal benefit of effort exceeds the marginal cost at three units of effort, but marginal cost exceeds marginal benefit at four units of effort, and the worker exerts three units of effort. Obviously, this does not yield the efficient level of effort, so we need to find the right piece rate. Because the piece rate is the worker's marginal benefit, and because the worker exerts effort as long as the marginal benefit exceeds the marginal cost, to get the efficient level of six units of effort the piece rate must lie between $220, the marginal cost of the sixth unit of effort, and $260, the marginal cost of the seventh unit of effort. For example, if the piece rate is $230 the worker will exert six units of effort, earning a total of 6 × $230 = $1,380. The worker's effort cost is $720, so the worker earns a net benefit of $660 from the employment relationship.

What about the firm? The firm earns $240 before labor costs for each unit but pays $230 in labor costs for each unit. Consequently, the firm earns profit of 6 × ($240 − 230) = $60. The worker earns a net benefit of $660, but the firm only earns $60. This piece rate system does much better for the worker than the firm. In fact, the very best the firm can do is by setting a piece rate of $221, which is the lowest piece rate it can set and still be sure that the worker exerts six units of effort. In this case the worker earns income of 6 × $221 = $1,326, yielding a net benefit of $1,326 − 720 = $606. The firm earns $240 − 221 = $19 per unit for a total profit of $114.

The firm would actually be better off with a lower piece rate. If the piece rate is $181, Table 4.2 shows that the worker exerts five units of effort. The worker earns a total of 5 × $181 = $905 and incurs an effort cost of $500, for a net benefit of $405. The firm earns 5 × $240 = $1,200 in net revenue and pays $905 to the worker, for a profit of $295. The firm earns higher profit by inducing the worker to exert less than the socially efficient level of effort. This raises the question of whether it is possible for the firm to earn more than $114 in profit while still getting the worker to exert six units of effort.

One method that is used in many industries is to have the worker pay a fee to the firm at the start and then earn a piece rate. For example, hair stylists rent their spaces from the owner of the shop and then keep all of the proceeds from haircuts. Some cabbies rent their cars from the cab company and then keep all of the proceeds from passengers. Accordingly, suppose that the firm charges the worker a $500 up-front fee and then pays a piece rate of $230. A comparison of marginal benefit and marginal effort cost using Table 4.2 suggests that the worker exerts six units of effort. The worker earns (6 × $230) − $500 = $880, with an effort cost of $720, for a net benefit of $160. Because this amount is positive, the worker is willing to take the job and exert six units of effort. The firm earns net revenue of 6 × $240 = $1,440, and its net payment to the worker is $880, for a profit of $560. By charging the up-front fee the firm is able to extract more of the surplus from the worker.

Of course, if the firm charges an up-front fee that is too high, the worker will choose not to work for the firm. Suppose, for example, that the firm charges a fee of $700 at the start and then pays a piece rate of $230. Comparing the worker's marginal benefit and marginal effort cost still suggests exerting six units of effort, but this time the worker's income of (6 × $230) − $700 = $680 does not cover the effort cost of $720, for a net benefit of −$40. By refusing to take the job, the worker exerts no effort at all and does not pay the up-front fee, in which case income is $0 but so is effort cost, yielding a net benefit of $0. The worker is better off not working when the up-front fee is too large.

Straight Salary

Firms often pay their workers a straight salary. Sometimes it takes the form of a fixed amount per month, and sometimes it takes the form of a fixed amount per hour, otherwise known as an hourly wage. Either way, it is based on time, not effort or output. Can a straight salary induce the worker to exert the Pareto efficient level of effort?

To ensure that the workers' effort costs are covered at the efficient level of effort, set the salary at $800. Thus, the workers are paid $800 no matter what, and the firm asks them to produce six units of effort. How much will the workers produce? The answer is nothing at all. If they exert six units of effort, their income is $800. If they exert five units of effort, their income is still $800. If they exert no effort at all, their income is still $800. No matter how much effort they exert, their income is $800. Because additional effort does not yield additional income, their marginal benefit from exerting effort is zero, so they will not exert any effort.

The workers benefit greatly from this compensation scheme. Their pay is $800, but they exert no effort and their effort cost is $0. Their net benefit is $800. On the other hand, the firm loses from this compensation scheme. It earns no revenue but still pays $800 in labor costs. The firm would not find a straight salary compensation scheme profitable.

Nevertheless, we see firms offering straight salary all the time, and you might object to the conclusion that workers do no work under this compensation scheme. In fact, workers on salary do work. Why? According to this analysis, some other motivating factor must be present. The most likely candidates involve consideration of the future: The workers work so they will not be fired or so they will not earn a bad reputation. We explore these issues further in Chapter 10. The scenario considered here does not incorporate any future, so it offers no motivation for the workers to exert any effort. They get their salary whether they exert any effort or not, and they get nothing extra for exerting effort, so they exert no effort.

DO WORKERS ON SALARY WORK LESS THAN THOSE WHO ARE PAID FOR PERFORMANCE?

Harry Paarsh of the University of Iowa and Bruce Shearer of Université Laval in Canada compared the productivity of tree planters in British Columbia, Canada, under two different pay systems. In one system the planters were paid by the hour, and in the other they were paid by the number of seedlings planted. Their statistical analysis shows that, on average, the piece rate system induced the average worker to plant about 173 more trees per day than the salary system did, an increase of 23 percent. However, because the piece rate system induced workers to work more quickly, it also induced them to take less care in planting the trees, and only about 109 of the 173 extra trees were planted well. (The issue of piece rates and the quality of performance is explored more thoroughly in Chapter 6.)

There has recently been a move in the legislature of British Columbia to require that tree-planters be paid a fixed wage rather than a piece rate. Not surprisingly, tree planting firms have resisted this move.

SOURCE: Paarsh, H. and B. Shearer, "Piece Rates, Fixed Wages, and Incentive Effects: Statistical Evidence from Payroll Records," *International Economic Review* 41 (February 2000), 59–92.

Quotas

In a quota system, workers must produce a certain amount before they get any money, and they get additional money for producing more than the required minimum. Thus, a quota system is similar to a piece rate system for high amounts of effort. As already discussed, in order to get the efficient amount of effort, the firm should set a piece rate between $220 (to guarantee that the worker exerts six units of effort) and $240 (so that the firm does not spend more than marginal net revenue on the sixth unit of output). Taking this as given, all we have left to specify is the quota and the payment made when the quota is reached.

First look at a compensation system in which the worker is paid nothing for the first five units of output and $230 per unit for every unit beyond the fifth. Thus, the quota is six units, and the payment for meeting the quota is the same as the payment for additional units, $230. The relevant information for analyzing the worker's response is contained in Table 4.3.

The benefit the workers derive from effort is income. When they exert six units of effort, marginal income exceeds the marginal cost of effort, as desired. However, at that level of effort, the workers' cost of effort is $720, but their income is only $230, for a net benefit of −$490. If, instead, the workers choose not to exert any effort at all, their income and effort cost are both zero, for a net benefit of $0. Under this compensation scheme, then, the workers will choose to exert no effort.

The problem with the compensation scheme in Table 4.3 is that it does not pay workers enough to cover their costs, so they did not work. We can fix this by raising the payment for meeting the quota.

TABLE 4.3 Worker Costs and Benefits Under a Simple Quota System

Units of Effort	Effort Cost	Marginal Effort Cost	Income	Marginal Income
0	$ 0	—	$ 0	—
1	20	20	0	0
2	80	60	0	0
3	180	100	0	0
4	320	140	0	0
5	500	180	0	0
6	720	220	230	230
7	980	260	460	230
8	1,280	300	690	230
9	1,620	340	920	230
10	2,000	380	1,150	230

Quota is 6 units; pay is $230 per unit for the sixth and every additional unit.

TABLE 4.4 Worker Costs and Benefits Under a Quota System

Units of Effort	Effort Cost	Marginal Effort Cost	Income	Marginal Income
0	$ 0	—	$ 0	—
1	20	20	0	0
2	80	60	0	0
3	180	100	0	0
4	320	140	0	0
5	500	180	0	0
6	720	220	750	750
7	980	260	980	230
8	1,280	300	1,210	230
9	1,620	340	1,440	230
10	2,000	380	1,670	230

Pay is $750 for meeting quota of six units, plus $230 for every additional unit.

Suppose that the quota is still six units of output, so that the workers are paid nothing for the first five units of output, but this time the firm pays $750 for the sixth unit and $230 per unit for each additional unit. The resulting payments are found in Table 4.4. Once again marginal analysis suggests exerting six units of effort. This time, however, the workers actually find it beneficial to exert the six units of effort because the income of $750 more than covers the effort cost of $720. It is also important to check that the firm is making a profit. The firm receives $240 in net revenue for each unit sold and pays $750, for a profit of $(6 \times \$240) - \$750 = \$690$, so the firm profits from the compensation scheme.

Both of these quota systems set the quota high. The system that worked, the one depicted in Table 4.4, used a high payment for meeting the quota. It is also possible to devise a workable quota scheme with a low quota. Suppose that the quota is three units, so that the worker is paid nothing for the first two units of output and is paid $230 per unit for the third unit of output and every subsequent unit of output. The payments are shown in Table 4.5. Once again, marginal analysis leads to an effort level of six units, as desired. Also, income at this effort level is $920, which more than compensates for the effort cost of $720, so the worker will choose to exert the efficient level of effort. As for the firm, its profit is $(6 \times \$240) - \$920 = \$520$.

A quota system shares the feature of a piece rate system of paying the worker by the unit. But compared to a straight piece rate system, the firm can earn additional profit when the worker is induced to exert the efficient amount of effort because the firm does not have to pay the worker for the output below the quota. The firm must,

TABLE 4.5   Worker Costs and Benefits Under System with a Low Quota

Units of Effort	Effort Cost	Marginal Effort Cost	Income	Marginal Income
0	$ 0	—	$ 0	—
1	20	20	0	0
2	80	60	0	0
3	180	100	230	230
4	320	140	460	230
5	500	180	690	230
6	720	220	920	230
7	980	260	1,150	230
8	1,280	300	1,380	230
9	1,620	340	1,610	230
10	2,000	380	1,840	230

Pay is $230 per unit for the third unit and every subsequent unit.

however, pay the worker enough to cover his effort costs or he will exert no effort.

Commission

Many salespeople are paid by commission; that is, they are paid a certain percentage of the dollar value of sales that they make. The purpose, of course, is to motivate salespeople to sell more of the product. Commissions are very similar to piece rates in that both relate the compensation directly to the amount of output, but commissions are more flexible because they allow for differences in the value of the product. For example, a car salesperson might earn a certain percentage of the dollar value of every car he sells. Because every car is different, the commission gives him an incentive to sell more expensive cars. A straight piece rate, in contrast, would pay the salesperson a fixed amount per car sold, regardless of the value of the car.

In the example we have been using, the price of the good is $800, so commissions should be computed as percentages of the $800 selling price. Also, the firm spends $560 per unit on materials, which amounts to 70 percent of the price. So, the highest commission the firm can pay without losing money on the unit is 30 percent.

If the firm sets the commission rate at 28.75 percent, it pays the worker $230 per unit produced, which is exactly the same as setting a $230 piece rate. As we saw in Table 4.2, this induces the worker to exert the efficient level of effort, six units, but it does not yield much profit for the firm. Commissions have exactly the same problems as piece rates, and for the simple example we considered here, every commission rate has a corresponding piece rate that induces the same behavior.

DO WORKERS REALLY WORK HARDER WHEN COMMISSION RATES GO UP?

Gerald Oettinger of the University of Texas, Austin, studied the response of baseball stadium vendors to changes in the commission rate. Stadium vendors walk through the stands at games and sell beer, soft drinks, or food. While an individual vendor has the same commission rate for the entire season, the commission rate depends on seniority, so different vendors receive different commission rates at the same time. Oettinger found that, after controlling for the fact that more senior vendors might be assigned higher-demand products or better parts of the stadium than newer vendors, higher commission rates do have a positive impact on the dollar amount of sales a vendor makes. For example, the highest commission rate is more than 20 percent higher than the lowest commission rate, and vendors making the highest commission rate sell about 2.4 percent more than the vendors making the lowest commission rate.

SOURCE: Oettinger, G., "Do Piece Rates Influence Effort Choices? Evidence from Stadium Vendors," *Economics Letters* 73 (October 2001), 117–123.

GENERAL LESSONS

The examples of compensation schemes in the preceding section illustrate three key lessons for using compensation to motivate performance.

Lesson 1

Workers exert no effort unless their pay increases with performance. This was illustrated by the straight salary example. In that example, pay was unrelated to effort, and because effort was costly to the workers, they exerted no effort. The key to getting workers to exert effort is to have a positive marginal benefit of effort, and because marginal benefit is the increase in the benefit as effort increases, the payoffs to effort must increase as effort increases.

Lesson 2

Workers exert no effort unless their benefit from exerting effort exceeds the cost. This is hardly a surprise, but it led to the failure of several of the compensation schemes in this chapter. For example, in the quota system, if the payment for meeting the quota was too low, the worker would earn a negative net benefit from exerting effort and consequently would exert no effort, as in Table 4.3.

The first two lessons identify two requirements that a compensation scheme must meet if it is to induce the worker to exert costly effort. It must tie pay to performance, and it must pay the worker enough to offset the effort costs. The second requirement has been given a name that will allow for a convenient reference. We say that the **worker's participation constraint is satisfied** if the worker's pay exceeds the sum of the worker's effort cost and opportunity cost at the relevant effort level. In this chapter we have assumed that workers receive a net benefit of zero from the next best alternative use of their time, so the opportunity cost is zero. The worker's participation constraint then reduces to the worker receiving nonnegative net benefit.

Lesson 3

The firm will not offer a compensation scheme unless it expects to profit from it. The firm also has a participation constraint. We say that the firm's participation constraint is satisfied if the firm earns nonnegative profit at the relevant effort level. A straight salary compensation scheme does not satisfy the firm's participation constraint because, as argued above, the worker exerts no effort, and the firm suffers a loss equal to the amount of the worker's salary.

All successful compensation systems must meet these three requirements. They also serve to highlight the goals of a successful compensation scheme.

Goal 1

A successful compensation scheme should induce the worker to exert the efficient level of effort. The opening section of this chapter argued that the appropriate level of effort is the efficient level because it maximizes the surplus available for the firm and the worker to share. For this to happen, however, the firm must tie pay to performance in the right way (according to Lesson 1) and the worker's participation constraint must be satisfied (according to Lesson 2).

Goal 2

A successful compensation scheme should enable the firm to keep as much of the surplus as possible. By exerting effort, the worker creates a surplus to be shared. The firm should choose a compensation scheme that keeps most, if not all, of the surplus as profit, leaving just enough of the surplus to ensure that the worker's participation constraint is satisfied.

The two goals work together. The compensation scheme should both make the surplus as large as possible and keep as much of the surplus as possible.

Homework Problems

1. Define Pareto efficiency.
2. Explain the relationship between revenue, net revenue, and profit.
   For problems 3 through 7, consider a worker and a firm with the following revenues and costs:

Units of Effort	Worker's Cost of Effort	Firm's Net Revenue from Effort
0	0	0
1	6	28
2	18	56
3	36	84
4	60	112
5	90	140
6	126	168
7	168	196
8	216	224
9	270	252
10	330	280

3. What is the optimal level of effort?
4. If the firm offers to pay the worker $15 per unit of effort, how much effort will the worker exert and how much profit does the firm make?
5. If the firm offers to pay the worker $10 plus $26 for each unit of effort past the second, how much effort will the worker exert and how much profit does the firm make?
6. If the firm requires the worker to pay the firm $20, and then the firm pays the worker $26 per unit of effort, how much effort will the worker exert and how much profit does the firm make?
7. If the firm offers to pay the worker $26 for each unit of effort past the fifth, how much effort will the worker exert and how much profit does the firm make?

CHAPTER

5 | PIECE RATES

The preceding chapter showed the importance of tying pay to performance. If the compensation scheme is designed correctly, it will induce the employee to exert the efficient amount of effort, and both the worker and the firm will benefit from the employment relationship. If it is designed incorrectly, the employee exerts an inefficient level of effort or perhaps no effort at all, and it is entirely possible that one of the parties is made worse off by the relationship.

The compensation scheme performs two tasks: It induces effort from the employee and it ensures that both parties benefit. In this chapter we look at one particular type of compensation scheme, a piece rate scheme in which the employee is paid by the unit of output. While this is not the only pay-for-performance scheme, it is a particularly important one. First, it has been used by a number of firms in a number of industries. In fact, about 15 percent of manual laborers are paid according to piece rate schemes. At the other end of the spectrum, some lawyers are paid by the number of hours they actually bill to clients, not by the total number of hours they work. Second, sales commissions are piece rates, and sales commissions are extremely common. Third, outside of the standard employment relationship, many contracts contain clauses that are essentially piece rates, with one party paying the other party based on the amount produced. Fourth and finally, piece rates are both simple to analyze and informative about the employment relationship.

PIECE RATES AT SAFELITE GLASS

The Safelite Glass Corporation is America's largest automobile glass service company, with its most familiar service being the replacement of damaged windshields. In 1994 and 1995, the company gradually changed the compensation plan for its auto glass installers, switching from hourly wages to a piece rate compensation scheme. The company used a sophisticated data management system that kept track of how many and what types of glass were installed by each installer every week, providing the basis for the piece rate pay.

A straight piece rate scheme would pay a certain amount for each piece of auto glass installed. Safelite did not use a straight piece rate system, however. Workers were guaranteed a minimum of $11 per hour and were paid about $20 for each unit installed. Thus, during a 40-hour work week, installers were guaranteed at least $440, which is the same amount they would earn from installing 22 units at the piece rate. If workers installed more than 22 units, they would be paid according to the piece rate and earn more than $440; however, if they installed fewer than 22 units, they would be paid the guaranteed wage of $440 for the week. This guaranteed minimum pay did two things. First, it reduced the fluctuations in installer's pay caused by fluctuations in demand, and second, it reassured workers who faced uncertainty because of the new pay system.

The theory tells us that under an hourly wage compensation scheme, workers would do the minimum amount of work required to keep their jobs, whereas under a piece rate system workers would be motivated to exert more effort. Edward Lazear of Stanford University obtained Safelite's pay records to determine whether the switch to piece rates had a positive impact on worker productivity.[1] He found that the switch to piece rates led to a 44 percent increase in output per worker. This is a significant increase, and it can be attributed to three factors. First, the piece rate system provided more incentives for workers, so they worked harder. This accounts for about half of the productivity increase. Second, the least productive workers did not fare very well under the piece rate system, so they left, raising the average productivity of the work force. Finally, the high pay available under the piece rate attracted new, highly productive workers, further raising the average productivity of the work force.

About half of the 44 percent productivity increase came from individual workers becoming more productive, and about half came from a change in the overall composition of the work force to more productive workers. The workers who became more productive earned more than they did under the hourly wage system, with their average weekly pay rising by about 11 percent. Thus, about half of the 44 percent productivity increase came from existing workers trying harder, and about half of that increase was paid to the workers. The rest was kept by the firm. Even though worker pay increased by about 11 percent, the firm's cost per unit installed fell by about 20 percent. Consequently, both the installers and the Safelite Glass Corporation benefited from the switch to a piece rate system.

---

[1]Lazear, Edward, "Performance Pay and Productivity," *American Economic Review* 90 (December 2000), 1346–1361.

OPTIMAL PIECE RATES

The example of Safelite Glass demonstrates that piece rate compensation schemes can both motivate workers and generate profit for the employer. It does not show, however, what the piece rate should be. Characterizing the optimal piece rate is the goal of this section.

A typical piece rate system consists of a piece rate, or an amount paid to the worker for every unit produced, and a salary component that the worker receives regardless of how much is produced. We denote the piece rate by b, output by q, and the salary component by s. If a worker produces q units of output, that worker's total compensation is given by

$$\text{Total compensation} = s + bq$$

Workers choose q to maximize their net benefit. Their benefit from producing q is their pay, $s + bq$, but they must exert effort to produce it. Their effort cost function is denoted by $C(e)$. In this chapter we assume that it takes exactly one unit of effort to produce one unit of output, so that we can also use C as a cost-of-output function, $C(q)$. We make three additional assumptions about the cost-of-effort function. First, it is nonnegative, so that exerting effort is always costly (as opposed to enjoyable). Second, more output requires more effort, which in turn entails greater cost. Put another way, the effort cost function is increasing in output. Third, each unit of output entails a greater cost than the previous unit, so that the marginal cost of output is increasing. The worker's net benefit is given by

$$\text{Net benefit} = s + bq - C(q)$$

If the workers produce any output at all, they produce an amount that equates marginal benefit and marginal cost. Their benefit from producing output is their compensation, $s + bq$, and the additional compensation for producing one more unit of output is simply the piece rate, b. Thus, marginal benefit is just the marginal compensation earned, which is the piece rate, b. Marginal cost is an upward-sloping function, as shown in Figure 5.1. The amount of output at which marginal benefit and marginal cost are equated is shown as q^* in the figure. Mathematically, if workers produce anything at all, they produce an amount of output q that solves

$$MC(q^*) = b$$

that is, the amount of output that equalizes marginal cost and the piece rate.

The firm's problem is somewhat different. The firm does not choose how much output is produced; it chooses the compensation scheme, that is, the salary component, s, and the piece rate, b. The firm's profit is its revenue from selling the q units of output less the costs of producing them. There are two types of production costs. One

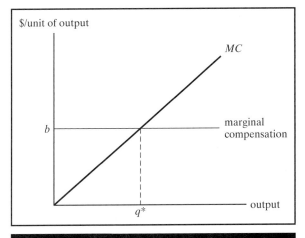

FIGURE 5.1   The Worker's Problem

MC is the worker's marginal cost-of-effort curve, and the worker's marginal compensation is simply the piece rate. The worker maximizes net benefit when marginal cost and marginal compensation earned are equalized, which is at point q^*.

is a labor cost, which is just the compensation paid to the worker, and the other is the cost of capital, materials, and so on. We use the term **net revenue** to mean revenue minus all nonlabor costs, so profit is simply net revenue minus labor costs. Letting the function $NR(q)$ denote the net revenue from selling q units, the firm's profit is given by

$$\pi(q) = NR(q) - [s + bq]$$

where $s + bq$ is the compensation paid to the worker.

The firm must pay the worker enough to ensure that the worker's participation constraint is satisfied. Suppose that there is some level of net benefit, u_0, such that if workers earn net benefit below this threshold, they will not take the job. Thus, the compensation scheme must allow workers to earn at least u_0. The workers' participation constraint is

$$s + bq^* - C(q^*) \geq u_0$$

meaning that the pay at the optimal effort level minus the cost of exerting the effort must be high enough to attract the workers to the job. The firm does not want to pay workers any more than it has to, so it pays just enough to satisfy the participation constraint exactly; that is, it sets pay low enough so that the workers earn net benefit exactly equal to u_0, or

$$s + bq^* = C(q^*) + u_0$$

Now go back to the firm's profit function. Because it sets pay low enough to barely satisfy the workers' participation constraint, after substituting $[C(q) + u_0]$ for $[s + bq]$ the profit function can be rewritten

$$\pi(q) = NR(q) - C(q) - u_0$$

The firm maximizes profit by equating marginal net revenue and marginal labor cost, which in this case means

$$MNR(q) = MC(q)$$

Note that u_0, the amount of net benefit a worker would receive at another job, does not depend on how much is produced at this job, and so does not factor into the marginal condition.

This tells us the profit-maximizing level of output but not the optimal compensation plan. To ascertain the optimal compensation plan, remember that the worker chooses an output level to make $MC(q) = b$. Substituting for the right side of the preceding equation yields

$$MNR(q) = b$$

Thus, the optimal piece rate is equal to the firm's marginal net revenue.

Figure 5.2 shows all of this graphically. The firm maximizes profit if it induces its workers to exert the amount of effort that equates the firm's marginal net revenue and the workers' marginal cost of effort. This is shown by output level q^{**} in the figure. The workers choose the output level that equates their marginal cost with the piece rate. If the

FIGURE 5.2 The Firm's Problem

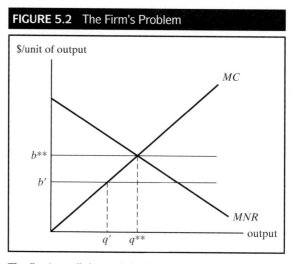

The firm's profit is maximized when output is q^{**}, where the firm's marginal net revenue equals the worker's marginal cost of effort. If the firm sets the piece rate at b', the worker exerts too little effort, producing q'. The optimal piece rate is b^{**}, which induces the worker to produce the profit-maximizing output level, q^{**}.

firm sets a low piece rate, such as b', workers exert too little effort, producing only q', which is where the horizontal piece rate line crosses the marginal cost line. The firm earns less than the maximal amount of profit. The optimal piece rate is b^{**}, which induces the workers to produce q^{**}, which is the profit maximizing amount of output.

We can now fully characterize the optimal piece rate compensation scheme. The optimal piece rate, b^{**}, is determined by the marginal condition

$$MNR(q^{**}) = MC(q^{**}) = b^{**}$$

The optimal salary component is set so that the worker's participation constraint is just satisfied:

$$s^{**} = u_0 - [b^{**}q^{**} - C(q^{**})]$$

The optimal salary component ensures that the workers' total net benefit is equal to u_0, the net benefit level required to attract them to the job.

GENERAL LESSONS

The construction of the optimal piece rate contains some important general results.

1. *Piece rates motivate workers.* As is always the case, workers equate their marginal compensation and their marginal effort cost as long as their participation constraint is satisfied. With a piece rate scheme, the piece rate *is* the marginal compensation. Higher piece rates induce workers to exert more effort and produce more output by moving them up their marginal cost-of-effort curve.

2. *The optimal piece rate is equal to the firm's marginal net revenue.* By setting the piece rate equal to marginal net revenue at the optimal output level, the firm induces the worker to exert the optimal amount of effort and produce the optimal amount of output, as in Figure 5.2. There are good reasons for this. For the firm to maximize profit, the worker must act in the best interest of the firm. The only way for this to happen is for the worker to have the same incentives as the firm, and the firm's incentives come from the fact that, for each additional unit produced, it earns a potential profit equal to marginal net revenue. To provide the worker with the same incentives, the firm must pay a piece rate equal to marginal net revenue.

3. *The salary component only impacts the distribution of the surplus.* Because the amount of salary does not depend on the amount the worker produces, it does not enter into the marginal analysis and has no effect on how much effort the worker exerts *if* the worker

exerts any at all. But it is an important determinant of whether the worker takes the job. At the same time, the firm wants the salary to be low because lower salary means more profit for the firm.

4. *The firm's profit must be at least zero.* Although this was not discussed in the preceding section, the firm has a participation constraint, too. The firm can earn zero profit if it does not hire the worker, so for the firm to hire the worker, the firm must make at least zero profit from the employment relationship. Because the firm's profit is given by $\pi(q^{**}) = NR(q^{**}) - [C(q^{**}) + u_0]$, the worker's cost of effort must be less than the firm's net revenue at the optimal output level, q^{**}.

5. *The optimal piece rate scheme leads to a Pareto efficient outcome.* An allocation is Pareto efficient (or socially efficient) if there is no other allocation that makes one party better off without making the other party worse off. The optimal piece rate scheme induces the worker to produce q^{**} units of output, which equalizes the firm's marginal net revenue and the worker's marginal effort cost. If the worker produced more than q^{**}, the firm would have to provide additional compensation that would exceed the firm's additional net revenue, so it is impossible to make both parties better off by increasing the piece rate to induce more production. If the worker produced less than q^{**}, the firm would be able to compensate the worker less, but its net revenue would fall by more than this amount, so at least one of the parties would be hurt by reducing output. Also, because both the worker's and the firm's participation constraints are satisfied, neither party can be made better off by terminating the employment relationship. Consequently, there is no way to make one party better off without hurting the other party. If chosen correctly, a piece rate compensation scheme can lead to a socially optimal outcome.

A CLOSER LOOK AT THE SALARY COMPONENT

As we have determined, the optimal salary component of the piece rate compensation scheme is set to exactly satisfy the worker's participation constraint. Let us take a closer look at exactly what this means.

Suppose that the firm sets the piece rate at b and the salary at s_1. Figure 5.3 shows the worker's compensation as a function of the amount of output produced. If the worker produces nothing, total pay is s_1, and each additional unit of output increases total pay by the piece rate, b. Consequently, total compensation is a line with intercept s_1 and slope b.

Figure 5.3 also shows the worker's costs. The worker faces two types of costs. The first is the effort cost, which is captured by the function $C(q)$. The other is an opportunity cost, the foregone net benefit the worker would have received had he not taken the job. The opportunity cost is u_0. The worker's total cost, then, is $u_0 + C(q)$, which is

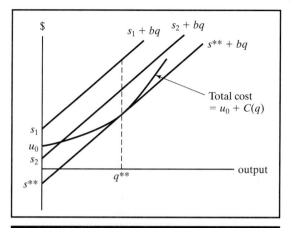

FIGURE 5.3 Finding the Profit-Maximizing Salary

The worker's compensation is given by $s + bq$, and cost is given by $u_0 + C(q)$, where u_0 is opportunity cost. The vertical distance between the compensation line and the cost curve is the worker's surplus from the employment relationship.

To maximize profit, the firm must give the worker as little surplus as possible. This is achieved by reducing the salary to s^{**}, so that the compensation line is tangent to the cost curve and the worker's surplus is zero.

also shown in the figure. Because net benefit is total compensation minus effort cost, the worker's optimal output level is the one at which the total compensation line is the farthest above the cost curve.

When the salary is set at s_1, the worker chooses to produce output q^{**}, and total compensation is above total cost. The worker earns strictly positive surplus. But remember, it is the firm that sets salary, not the worker. Is this the best the firm can do? The answer is no. The worker does not need this much surplus in order to take the job and would still take the job if the surplus was lower. So the firm could cut the salary to s_2, which shifts the total compensation curve downward. Cutting the salary would reduce the worker's surplus but still leave it positive. By cutting the salary, the firm can keep more of the surplus for itself. However, when the salary is s_2, the worker's surplus is still positive, and the firm can still do better. The firm can keep cutting salary until it is equal to s^{**}, at which the total compensation curve is tangent to the total cost curve. At this point the worker's surplus is zero and the participation constraint is exactly satisfied. This is the optimal salary computed earlier.

The optimal salary shown in Figure 5.3 is negative. We discussed negative salary components in Chapter 4. There are also ways around the negative salary component. Figure 5.4 shows an alternative

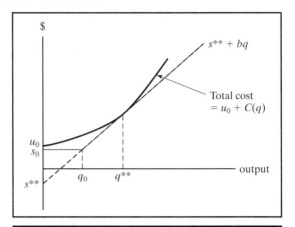

FIGURE 5.4 Piece Rates with a Quota and a Positive Salary

The firm can achieve exactly the same results as setting the negative salary s^{**} through a different compensation scheme without the negative salary component. The firm pays the worker a salary of s_0 and sets a quota of q_0. The worker earns an additional b per unit for each unit above the quota. The worker's compensation curve is now kinked, being horizontal at s_0 for output levels below q_0 and rising for output levels above q_0.

compensation scheme. In this compensation scheme the worker earns salary s_0 and receives a piece rate, but does not get paid for every unit of output produced. Instead, the worker receives nothing for the first q_0 units and then receives the piece rate b for every unit above that. In other words, the worker has a quota of q_0 and receives no additional pay until the quota is met. The worker gets paid an additional amount b for each unit produced above the quota. This is a realistic compensation scheme, and it allows the firm to keep all of the surplus without using a negative salary component.

MOTIVATING THE WRONG BEHAVIOR

The theory predicts, and the evidence shows, that piece rates motivate workers and that properly-set piece rates induce behavior that maximizes the firm's profit. Sometimes, however, the system is poorly designed, so that it motivates the wrong behavior. This section presents a few examples.[2]

---

[2]Unless otherwise noted, these examples are from Prendergast, Canice, "The Provision of Incentives in Firms," *Journal of Economic Literature* 37 (March 1999), 7–63.

In 1992, Sears Auto Centers in California and New Jersey were caught selling unnecessary repairs. With many documented instances of replacing good parts, Sears eventually agreed to pay $8 million to settle the California charges and to make restitution to customers nationwide. One of the major causes of the problem was the way Sears compensated its mechanics. They were paid in part on commission, so higher repair bills meant higher pay. Not surprisingly, this motivated the mechanics to perform more repairs, whether they were needed or not. After getting caught and paying restitution, Sears ended the practice of paying mechanics on the basis of commissions.

Since 1988 it has been illegal for the Internal Revenue Service to use any sort of revenue-based performance measure for evaluating auditors. After all, if auditors are evaluated and paid based on the revenue they collect from audits, their incentives change dramatically. They should avoid wealthy taxpayers, who will have complicated returns and the backing of lawyers and accountants, and instead target less wealthy taxpayers who are unlikely to put up a fight. Also, they should more readily use the agency's property-seizure authority to ensure that the revenue is collected.

In 1997 a document from the Las Vegas office of the IRS was uncovered that listed performance quotas for that office's auditors, and in 1998 it was discovered that poor people in Nevada were twice as likely to be audited as poor people anywhere else in the country. Also in 1998 the Arkansas-Oklahoma district was found to have used revenue statistics in employee performance evaluations, and that district's property-seizure rate was more than twice the national average.

These two examples show that a poorly-conceived incentive pay system can lead to unwanted results, not because the employees are breaking the rules but merely because they are responding to the incentives they face. This happens in a number of ways that are not as nationally prominent as the first two examples. For instance, a company decided that secretaries should be paid on the basis of how much they type and installed a device to measure keystrokes on keyboards. They later discovered that one of the secretaries ate lunch in her office, eating with one hand and typing nonsense as fast as she could with the other.

Scott Adams, in his book *The Dilbert Principle*, reports the following story that was sent to him by one of his readers[3]:

> A manager wants to find and fix software bugs more quickly. He offers an incentive plan: $20 for each bug the Quality Assurance people find and $20 for each bug the programmers fix. (These are the same programmers who create the

---

[3] Adams, Scott, *The Dilbert Principle* (New York: HarperBusiness, 1996), 12.

bugs.) Result: An underground economy in "bugs" springs up instantly. The plan is rethought after one employee nets $1,700 the first week.

Essentially, the incentive plan provides a $20 piece rate for easily detectable software bugs and, not surprisingly, the programmers produced more easily-detectable bugs.

Occasionally penalties, or negative piece rates, are used as motivation. Incentive clauses are very common in team sports in the United States. Ken O'Brien, an NFL quarterback in the 1980s, had a problem early in his career with throwing too many interceptions. To combat this, he was given a contract that penalized him for every interception. This did result in his throwing fewer interceptions, but it also resulted in his throwing fewer passes, even in situations when he should have thrown, to the detriment of the team. A similar problem arises with surgeons in New York, who are penalized if their mortality rates get too high. Surgeons respond by taking less risky cases.

OPTIMAL SALES COMMISSIONS

Sales commissions are a very common form of piece rate, covering sales of virtually all big-ticket items, including real estate, cars and trucks, and most industrial sales. They work in basically the same way as the piece rate schemes discussed earlier but with a difference in that the dollar amount of the commission is tied directly to the price of the good in a way that the piece rate is not.

To make this more concrete, suppose that the firm faces a downward-sloping demand curve and that the price at which it can sell q units of the good is given by the function $P(q)$. Further suppose that all nonlabor costs are constant per unit of output and given by c. The firm's total revenue is the amount it sells times the price per unit, or $P(q)q$, and net revenue is $NR(q) = P(q)q - cq$.

The firm's salesperson is paid on commission. The commission contract consists of two parts. The first is a salary component, s. The second is a commission rate, r, which is the fraction of the sales price the salesperson receives for each unit sold. If the salesperson sells q units, total pay is $s + rP(q)q$. The salesperson sells q units at a price $P(q)$ each and so receives a commission in the amount $rP(q)$ for each unit.

To determine how many units the salesperson will sell, we need to perform marginal analysis. It is helpful to start with marginal revenue, as opposed to marginal net revenue. Marginal total revenue is the slope of the total revenue function, $TR(q) = P(q)q$, where the notation $TR(q)$ is used to differentiate it from net revenue, $NR(q)$. Net revenue differs from total revenue in that the cost of nonlabor inputs is subtracted, and these nonlabor inputs cost c per unit of output. Thus, marginal net revenue is given by

$$MNR(q) = MTR(q) - c$$

The sales commission is given by the function $SC(q) = rP(q)q = rTR(q)$. Consequently, the sales commission is a fraction r of total revenue, and the marginal sales commission is a fraction r of marginal total revenue:

$$MSC(q) = rMTR(q)$$

We can now graph the marginal net revenue and marginal sales commission curves. We begin with the graph of the marginal sales commission curve shown in Figure 5.5. Start with the MTR curve, which is downward sloping because demand is downward sloping. The marginal sales commission curve, labeled MSC, is obtained by taking a fraction r of the MTR curve, which rotates the curve inward from the horizontal intercept. Lower commission rates lead to lower MSC curves.

The salesperson sells until the marginal cost of effort equals the marginal benefit. When the commission rate is r, the marginal benefit of sales is shown by the MSC curve and the marginal cost is shown by

FIGURE 5.5 The Salesperson's Problem

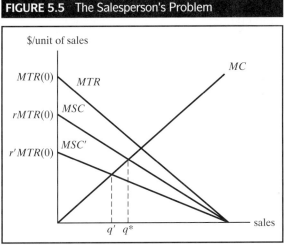

To get the MSC curve from the MTR curve, rotate it downward holding the horizontal intercept fixed. Lower commission rates lead to lower MSC curves, as shown by the diagram with $r' < r$.

When the commission rate is r, the salesperson exerts effort until the marginal sales commission equals the marginal cost of effort, which is q^*. A reduction in the commission rate r rotates the MSC curve inward to MSC', which leads to fewer sales at q'.

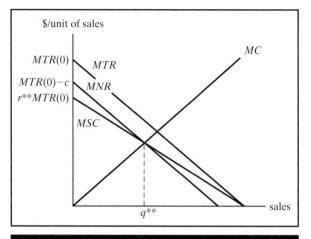

FIGURE 5.6   Optimal Sales Commission

The optimal sales commission makes the *MSC* curve pass through the intersection of the *MNR* and *MC* curves.

the *MC* curve, so the salesperson sells the amount q^*. A decrease in the commission rate, r, rotates the *MSC* curve inward, leading to fewer sales. All of this is just like the analysis of piece rates, except there the marginal compensation curve was horizontal and here it is downward sloping.

The *MNR* curve is derived from the *MTR* curve by shifting it downward by the amount of the per-unit nonlabor cost, c, as shown in Figure 5.6. The firm maximizes profit when the salesperson sells q^{**}, where $MNR(q^{**}) = MC(q^{**})$. To achieve this, the firm should set the commission rate, r^{**}, so that

$$MSC(q^{**}) = r^{**}MTR(q) = MNR(q)$$

If we think of $r^{**}MTR(q)$ as the salesperson's piece rate, we get the standard result that the optimal piece rate equals the firm's marginal net revenue. This means that the firm should pay a commission to the salesperson equal to the entire net revenue on the marginal unit sold. To put it another way, even though salespeople should receive a commission rate that is a small fraction of the price of the good, they should receive one that is 100 percent of the marginal net revenue.

Homework Problems

Problems 1 through 4 use the following information:
Workers are paid using a piece rate scheme with piece rate b and salary s. The workers' cost of effort is $C(q) = 2q^2$, and their marginal cost is $MC(q) = 4q$.

Each unit of effort generates one unit of output. The firm's net revenue is $NR(q) = 80q$, and marginal net revenue is $MNR(q) = 80$. The workers' net benefit at the next best alternative employer is zero.

1. Assume that the salary is high enough for the participation constraint to hold. Find how much output a worker produces as a function of the piece rate.
2. Find the profit-maximizing level of output.
3. Find the profit-maximizing piece rate.
4. Find the profit-maximizing salary.

Problems 5 through 7 use the following information:

Workers are paid using a commission scheme with commission rate r and salary s, so their total pay from selling q units of output is $r \cdot TR(q)$, where $TR(q)$ is the total revenue when output is q. The firm's total revenue function is $TR(q) = 200q - 2q^2$, and nonlabor costs are 40 per unit. Marginal total revenue is given by $MTR(q) = 200 - 4q$. The workers' effort cost function is $C(q) = 40q + 3q^2$, and their marginal cost function is $MC(q) = 40 + 6q$. The worker's net benefit at the next best alternative employer is zero.

5. Find the net revenue and marginal net revenue functions.
6. Find the profit-maximizing level of output.
7. Find the profit-maximizing commission rate.

6 | PROBLEMS WITH PIECE RATES

Piece rate compensation schemes can be powerful motivational devices. Not only can they be used to entice workers to exert more effort, but they can be fine-tuned to induce workers to exert the *optimal* amount of effort, both from the firm's point of view and from a social welfare point of view. The end of Chapter 5 contained some examples of situations in which the use of piece rate systems led to bad, but predictable, outcomes. These bad outcomes arose because piece rates led to situations in which workers exerted more effort than the firm would have liked and in ways that were detrimental to the firm. These are not the only problems with piece rates, however. This chapter further explores some of the potential problems.

SHOULD TEACHERS BE PAID FOR PERFORMANCE?

The current pay system for teachers is based on two factors: how long the teacher has been teaching and how many graduate courses the teacher has taken. By and large the public has been in favor of changing the system so that raises are based on what students learn, not how long the teacher has been teaching. Besides, there are problems with the incentives in the current system. Teachers who have taught for a long time have no incentive to leave because they are being paid at the top of the scale, whereas new teachers have little incentive to stay because they are paid at the bottom of the scale. Also, because teachers are paid more for having taken additional graduate courses, the incentive is to take a large number of those courses whether or not they enhance the teacher's effectiveness.

Why not link teachers' raises to their students' performance? This allows the system to reward teachers who do well and punish teachers who do not. It also provides teachers with the incentive to exert extraordinary effort, which the current system does not because it pays all teachers the same way. Moreover, the theory says that paying for performance can be an exceptional motivational tool. School districts in more than half of the states in the United States, including New York City, Los Angeles, and all of Florida, have implemented or have considered implementing merit pay programs for teachers for just these reasons. The British government has attempted to tie raises to performance throughout England.

The 4,700-student Colonial School District in a prosperous suburb of Philadelphia has already begun a performance pay system for their teachers. Individual teachers are paid bonuses of up to $2,500 based on their students' standardized test scores. The public tends to favor such changes. Teacher unions do not, and neither do a number of analysts. They cite several reasons, such as the demoralizing nature of the program because it implies that teachers are not already doing all they can.

Three of the reasons that many are opposed to basing pay on standardized test performance are of particular importance here. One is that the tests capture only part of what a student is supposed to learn, and teachers will have an incentive to "teach to the test." Standardized test scores can be improved when students learn certain strategies, which is the basis for many SAT preparation courses. Scores can also be improved if the material covered is restricted to the material on the tests and if assignments mirror the types of tasks on the tests. Critics argue that this leaves out other parts of the educational process, such as research projects, laboratory work, and similar activities. If a teacher's performance is measured on only one set of tasks, teachers will focus all of their efforts on those tasks that are rewarded.

A second reason is that making teachers compete for raises will reduce their cooperation among themselves. Education is, ideally, a cooperative exercise, with teachers in one class reinforcing material taught in another class. Also, teachers with good ideas should share them. Under the performance pay plan, however, sharing might cost a teacher money, so it is less likely to occur.

A third reason given by the opposition, especially teachers unions, is that teachers have very little control over how well their students do on the standardized tests. They are at the mercy of their class assignments. A good teacher with low-achieving students will do worse than a poor teacher with high-achieving, highly motivated students. Also, the tests were designed to give an indication of a student's aptitude and development, not the teacher's performance, so test scores may or may not be a reliable measure of what the teacher is accomplishing. Finally, test scores can be influenced by many things beyond the teacher's control, especially the student's home life. Doug McAvoy, the general secretary of England's National Union of Teachers, states, "Linking pay to pupils' performance in tests or exams is unfair. There are so many external factors beyond the teachers' control that affect how pupils perform in school that any system of measurement will always be crude no matter how much the government denies this."[1]

---

[1]BBC News, July 8, 1999.

This example suggests two problems with merit pay. First, programs lead workers to focus on tasks that are rewarded and ignore tasks that are not. In Chapter 5 workers only had one task, so this was not an issue, but critics of incentive pay for teachers suggest that because teachers are supposed to perform several tasks, such as preparing students for standardized tests, teaching them additional material, and cooperating with other teachers, it becomes an issue in the real world. Second, teacher performance is not measured perfectly, so teachers might earn more or less than they deserve. In the remainder of this chapter we move away from the world of public education and into the world of profit-maximizing firms to see whether these problems exist there and what firms should do about them.

DO INCENTIVES LEAD TO "TEACHING TO THE TEST?"

For many years, public school students in Texas were required to take the Texas Assessment of Academic Skills, or TAAS. This standardized test was used to evaluate schools throughout the state. Schools were placed into different categories based on the percentage of the students at the school who passed the test. Even though the state provided only very small monetary rewards when a school performed well according to the test, school boards and parents placed a great deal of pressure on principals and teachers to get the highest ratings.

Donald Deere and Wayne Strayer of Texas A&M University looked at the data from TAAS to determine whether there is evidence that schools teach to the test in order to get higher evaluations.

Their work uncovers three facts. First, passing rates grew substantially through time. Over a six-year period, the fraction of students passing the math test increased from 58 percent to 85 percent, and the fraction passing the reading test grew from 74 percent to 86 percent. Second, the same students' performances on other standardized tests showed nowhere near this growth rate. Third, the biggest gains in test scores came for students who were close to or below the passing level, probably because schools concentrated their efforts on getting the children who were close to passing to increase their scores. All of this points to the conclusion that when incentives are based on standardized test scores, teachers respond to the incentives and teach to the test.

SOURCE: Deere, Donald and Wayne Strayer, "Putting Schools to the Test: School Accountability, Incentives, and Behavior," Texas A&M University working paper, March 2001.

MULTIPLE TASKS

One of the major concerns about piece rate systems is that they promote quantity at the expense of quality. Suppose, for example, that workers at a manufacturing company are paid according to the number of units of output they produce. They can increase their output by speeding their production, but then they take less care and the items they produce have more defects. If they slowed down they would produce fewer items but with higher quality. Firms care about the quality of their output because defects lead either to customers returning items or deciding to buy from someone else in the future. If the workers are rewarded only for quantity and not quality, they will produce a large amount of output with very little attention to quality, and the firm's long-term profits might fall.

If the firm wants workers to devote effort to both quantity and quality, how should it set up its pay scheme? More generally, how should a firm set up its compensation scheme when a worker has two tasks? Consider a worker who can apply effort to two tasks that take different amounts of time. It takes h_1 hours to produce a unit of output 1, and the worker is paid a piece rate b_1 for each unit of output 1 produced. Similarly, it takes h_2 hours to produce a unit of output 2, which earns the piece rate b_2. If the worker produces q_1 units of output 1 and q_2 units of output 2, the worker's total income is

$$s + b_1 q_1 + b_2 q_2$$

where s is the salary component of compensation.

The worker gets disutility from exerting effort, and disutility depends on the amount of time spent producing output. Producing q_1 units of output 1 takes $h_1 q_1$ hours, and producing q_2 units of output 2 takes $h_2 q_2$ hours, for a total of $h_1 q_1 + h_2 q_2$ hours. The disutility of effort is captured by the cost function $C(h_1 q_1 + h_2 q_2)$, which should be thought of as the disutility of the time spent working. The marginal cost of producing output 1 is the additional cost of producing one more unit, which requires h_1 additional hours of work. The additional cost from one more hour of work is MC, so the marginal cost of output 1 is $h_1 MC$. Similarly, the marginal cost of output 2 is $h_2 MC$.

A worker's net benefit is given by

$$s + b_1 q_1 + b_2 q_2 - C(h_1 q_1 + h_2 q_2)$$

Workers choose how much output of each type to produce to maximize their net benefit, and we are interested in how much time is spent on each of the two tasks. In particular, do the workers produce both types of output or spend all of their time on one type of output and ignore the other? We can answer this by rephrasing the question in the following way: If workers decide to spend a total of H hours producing output, how should they allocate the time between the two types of output?

Suppose that a worker has decided to spend H hours producing output, split in some way between the two different types of output. Let us begin by assuming that the worker decides to produce q_1 units of output 1 and q_2 units of output 2. What would happen if the worker produced one more unit of output 1? First, because the worker is only spending a total of H hours producing, the worker would have to reduce production of output 2. Producing one more unit of output 1 requires an additional h_1 hours, and producing one less unit of output 2 frees up h_2 hours. To free up the h_1 hours needed to produce the additional unit of output 1, the worker must cut production of output 2 by h_1/h_2 units, because that takes $(h_1/h_2) \cdot h_2 = h_1$ hours, as desired.

Producing one more unit of output 1 affects the worker's pay. The extra unit of output 1 raises pay by b_1, the piece rate for output 1. But cutting production of output 2 by h_1/h_2 units reduces pay by $(h_1/h_2) \cdot b_2$. Producing one more unit of output 1 is worthwhile if the increase in pay from producing additional output 1 exceeds the decrease in pay from producing less output 2 or if $b_1 > (h_1/h_2) \cdot b_2$. We can rearrange this to

$$\frac{b_1}{h_1} > \frac{b_2}{h_2}$$

The fraction b_1/h_1 is the pay per hour spent producing output 1, and b_2/h_2 is pay per hour spent producing output 2. The above condition states that an hour spent producing output 1 pays better than an hour spent on output 2. If this condition holds, the worker should only produce output 1. Time spent on output 1 always pays better than time spent on output 2, so workers should increase the amount of time devoted to output 1 and decrease the time devoted to output 2 until they spend all of their time on output 1 and none on output 2.

If the opposite condition holds, $b_1/h_1 < b_2/h_2$, the worker should produce only output 2. *The only way that the firm can get the worker to produce both types of output is if $b_1/h_1 = b_2/h_2$*, so that an hour spent producing output 1 pays exactly the same as an hour spent on output 2. Otherwise, the workers spend all their time on the activity that pays better.

We have not yet said anything about the firm's part of the problem. We do not need to. The important point here is that if the firm wants the worker to exert effort to produce both types of output it must reward both types of output equally; otherwise, the worker only exerts effort in the task that pays better. It is easy to think of situations in which one task pays better and the other task is ignored. For example, sales clerks in clothing stores are often paid by commission. They get paid for dealing with customers, not for hanging up clothes or helping their coworkers, so these other important tasks are often not performed. For another, perhaps more immediate example, students can learn from going to class and from reading the book. But if tests do not cover both, students will only do one of the two.

We close this section with three examples of how paying according to one measure can lead employees to ignore another measure.[2] A long time ago, before telephone service was deregulated, when you called information you would be connected to someone who was employed by the local phone company and paid by the hour. These operators were instructed to handle calls accurately, and they did. Then deregulation came, and information services were contracted out to large centralized banks of operators who were paid by the number of calls they handled. This was a piece rate. The ensuing behavior was just what we would expect: Speed increased but accuracy decreased. The operator's goal was to give out a number quickly and not necessarily to give it correctly.

It is also possible to stress accuracy at the expense of speed. Scott Adams, the creator of Dilbert, once worked as a teller at a bank. Management only cared about the number of mistakes made. Obviously, the best way for a teller to cut down the number of mistakes is to cut down the number of transactions handled. So tellers had the incentive to go slower, talk to customers longer, and otherwise waste time. They also became adept at spotting the customers who would have long, complex transactions that might be more likely to entail errors. When those customers came to the front of the line, tellers would hang onto their current customers as long as possible hoping that the difficult customer would go to someone else.

One final tale shows how paying according to output leads to speed over quality. Phone installations are done in homes and businesses, so they are difficult to supervise. What would happen if installers were paid strictly by the job and not by the successfully completed job? Then installers would do the easy jobs quickly and well but the difficult ones quickly and poorly because doing the difficult ones well would take too long and be too costly (in terms of opportunity costs) for the installers. They would still get paid for the faulty installations, but the company would have to pay for someone to go out and fix the problems.

IMPERFECTLY-OBSERVABLE EFFORT

Up to this point we have assumed that effort and output were perfectly correlated and the firm could observe how much effort a worker exerted by simply counting the worker's units of output. This is unrealistic.

---

[2]These anecdotes are from Lawler, Edward E. III, *Rewarding Excellence: Pay Strategies for the New Economy*, Jossey-Bass, Inc., 2000; and Adams, Scott, *The Joy of Work: Dilbert's Guide to Finding Happiness at the Expense of Your Co-Workers*, HarperBusiness, 1998.

Sometimes workers work very hard with little to show for it, and sometimes they do not have to work much at all to produce a lot. Think about the case of car salespeople. Some days no serious buyers come on the lot, and no matter how hard the salespeople work with those they do see they are unable to sell any cars. Other days they might see several buyers who have already decided to buy a car, and they make sales without much effort at all. The flow of customers is beyond the salespeople's control, but the firm cannot base their pay on the amount of effort they exert because that amount could never be verified in a court of law. The number and value of the cars they sell is verifiable in court, however. If the salespeople's pay is based on their performance, that is, the number of cars they sell, their pay is not perfectly correlated with their effort.

This raises some issues for how the optimal piece rate should be set. The key issue here is that the workers face income risk. The salespeople's income was risky because it depended in part on the flow of customers, which was beyond their control. In general, people are **risk averse**, meaning that they would rather have the expected amount of income for sure rather than face a risk. For example, a risk averse individual would rather have $1,000 for sure than play a bet that pays $2,000 with probability 1/2 and pays $0 otherwise. Similarly, a risk averse individual would prefer to have $0 for sure rather than play a bet that pays $500 if a coin lands heads and pays –$500 if it lands tails. In fact, the person would even be willing to pay to avoid this bet. The amount that a risk averse individual is willing to pay to avoid randomness and receive the expected value of the gamble for sure is called a **risk premium**. We can think of this as an alternative definition of risk aversion: A risk averse individual is one who is willing to pay a positive risk premium to avoid randomness and receive the expected value of the gamble for sure.

Risk averse workers would prefer not to have any income risk. Of course, the firm could remove all income risk by simply paying the worker a straight salary, but this does not motivate the worker to exert any effort. Furthermore, since workers do not like risk, they must be compensated for facing it; otherwise, they would work somewhere else. The problem of finding the optimal piece rate, then, is one of trading off the motivation provided by the piece rate with the income risk inherent in performance pay.

To model the firm's choice of a piece rate, we must distinguish between effort and output. Let e denote the amount of effort exerted by the worker, and let q denote the amount of output the worker produces. The two are related, with

$$q = e + \tilde{\varepsilon}$$

where the tilde above the epsilon denotes that it is random. The random variable $\tilde{\varepsilon}$ is assumed to be a **noise variable**; that is, it is a random variable with a mean of zero. The noise variable has an average value of zero, which means that on average the amount of output produced by the worker is equal to the amount of effort exerted. Put another way, on average each unit of effort yields one unit of output. In any given time period, however, actual output could be higher or lower than the amount of effort exerted. Thus, the worker could have a day that was more productive than usual or one that was less productive than usual. That is the source of risk.

The worker's income is based on a salary component s and a piece rate b paid for each unit of output, so that total income is

$$s + bq = s + be + b\tilde{\varepsilon}$$

The worker's cost of effort depends on the amount of effort exerted, and it is given by $C(e)$. The worker has one more cost, however, the cost of bearing risk. Like the cost of effort, it is not an out-of-pocket cost, but it is still a cost because bearing risk reduces the worker's utility, just as an out-of-pocket cost would. The size of this risk cost is affected by several factors. First, it depends on how much the worker dislikes risk. The more the worker dislikes risk, the higher the risk cost. Second, it depends on the piece rate. The risky component of the worker's income is $b\tilde{\varepsilon}$. If the piece rate b is zero, the risky component disappears, and the worker bears no risk cost. If b is positive, however, there is risk, and the worker faces a risk cost. The larger b is, the larger the risky component of income is, and the more risk the worker faces. Consequently, the risk cost increases with the piece rate. Finally, the risk cost depends on the amount of variation in the noise variable $\tilde{\varepsilon}$. The more it fluctuates, the more risk the worker faces and the higher the risk cost.

Let $RC(b)$ denote the worker's risk cost; it is a function of b because increases in the piece rate increase the risk cost. The worker's net benefit, then, is given by

$$s + bq - C(e) - RC(b) = s + be + b\tilde{\varepsilon} - C(e) - RC(b)$$

Because of the randomness of the noise variable, workers do not maximize net benefit. Instead, they maximize *expected* net benefit, or the average value of net benefit over a large set of observations. Remember that the expected value of the noise variable is zero, so it disappears from the expected net benefit term. This leads to the formula for expected net benefit:

$$s + be - C(e) - RC(b)$$

The workers have a participation constraint governing when they will choose to work for the firm. The participation constraint sets a lower bound on expected net benefit:

$$s + be - C(e) - RC(b) \geq u_0$$

where u_0 is the worker's net benefit from the next best alternative use of his time.

As long as the participation constraint is satisfied, the worker chooses the effort level that maximizes expected net benefit. Because, like the salary component, the risk cost is not a function of e, it does not figure into the marginal condition for maximizing net benefit. We are left with the standard marginal condition from Chapter 5:

$$MC(e^*) = b$$

or the marginal cost of effort equals the marginal benefit of effort, which is the piece rate. Thus, the presence of the noise variable has no effect on the worker's marginal condition. It does, however, show up in the worker's participation constraint. Consequently, it may have an impact on whether workers choose to work for the firm, but if they do choose to work for the firm, the noise variable has no impact on how hard they work.

The noise variable does impact the *firm's* choice of the optimal piece rate, however. The noise variable enters into the worker's participation constraint, so the firm must pay the worker more to compensate for the risk induced by the piece rate system. Consequently, the firm faces a trade-off when determining the optimal piece rate: A higher piece rate induces workers to exert more effort, but it also increases the amount of risk workers face and for which they must be compensated.

When the firm maximizes profit, it sets total compensation so that the worker's participation constraint is met exactly, or

$$s + be = C(e) + RC(b) + u_0$$

The left-hand side of the equation is expected total compensation when the worker exerts effort e, and the right-hand side is the cost of that effort plus the cost of bearing the risk, plus the opportunity cost of the next-best alternative use of the worker's time. The firm's profit is then given by

$$\pi(b) = NR(e^* + \tilde{\varepsilon}) - (s + b[e^* + \tilde{\varepsilon}])$$

where e^* is the effort level chosen by the worker when the piece rate is b and NR is the net revenue function. The first term on the right-hand side is the firm's net revenue (revenue minus nonlabor costs), and the second term is the labor cost.

There is noise in the firm's profit function, so we take the expected value. Because the expected value of the noise variable $\tilde{\varepsilon}$ is zero, expected profit is given by

$$E\pi(b) = NR(e^*) - [s + be^*]$$

where the first term on the right is expected net revenue and the term in brackets is the labor cost. Substituting from the worker's participation constraint yields

$$E\pi(b) = NR(e^*) - [C(e^*) + RC(b) + u_0]$$

The firm chooses the piece rate b to maximize expected profit.

The first question we want to ask is, does the firm set the piece rate higher or lower than it would if there were no noise? If there were no noise, the worker would face no income risk, causing $RC(b) = 0$ and

$$\pi_0(b) = NR(e^*) = [C(e^*) + u_0]$$

where π_0 denotes profit in the noiseless case. The first term is the firm's benefit and the second is the cost. Let b_0 denote the optimal piece rate when there is no noise, and let e_0 denote the level of effort induced. Then b_0 makes the marginal profit zero, which is another way of saying that it equates the marginal benefit of increasing the piece rate with the marginal cost. To distinguish the firm's benefit and cost functions from the worker's, let $\mathcal{B}_0(b)$ denote the firm's benefit when the piece rate is b and there is no noise, and let $\mathcal{C}_0(b)$ denote the firm's cost when the piece rate is b and there is no noise. Then the piece rate b_0 satisfies

$$M\mathcal{B}_0(b_0) = M\mathcal{C}_0(b_0)$$

Figure 6.1 shows the marginal benefit and marginal cost curves. The optimal piece rate when there is no noise is found at the intersection of the curves $M\mathcal{B}_0$ and $M\mathcal{C}_0$.

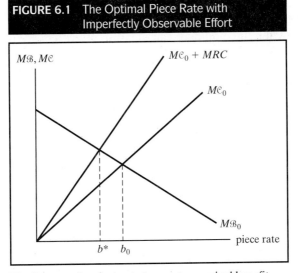

FIGURE 6.1   The Optimal Piece Rate with Imperfectly Observable Effort

The firm sets the piece rate to equate marginal benefit and marginal cost. When there is no noise the marginal cost curve is $M\mathcal{C}_0$ and the optimal piece rate is b_0. When there is noise the marginal cost curve rotates upward to $M\mathcal{C}_0 + MRC$ because of the worker's cost of bearing risk, and the optimal piece rate falls to b^*.

But what if the firm faces noise? Then the marginal cost of increasing the piece rate rises because increasing the piece rate increases $RC(b)$, the amount the firm must compensate workers for facing income risk. The firm's marginal cost rises to $MC_0(b) + MRC(b)$. To see whether the firm wants to set the piece rate higher than, lower than, or equal to b_0, look back at Figure 6.1. The marginal cost curve rotates upward to $MC_0 + MRC$ because of the risk cost borne by workers. The optimal piece rate is found at the intersection of $MC_0 + MRC$ and MB_0, which is at b^*. The optimal piece rate is lower in the presence of noise than it is in the absence of noise.

The intuition behind this result is fairly straightforward. When firms base pay on output but output does not perfectly reflect effort, workers face income risk. Because workers do not like income risk, they must be compensated for facing it. Furthermore, the higher the piece rate, the more risk workers face, and the more they must be compensated. The presence of noise, therefore, leads the firm to set a lower piece rate so that it does not have to compensate workers as much for facing income risk. When it sets the piece rate lower, it must raise the salary component of pay so that the worker's participation constraint is still met. Thus, when firms cannot measure effort perfectly, they respond by putting less of the worker's income at risk, offering a higher salary and a lower piece rate.

We can also examine the effects of some changes in the environment. When workers become more risk averse, they must be compensated even more for facing income risk. This raises MRC further and reduces the optimal piece rate even more. Hence, when employees become more risk averse, the optimal piece rate falls.

When the employer can measure effort less accurately, the noise term has more fluctuations. As stated earlier, this increases the amount of income risk faced by the worker. Because workers do not like income risk, they must be compensated more for facing the income risk when output is measured less accurately. This also causes MRC to rise and induces the firm to reduce the piece rate.

FAIRNESS

When output is not a perfect measure of effort, two employees who are paid with piece rates can exert the exact same amounts of effort but receive different incomes. This is unfair. If this lack of fairness does not bother the employees, then the firm should not be concerned, and it can set the piece rate the same way it did in the preceding section. If workers care about fairness, however, the firm should set the piece rate lower.

Incentive pay naturally makes wages unequal when the firm cannot measure effort precisely. Suppose there are two workers. Worker

1's output q_1 is given by $q_1 = e_1 + \tilde{\varepsilon}_1$, and worker 2's output is given by $q_2 = e_2 + \tilde{\varepsilon}_2$. Further assume that the two workers exert the same amount of effort, $e_1 = e_2$, so that if effort were measured perfectly they would be paid exactly the same amount. If worker 1 is lucky so that the outcome of the noise variable $\tilde{\varepsilon}_1$, is high, and if worker 2 is unlucky so that the outcome of the noise variable $\tilde{\varepsilon}_2$, is low, then worker 1 produces more output and is paid more than worker 2 even though they exert exactly the same amount of effort. If worker 2 had been lucky and worker 1 had been unlucky, then worker 2 would have been paid more. What matters here is that the only reason that the two workers are paid differently is that one is luckier than the other.

If workers do not like it when different workers who exert the same effort are paid differently, then they must be paid more for putting up with income inequality. This is exactly the same as the firm having to compensate workers for bearing income risk in the preceding section. The higher the piece rate, the more incomes fluctuate, and the more potential inequality there is. Thus, the higher the piece rate, the more the firm must compensate workers for putting up with income inequality. It is, therefore, in the firm's best interest to set the piece rate lower so that it does not have to compensate the workers as much.

GENERAL LESSONS

The results of this chapter can be summarized by two principles for using incentive pay.

1. *The Equal Compensation Principle.* If the firm's profit is maximized when the employee undertakes more than one costly activity, all of the valuable activities must be compensated equally at the margin; otherwise the employee undertakes only those activities that are rewarded most highly.
2. *The Incentive Intensity Principle.* The optimal piece rate (or the optimal sales commission rate) is higher when:
   - The firm's marginal net revenue is higher
   - Employees are less risk averse
   - The employer can measure effort more accurately
   - Employees are less concerned with fairness

In this chapter's discussion of the Equal Compensation Principle, we saw that given a choice between two tasks employees will undertake the one that pays better. To get employees to engage in both activities, the two activities must be rewarded equally at the margin.

In Chapter 5's discussion of the Incentive Intensity Principle, we learned first that in the absence of noise the optimal piece rate is equal to the firm's marginal net revenue. This is the first point in the Incentive

Intensity Principle. In this chapter we learned that if firms cannot measure effort accurately, the use of incentive pay makes workers' incomes risky. Because workers do not like income risk, they must be compensated for bearing that risk. The amount of compensation rises when workers become more risk averse and when the firm's measurements become less accurate. To reduce the amount it must compensate the workers for facing risk, the firm sets the piece rate lower. Or, put the opposite way, as workers become less risk averse or as measurements become more accurate, the firm's optimal piece rate rises.

Finally in this chapter we found that if workers are concerned with fairness they do not like the pay inequality that arises from the use of incentive pay, and they must be compensated for putting up with the inequality. The higher the piece rate, the more compensation they require. The firm should reduce the piece rate in order to reduce the amount of inequality compensation it must pay. Or, put the opposite way, as workers become less concerned with fairness, the firm's optimal piece rate rises.

How do these principles affect the debate about teacher compensation discussed in the beginning of this chapter? The proposal being made specifically in the Colonial School District was to reward teachers based on their students' performance on standardized tests. The complaints were that teachers would focus on the material covered on the standardized tests at the expense of other material; teachers would no longer cooperate in the best interests of the children; and teachers ultimately have little control over how their students do on the tests. The first two complaints relate to the Equal Compensation Principle. If teachers are rewarded for one activity only, they will concentrate on that one activity at the expense of others. The third complaint relates to the Incentive Intensity Principle. If student test scores are not an accurate measure of teacher effort, performance pay should be minimal. Based on these two principles, the complaints about rewarding teachers according to their students' test scores are valid.

When should piece rates or sales commissions be used? According to the Incentive Intensity Principle and Equal Compensation Principle, they should be used when employees perform a single, well-defined task that allows for easy, accurate measurement. Such a case was discussed in Chapter 5. Safelite Glass pays its windshield installers by the installation. Successful installations are easy to measure, and there are no other activities that installers should undertake.

Homework Problems

1. What general rule do workers follow when choosing which task to perform?
2. What tradeoff does a firm face when it wants to pay its employees using a piece rate but cannot measure effort perfectly?

3. A worker is supposed to perform three tasks. The effort requirements and piece rates are contained in the following table. Which
tasks (or combination of tasks) does the worker perform? Provide
a combination of piece rates that makes the worker indifferent
between all three of the tasks.

Task	Effort Required	Piece Rate
A	2	$12
B	3	15
C	5	24

4. A worker is called upon to produce two types of output. Output 1
requires 1 unit of effort to produce, and output 2 requires 4 units of
effort to produce. The worker is paid a piece rate of 10 for each unit
of output 1 and a piece rate of b_2 for each unit of output 2. The
worker's cost function is $C(e) = e^2$ and the marginal cost function is
$MC(e) = 2e$, where e denotes the amount of effort expended by the
worker. Find the piece rate for output 2 that makes the worker willing to produce both types of output.

5. A firm hires students to be telemarketers. One group of students
makes their calls from a supervised office, and another group of students makes their calls from home. Explain why it makes sense to
pay the first group according to the number of calls made but not the
second group, referring to the Incentive Intensity Principle.

6. Draw a graph showing what happens to the optimal piece rate when
the price of the firm's output rises.

7 | MOTIVATING MULTIPLE TYPES

Each of the last three chapters was about motivating workers. They all made the hidden assumption that either there is only one worker or, if there are many workers, they are all identical. There was a good reason for making this assumption because it simplifies the analysis, which is important when introducing concepts.

In this chapter we discard that hidden assumption and assume that workers are not identical. In particular, some workers are better at producing than others, but both the high-productivity workers and the low-productivity workers work for the same firm in the same job. Two central issues must be addressed. First, if the firm cannot tell which type is which, how should it set the piece rates to motivate both? Second, which type of worker—high-productivity or low-productivity—fares better? In other words, does it pay to have talent, or are the skills and knowledge that make someone a high-productivity worker wasted in this setting?

THE FULL-INFORMATION CASE

Before tackling the setting in which the firm cannot tell whether a worker has high productivity or low productivity, we will consider the setting in which it can. We have two reasons for doing so. First, this provides a benchmark against which we can compare the results for the setting in which we are interested. Second, it helps introduce some of the concepts.

Begin by thinking about what makes one worker a high-productivity worker and another one a low-productivity worker. Given a particular set of incentives, the high-productivity worker should produce more output than the low-productivity worker. One way to approach this is to assume that one worker has lower effort costs than the other. The one with the lower effort costs exerts more effort than the other, thereby producing more. Our assumption is that the high-productivity worker has lower effort costs than the low-productivity worker.

To make this more concrete, let us use some specific cost functions. High-productivity (low effort cost) workers have cost function $C_H(q) = q^2$, while low-productivity (high effort cost) workers have cost function $C_L(q) = 2q^2$. The corresponding marginal cost functions are $MC_H(q) = 2q$ for high-productivity workers and $MC_L(q) = 4q$ for low-productivity workers.[1] It costs the low-productivity worker twice as much to produce a given amount of output as it costs the high-productivity worker. The low-productivity worker's marginal cost is also doubled.

Both workers have a reservation utility of zero. The firm earns marginal net revenue of 12 for every unit of effort exerted by the workers. The firm offers standard piece rate compensation packages that consist of a salary component, s, and a piece rate, b, so that a worker who produces output q earns a total of $s + bq$. Finally, the two types of workers are equally prevalent in both society and the firm. This means that any particular worker is equally likely to have high or low productivity.

The assumption in this section is that the firm can look at a worker and tell whether that worker has high productivity or low productivity; in the next section we will assume that the firm cannot tell the worker's type. When the firm can tell the two types of workers apart, it should offer the profit-maximizing compensation package to each type. These packages were discussed thoroughly in Chapter 5, so only a brief outline is given here. Start with the high-productivity workers and assume that the firm offers them a compensation package with salary s_H and piece rate b_H. The marginal condition for the worker is to produce output until the marginal benefit equals the marginal cost:

$$MC_H(q) = 2q = b_H \qquad (7.1)$$

if the worker's participation constraint is satisfied:

$$s_H + b_H q - C_H(q) \geq 0 \qquad (7.2)$$

From (7.1) the worker produces $q_H = b_H/2$ if the participation constraint is satisfied.

The marginal condition for the firm is to set the piece rate equal to marginal net revenue so that $b_H = 12$. From the worker's marginal condition (7.1), output is $q_H = b_H/2 = 6$. The salary component is set as

---

[1]There is a simple rule for finding marginal functions. If the original function takes the form of $a + bx$, the marginal function is b. If the original function takes the form $a + bx + cx^2$, the marginal function is $b + 2cx$. Thus, if the cost function takes the form of $2q^2$, the marginal cost function is $4q$. You probably learned this in a calculus class, and it is a simple rule that we use again in this chapter.

low as possible so that the participation constraint (7.2) holds with equality. Plugging $q_H = 6$, $b_H = 12$, and $C_H(q) = q^2$ into (7.2) yields:

$$NB_H = s_H + b_H q_H - C_H(q_H) = s_H + 12 \cdot 6 - 6^2 = s_H + 36 = 0$$

where NB_H is the high-productivity worker's net benefit, and it is set equal to zero (at the end) because that is the worker's reservation utility. Solving yields $s_H = -36$. The worker's pay is $-36 + 12 \cdot 6 = 36$, but effort cost is $6^2 = 36$, yielding a net benefit of zero. The firm's net revenue is $12 \cdot 6 = 72$, and its labor cost is 36 for a profit of 36.

Now consider the low-productivity worker. The firm's marginal condition is to set the piece rate equal to marginal net revenue, so the low productivity piece rate is $b_L = 12$. The worker's marginal condition is to produce until marginal cost equals the piece rate:

$$MC_L(q) = 4q = 12 = b_L$$

so that $q_L = 3$. The firm sets s_L so that the low-productivity worker's participation constraint is just satisfied:

$$NB_L = s_H + b_L q_L - C_L(q_L) = s_L + 12 \cdot 3 - 2 \cdot 3^2 = s_L + 18 = 0$$

which yields $s_L = -18$. The worker is paid $-18 + 12 \cdot 3 = 18$, but receives zero net benefit. The firm earns a profit of 18.

If the firm hires a random worker before determining whether the worker has high or low productivity and then offers the optimal piece rate contract for whichever type the worker turns out to be, the firm's expected profit is $(1/2)(36) + (1/2)(18) = 27$. To facilitate comparison with the setting in which the firm cannot tell the worker's type, these results are summarized in Table 7.1.

One more thing should be said about the full-information setting. As we learned in Chapter 5, when the firm sets the piece rate and the salary to maximize profit, its workers produce the Pareto efficient amount of output. This is also true here, so the output levels in Table 7.1

TABLE 7.1 Full Information Setting		
	High-Productivity	*Low-Productivity*
Output	6	3
Pay	36	18
Net benefit	0	0
Profit	36	18
Expected profit:	27	

Contract: $-18 + 12q$ for low-productivity workers, $-36 + 12q$ for high-productivity workers.

are also the Pareto efficient output levels. This is one reason why the full-information setting is such a useful benchmark; it allows us to determine the efficient levels of output so that we can determine whether the presence of hidden information leads to inefficient outcomes.

MORAL HAZARD

Now suppose that the firm cannot tell what type a worker is, in which case the firm no longer knows which contract to offer the worker. What would happen if the firm offered the worker a choice between the two contracts we found in the last section? Would the two types of workers take the appropriate contracts, or would something else happen?

This is a fairly easy question to answer: Something else would happen. Look back at Table 7.1. Both contracts have the same piece rate, but the contract designed for low-productivity workers has a higher salary. So, both types of workers prefer the low-productivity contract.

Because that was too easy and did not induce workers to choose the appropriate contracts, let us try something else. Suppose that the firm offers workers the following choice. Either (1) produce 3 units or less of output and be paid a piece rate of 12 and a salary of –18, or (2) produce more than 3 units of output and be paid a piece rate of 12 and a salary of –36. Now the only choice for the workers is how much to produce.

The low-productivity workers satisfy their marginal condition by producing 3 units of output, and their participation constraint is satisfied, so they will produce 3 units of output. Figuring the output of the high-productivity workers takes a bit more work. First, if they produce more than 3 units, then they should produce 6 because that is where the marginal condition is satisfied. If they produce 6 units of output, then from Table 7.1 we know that their net benefit is zero. What if they produce 3 units of output? They get paid $-18 + 12 \cdot 3 = 18$, but their effort costs are given by $C_H(3) = 3^2 = 9$. Their net benefit is the pay minus the effort cost, or 9. This is better than the zero net benefit they get from producing 6 units of output, so the high-productivity workers produce 3. But this is the same as the output of the low-productivity workers. What we find is that high-productivity workers benefit from mimicking the low-productivity workers.

This pattern in which the high-productivity types mimic the low-productivity types is known as **moral hazard**. Moral hazard occurs here because the high-productivity workers benefit from pretending to be low-productivity workers. Even though they produce fewer units than they otherwise would, they can exploit their cost advantages to generate greater net benefit.

Low-productivity workers are no better or worse off than they were in the full information setting, but high-productivity workers gain and the firm loses. High productivity workers get a net benefit of 9, as

TABLE 7.2 Hidden Information Setting		
	High-Productivity	*Low-Productivity*
Output	3	3
Pay	18	18
Net benefit	9	0
Profit	18	18
Expected profit:	18	

Contract: $-18 + 12q$ for up to 3 units of output, $-36 + 12q$ for more than 3 units of output.

opposed to a net benefit of zero in the full information setting. The firm still earns a profit of 18 when it employs a low-productivity worker, but because high-productivity workers mimic the low-productivity workers, the firm also earns a profit of 18 from employing a high-productivity worker. Compare this to the full-information case, in which a high-productivity worker generated a profit of 36. The firm's expected profit is now 18. This is summarized in Table 7.2.

Moral hazard also leads to a loss of efficiency. Comparing Table 7.2 to Table 7.1, we see that the low-productivity workers still produce the efficient level of output, but the high-productivity workers produce less.

THE OPTIMAL CONTRACT FOR THE HIDDEN INFORMATION SETTING

Because of moral hazard, the high-productivity workers have an incentive to imitate the low-productivity workers, which reduces the firm's expected profit. The firm can counter this effect in two ways, both of which involve making imitating the low-productivity workers less attractive. First, it could pay the low-productivity workers less, so that imitation does not generate as much net benefit. Second, it could pay high-productivity workers more for producing more, so that the opportunity cost of imitation is higher. In this section we will construct the optimal contract for the firm, and we will find that it has both of these features.

Let us start with a general contract. The firm sets five numbers:

s_L = salary for low-productivity contract
s_H = salary for high-productivity contract
b_L = piece rate for low-productivity contract
b_H = piece rate for high-productivity contract
$\bar{q}$ = output level that determines which contract is in effect

Workers who produce $\bar{q}$ or fewer units of output are governed by the low-productivity contract with salary s_L and piece rate b_L, but those who produce more than $\bar{q}$ units of output are governed by the high-productivity contract.

The contract only makes sense if both parts of it are used, that is, if the high-productivity workers produce $q_H > \bar{q}$ and the low-productivity workers produce $q_L \leq \bar{q}$. This leads to our first constraint. The low-productivity workers must be willing to produce q_L, which means that their participation constraint must be satisfied:

$$s_L + b_L q_L - 2q_L^{\,2} \geq 0$$

We want the high-productivity workers to produce $q_H > \bar{q}$. To do so, they must be better off producing q_H than producing q_L. Economists call this condition an **incentive compatibility constraint** because it says that the high-productivity types must have an incentive not to imitate the low-productivity types:

$$s_H + b_H q_H - q_H^{\,2} \geq s_L + b_L q_L - q_L^{\,2}$$

The left-hand side of the expression is the high-productivity worker's net benefit from producing q_H, and the right-hand side is the high-productivity worker's net benefit from producing q_L, the low-productivity worker's output. The expression states that producing q_H must generate at least as much net benefit as producing q_L.

When the firm maximizes profit, it gives as little of the surplus as possible to the workers. This means that it should pay low-productivity workers no more than it has to in order to just satisfy their participation constraint, and so it must hold with equality. Also, the firm should pay high-productivity workers no more than is necessary to just satisfy their incentive compatibility constraint, so it must also hold with equality. Letting LP denote the low-productivity worker's participation constraint and HIC denote the high-productivity worker's incentive compatibility constraint, we have:

LP: $\qquad\qquad s_L + b_L q_L - 2q_L^{\,2} = 0$

HIC: $\qquad\qquad s_H + b_H q_H - q_H^{\,2} = s_L + b_L q_L - q_L^{\,2}$

Now that they hold with equality, the LP and HIC constraints make it possible to write the firm's profit function. If the firm faces a low-productivity worker, its profit is

$$\pi_L = 12q_L - (s_L + b_L q_L)$$

because the firm earns net revenue of 12 for every unit produced and it pays the low-productivity worker $s_L + b_L q_L$. Rearranging the LP constraint yields

$$s_L + b_L q_L = 2q_L^{\,2} \qquad\qquad (7.3)$$

Substituting this into the expression for profit yields

$$\pi_L = 12q_L - 2q_L^2$$

When the firm faces a high-productivity worker, its profit is

$$\pi_H = 12q_H - (s_H + b_H q_H)$$

Rearranging the HIC constraint gives us

$$s_H + b_H q_H = s_L + b_L q_L - q_L^2 + q_H^2$$

Substituting in (7.3) from the LP constraint allows us to further simplify this to

$$\begin{aligned} s_H + b_H q_H &= s_L + b_L q_L - q_L^2 + q_H^2 \\ &= 2q_L^2 - q_L^2 + q_H^2 \\ &= q_L^2 + q_H^2 \end{aligned} \tag{7.4}$$

Now substitute this into the expression for profit to get

$$\pi_H = 12q_H - q_L^2 - q_H^2$$

The next step is to find the profit-maximizing levels of q_L and q_H. First, though, because the firm cannot tell which type of worker it faces, we must find expected profit. When the firm employs a worker, it is equally likely to get a low-productivity worker who generates profit π_L and a high-productivity worker who generates profit π_H. Expected profit is then given by

$$\begin{aligned} \pi &= \tfrac{1}{2}H\pi_L + \tfrac{1}{2}\pi_H \\ &= \tfrac{1}{2}(12q_L - 2q_L^2) + \tfrac{1}{2}(12q_H - q_L^2 - q_H^2) \\ &= \tfrac{1}{2}(12q_L - 3q_L^2) + \tfrac{1}{2}(12q_H - q_H^2) \end{aligned}$$

where the last line comes from rearranging the second line.

The firm chooses q_L and q_H to maximize expected profit. The marginal condition for q_L (see footnote 1) comes from taking the marginal expected profit with respect to q_L and setting it equal to zero:

$$\tfrac{1}{2}(12 - 6q_L) = 0$$

Solving for q_L yields $q_L = 2$. Now do the same for q_H, and the marginal condition is

$$\tfrac{1}{2}(12 - 2q_H) = 0$$

The optimal output for the high-productivity worker is $q_H = 6$.

This involves a lot of math, but it gives us something to talk about. In the full information setting we found that the high-productivity workers produce 6 units and the low-productivity workers produce 3, and these were the efficient levels of output. In the hidden information setting the high-productivity workers still produce 6, but the low productivity workers only produce 2. The high-productivity workers still produce the efficient level of output, but the low-productivity workers produce less. Why do we lose efficiency in the hidden information setting?

The answer requires thinking about moral hazard. The natural tendency is for the high-productivity workers to mimic the low-productivity ones in order to exploit their cost advantages. When the low-productivity workers produce 3, as in the full information case, they have an effort cost of 18. When high-productivity workers produce 3, their effort costs are only 9, allowing them to earn a net benefit of $18 - 9 = 9$. But, when low-productivity workers produce only 2 , their cost is 8, and when high-productivity workers produce 2, their cost is 4. Thus, when low-productivity workers produce only 2 the high-productivity workers are only able to earn a net benefit of $8 - 4 = 4$. By getting the low-productivity workers to produce only 2 units of output, the firm makes imitation a less-attractive alternative for the high-productivity workers.

Now let us find the details of the compensation package. To find the piece rates, remember that workers choose their output so as to equate marginal cost with the piece rate. The marginal cost function for high-productivity workers is $MC_H(q) = 2q$, so when they produce 6 units of output their marginal cost is $2 \times 6 = 12$, and this must be the piece rate b_H. The marginal cost function for low-productivity workers is $MC_L(q) = 4q$. When they produce 2 units of output their marginal cost is $4 \times 2 = 8$, and this is the piece rate b_L.

The low-productivity workers' salary is determined by their participation constraint, LP. Rearranging yields

$$s_L = 2q_L{}^2 - b_Lq_L = 2 \cdot 2^2 - 8 \cdot 2 = -8$$

after plugging in the values we have already found, $b_L = 8$ and $q_L = 2$. The high-productivity worker's salary is determined by his incentive compatibility constraint, HIC. Rearranging (7.4) yields

$$s_H = q_L{}^2 + q_H{}^2 - b_Hq_H = 2^2 + 6^2 - 12 \cdot 6 = -32$$

after substituting the known values $q_L = 2$, $q_H = 6$, and $b_H = 12$.

We can complete our calculations by computing the workers' net benefits and the firm's expected profit. The low-productivity workers get

$$NB_L = s_L + b_Lq_L - C_L(q_L) = -8 + 8 \cdot 2 - 2 \cdot 2^2 = 0$$

and the high productivity workers get

$$NB_H = s_H + b_Hq_H - C_H(q_H) = -32 + 12 \cdot 6 - 6^2 = 4$$

	High-Productivity	Low-Productivity
TABLE 7.3 Optimal Contract with Hidden Information		
Output	6	2
Pay	40	8
Net benefit	4	0
Profit	32	16
Expected profit:	24	

Contract: $-8 + 8q$ for up to 2 units of output, $-32 + 12q$ for more than 2 units of output.

Finally, the firm's expected profit is given by

$$\pi = \frac{1}{2}(12q_L - 3q_L^2) + \frac{1}{2}(12q_H - q_H^2)$$
$$= \frac{1}{2}(12 \cdot 2 - 3 \cdot 2^2) + \frac{1}{2}(12 \cdot 6 - 6^2)$$
$$= 24$$

The firm does worse than in the full-information case but better than it did when it offered the contract in Table 7.2.

We can now fully specify the optimal contract. The firm pays a salary of –8 and a piece rate of 8 if the worker produces no more than 2 units of output, and it pays a salary of –32 and a piece rate of 12 if the worker produces more than 2 units of output. The results are summarized in Table 7.3.

Table 7.3 reveals several important pieces of information. First, the high-productivity workers produce the efficient level of output, but the low-productivity workers do not. The reason that the low-productivity workers produce less than in the full information case is that the firm lowers the piece rate in order to diminish the incentive for high-productivity workers to imitate low-productivity workers.

Second, the low-productivity workers earn zero net benefit, as usual, but the high-productivity workers earn positive net benefit. The net benefit of 4 that the high-productivity workers earn is exactly the same as what they would earn if they imitated the low-productivity workers and produced only 2 units of output. The firm must give the high-productivity workers at least this much net benefit to keep them from imitating the low-productivity workers. The source of this positive net benefit for high-productivity workers is the information that they have and the firm wants; if the firm knew that they were high-productivity workers, it could offer them separate contracts and extract all of the net benefit, as it did in the full-information case. The net benefit of 4 that the high-productivity workers earn is their payment for revealing their information, and is known as an **information rent**.

Third, the firm's expected profit is higher than it was in Table 7.2 but lower than in Table 7.1. The firm does not do as well as in the full information setting for two reasons: The low-productivity workers do not produce as much as in the full information case (2 units instead of 3), and the high-productivity workers extract information rents. The firm does do better than in Table 7.2, however, because it offers a contract that induces the high-productivity types to produce more than the low-productivity types.

GENERAL LESSONS

Although it was highly mathematical, the analysis in this section yields some important information.

1. *If the firm can tell the different types of workers apart, it can offer them different compensation schemes.* The firm sets a high piece rate to both types of workers but a low salary for the high-productivity workers and a high salary for the low-productivity workers. Because their costs are lower, high-productivity workers ultimately produce more than low-productivity workers. Both types get zero net benefit, however.

2. *If the firm can tell the different types of workers apart, it can induce them to produce the efficient levels of output.* Full information leads to a Pareto efficient allocation. Also, because the workers receive zero net benefit, the firm's profit is as high as possible in the full information case.

3. *If the firm cannot tell the different types of workers apart, high-productivity workers have an incentive to imitate low-productivity workers.* This is moral hazard, and it reduces the firm's profit. High-productivity workers enjoy a cost advantage over the low-productivity workers, and they can exploit this advantage by mimicking the low-productivity workers.

4. *If the firm cannot tell the different types of workers apart, it should offer a menu of compensation schemes to the workers.* The menu of compensation schemes should state how much the worker will be paid for different output ranges, with higher salary and a lower piece rate for low output levels and a lower salary and a higher piece rate for high output levels. If the firm constructs the menu of compensation schemes correctly, the high-productivity workers will produce more and be paid more than the low-productivity workers, thereby solving the moral hazard problem.

5. *If the firm cannot tell the different types of workers apart, low-productivity workers will produce less than the efficient level of output and earn zero net benefit.* The firm sets a lower piece rate than in the full information setting, and because their incentives are reduced, low-productivity workers produce less than in the full information setting. The firm is still able to extract all of the surplus, however.

6. *If the firm cannot tell the different types of workers apart, high-productivity workers produce the efficient level of output but earn positive net benefit.* High-productivity workers must be compensated for not imitating low-productivity workers, which leads them to earn positive net benefit. This positive net benefit is a result of the high-productivity types having information that the firm would like to extract and is called an information rent.

At the beginning of this chapter we posed two questions. If the firm cannot tell which type of worker is which, how should it set the piece rates to motivate both types? And which fares better, the high-productivity worker or the low-productivity worker? We now know the answers. Regarding the first question, the firm uses the same piece rate for the high-productivity workers as it would use if it knew the workers' types, but it must set a lower piece rate for the low-productivity workers. Regarding the second question, the high-productivity workers definitely fare better because they earn information rents.

Homework Problems

For the following problems assume that a high-productivity worker has cost function $C_H(q) = q^2$ and marginal cost function $MC_H(q) = 2q$ and a low-productivity worker has cost function $C_L(q) = 3q^2$ and marginal cost function $MC_L(q) = 6q$. The two types are equally likely, and both types of worker have reservation utility of zero. The firm earns net revenue of 60 for each unit of output produced by the workers.

1. Find the optimal contract for the two types of workers in the full information setting.
2. Now consider the hidden information setting. Write the low-productivity worker's participation constraint and the high-productivity worker's incentive compatibility constraint using the notation from the section on the optimal contract for the hidden information setting.
3. Write the profit the firm receives from both types of workers.
4. Use the low-productivity worker's participation constraint to write π_L as a function of q_L.
5. Use the low-productivity worker's participation constraint and the high-productivity worker's incentive compatibility constraint to write π_H as a function of q_H and q_L.
6. Write the firm's expected profit as a function of q_H and q_L.
7. Find the optimal output levels for the two types of workers in the hidden information setting.
8. Find the optimal piece rates for the two types of workers in the hidden information setting.
9. Find the optimal salary levels for the two types of workers in the hidden information setting.
10. Find the high-productivity worker's information rent.

CHAPTER

8 | GAME THEORY

S o far in this book we have explored (thoroughly) the use of piece rate systems to motivate workers. Piece rates are not the only way to induce workers to exert effort, however, and we will examine two others in the next two chapters. In Chapter 9 we look at a situation in which workers compete with each other for raises or bonuses, and in Chapter 10 we look at a situation in which the firm and the worker cooperate with each other to increase the surplus from the employment relationship. The work on piece rates relied primarily on marginal analysis, but that standard tool is insufficient for studying the new problems. This chapter provides the necessary new tool.

Game theory is the study of strategic interactions between small numbers of actors. In the case of workers competing with each other for a raise, the actors are the individual workers, and they must determine how hard to work so that they can outperform their rivals. In the case of a worker and a firm cooperating to increase the surplus, the actors are the worker and the firm, and they must ascertain a way of cooperating without allowing the other party to take advantage of them.

The purpose of this chapter is to develop a tool that is used later in the book. In this book we use three types of games, and because the different games call for different techniques, the chapter is organized around those three types of games.

WHAT IS A GAME?

In the language of economics, a **game** is a situation in which two or more parties interact to jointly determine their payoffs. This definition includes several terms, but the one that distinguishes games from other types of economic interactions is the last, jointly-determined payoffs. To see how games differ from other situations, it is helpful first to look at a situation that is not a game.

Think about a firm in a perfectly competitive industry. The assumptions of perfect competition say that each firm in the industry is so small that it has no effect on the market price. A firm's payoff is its profit, which is the market price times the amount it produces, less production costs. Because no single firm can impact the market price, no firm can have any impact on any other firm's profit. Because payoffs are not jointly determined, we do not consider perfect competition to be a game.

Contrast this with a duopoly, which is a market with only two firms. Each firm is large enough to affect the market price, and the more a firm produces, the lower the market price is. More to the point, if firm A increases its output, the market price falls, making firm B's output less valuable and causing its profit to fall. Here firm A's choice impacts firm B's payoff, so this is considered a game. Payoffs are jointly determined.

In fact, the piece rate scheme in Chapter 5 is the solution to a game. In that game the firm sets the worker's salary and piece rate, which, of course, have an impact on the worker's payoff. The worker decides how much to produce, which has an impact on the firm's payoff. The payoffs are jointly determined, and we have been analyzing games for the last four chapters. They were particularly simple games, however, and solving them did not require any unusual techniques. The games in the next two chapters are different and require some new techniques to solve.

Returning to the definition of a game, the different parties in a game are called players; they could be individual people, groups of people, individual firms, government organizations, or any other entity that makes decisions. In this book, payoffs are monetary, providing additional profit to a firm or additional utility to a worker. The choices players can make are called **strategies**. The payoffs are determined by the combination of strategies chosen by all of the different players. This is what makes game theory different from other areas of economics. When one player changes his strategy, the payoffs change for all of the players, not just the one who changes his strategy. The purpose of game theory is finding a **solution** to a game, that is, a prediction of what strategies the different players will choose.

Before we can solve a game, we must first identify the players, their strategies, and how those strategies determine the payoffs. The best way to do this depends on the particulars of the game being studied. In some games players make their choices at the same time, such as when the offense and defense in a football game must choose their plays before they know what their opponents are going to do. In other games players make their choices sequentially, so that the second mover gets to see what the first mover did before making a choice. The piece rate game had this feature, with the firm moving first, setting the salary and piece rate, and the worker moving second after learning the compensation scheme. Some games give players only a small set of options, such as when two parties have the choice of either cooperating with each other or not. Other games give players a wide range of choices, such as in a duopoly when a firm can choose any level of output.

The next section expands on what we mean by a solution to a game. The remainder of the chapter is divided into three sections. We first study simultaneous games in which players have only a small number of strategies from which they can choose. We then move on to simultaneous games with a large number of possible strategies, and we conclude with the study of sequential games. Each game has a different way of relating payoffs to strategies, and each has a different method for finding a solution.

THE CONCEPT OF EQUILIBRIUM

One "solves" a game by making a prediction about which strategies the players will choose. But how exactly does one do this? There must be some basis for making the prediction. To find such a basis, let us look at another area of economics in which interactions occur, namely the market.

In a market economy, consumers observe the prices of goods and determine the quantities of the goods that they would like to buy. At the same time, producers observe the prices and determine the quantities of the goods that they would like to sell. The market for a particular good is in equilibrium if the quantity demanded by consumers exactly equals the quantity supplied by producers, and the equilibrium price is the price that makes quantity demanded equal quantity supplied. This is the entire basis of supply and demand.

Let us look a bit closer at what is meant by an equilibrium here. An **equilibrium** is a situation in which there is no pressure for anything to change. If the market is in equilibrium, all consumers can buy their desired amounts of the good at the market price, so there is no pressure for them to bid up the price so that they can buy more goods. Furthermore, all producers can sell their desired amounts of the good at the market price, so there is no pressure for producers to bid down the price in order to sell more goods. There is no pressure for the price to change, and there is no pressure for consumers and producers to change their behavior in any way. This is what we mean when we say that the market is in equilibrium.

We can use the same concept to solve games. An equilibrium in a game is a situation in which neither player wants to change his strategy. Think about a game with two players. If player 1 does not want to change his strategy, it must be the case that the strategy is a best response to the opponent's strategy. After all, if it were not a best response, player 1 would have an incentive to change his strategy. At the same time, in equilibrium player 2's strategy must be a best response to player 1's strategy; otherwise, player 2 would want to change. In equilibrium, then, both players must choose strategies that are **mutual best responses**; that is, the strategies must be best responses to each other. *An equilibrium of a game is a combination of strategies that are mutual best responses to each other.*

A combination of strategies that have the mutual best response property is called a **Nash equilibrium** of the game. The concept is named after John Nash, the Princeton mathematician who devised it. Nash received a Nobel Prize for the contribution, and he also may be familiar from the book and movie *A Beautiful Mind*.

SIMULTANEOUS GAMES

In this section we look at games in which the players choose between a small number of strategies and must do so all at the same time. Let us begin with an example. There are two players, call them 1 and 2. They each have two choices. Player 1 chooses between A and B, and player 2 chooses between X and Y. If 1 chooses A and 2 chooses X, they both receive payoffs of $20. If 1 chooses B and 2 chooses Y, they both receive $10. If 1 chooses A and 2 chooses Y, player 1 gets $30 and player 2 gets $5. Finally, if 1 chooses B and 2 chooses X, player 1 gets $5 and player 2 gets $30. What will happen in this game?

This is an example of a **simultaneous game**, that is, a game in which the players make their choices at the same time. Because they move at the same time, neither player gets to see what the other player is doing before making his own choice. Later in this chapter we look at games where one player moves first and the other player gets to observe the move before choosing.

The first step in solving the game is to find a simple way to present the information provided. We do this using a **payoff matrix**, as shown in Game 8.1. The game has four possible outcomes corresponding to the four possible combinations of strategies chosen by players 1 and 2, and the numbers in the table are the payoffs to the two players. Player 1 chooses the row of the table and the payoff is the first number in each cell, whereas player 2 chooses the column and the payoff is the second number in each cell. If player 1 chooses A and player 2 chooses Y, the payoffs are found in the first row (corresponding to 1 playing A) and the right column (corresponding to 2 playing Y), in which case player 1 receives a payoff of $30 and player 2 receives a payoff of $5.

GAME 8.1

Player 2

		X	Y
Player 1	A	20, 20	30, 5
	B	5, 30	10, 10

To solve this game we look for a Nash equilibrium, that is, a pair of strategies that are mutual best responses. Given that player 1 can only choose the row and player 2 can only choose the column, finding a Nash equilibrium boils down to two things occurring simultaneously: The row chosen by 1 must be a best response to the column chosen by 2, and the column chosen by 2 must be a best response to the row chosen by 1. We can find the Nash equilibrium of the game using Table 8.1. The first column of the table lists each of player 1's possible strategies. The second column is player 2's best response to each of those strategies. If player 1 plays A, 2 gets 20 for playing X and 5 for playing Y, so X is the best response to A. If 1 plays B, 2 can get 30 from playing X or 10 from playing Y, so X is the best response to B.

The third column of Table 8.1 is player 1's best response to the strategy in the second column. In other words, it is 1's best response to 2's best response. In the first row, when player 1 plays A, player 2's best response is X. Player 1's best response to that is A because when 2 plays X player 1 can get 20 from playing A or 5 from playing B. Playing A generates a higher payoff, so it is the best response. In the second row of Table 8.1, when player 1 plays B, player 2's best response is X. Once again, player 1's best response to X is A.

If the first and last columns of the table match, the strategy combination is a Nash equilibrium. This occurs in the first row of the table. When player 1 plays A, player 2's best response is X, and player 1's best response to that is A. Thus, X is a best response to A, and A is a best response to X. We have a Nash equilibrium in which player 1 plays A, player 2 plays X, and both players receive payoffs of $20.

TABLE 8.1 Best Responses for Game 8.1

Strategy Played by Player 1	*Player 2's Best Response*	*Player 1's Best Response*
A	X	A
B	X	A

Notice that there is not a Nash equilibrium when player 1 plays B. The best response to B is X, but the best response to X is A, so B and X are not mutual best responses.

Now look back at the original game. Is there any way to tell that the combination of A and X is a Nash equilibrium? Recall that in a Nash equilibrium neither player wants to change strategy given what the other player is doing. When player 2 plays X, player 1 does not want to change from playing A to playing B because his payoff is 20 when he plays A but only 5 when he plays B. When player 1 plays A, player 2 does not want to change from playing X to playing Y because X pays 20 but Y only pays 5. Thus, we really do have an equilibrium.

The combination of B and Y is not a Nash equilibrium. If player 2 plays Y, player 1 would like to change from playing B to playing A because A pays 30 but B pays only 10. This is enough to tell that the combination of B and Y does not constitute a Nash equilibrium because one of the players wants to change. It turns out that player 2 would also want to change from Y to X because when player 1 plays B, playing X pays 30 whereas playing Y pays only 10.

Game 8.2 is more complicated. The two players are named Row and Column. Row can choose among the three strategies A, B, and C, and Column can choose among the strategies X, Y, and Z. Just as before, when choosing a strategy Row chooses the row that determines the payoffs, and Column chooses the column that determines the payoffs. The payoff matrix shows the payoffs that correspond to the nine possible strategy combinations, with the first number in each pair representing Row's payoff and the second number representing Column's payoff. So, for example, if Row plays B and Column plays X, Row's payoff is 7 and Column's payoff is 0.

GAME 8.2

Column

		X	Y	Z
	A	12, 12	6, 14	19, 8
Row	B	7, 0	13, 2	6, 6
	C	15, 6	8, 2	4, 4

Once again we wish to find a Nash equilibrium. The best responses are shown in Table 8.2. Notice from the table that X is a best response to C and that C is a best response to X, so that there is a Nash equilibrium in which Row plays C and Column plays X. In equilibrium Row receives a payoff of 15 whereas Column receives a payoff of 6.

TABLE 8.2   Best Responses for Game 8.2

Strategy Played by Row	Column's Best Response	Row's Best Response
A	Y	B
B	Z	A
C	X	C

The Nash equilibrium in this game is not Pareto efficient. Remember that an allocation is Pareto efficient if there is no other allocation that makes one party better off and no one worse off. In the Nash equilibrium, Row receives a payoff of 15 and Column receives 6, but if Row plays A and Column plays Z, Row gets 19 and Column gets 8. Both players would be better off than they are in equilibrium, and so the equilibrium is not Pareto efficient. Why cannot the two players get the higher payoffs? If Row plays A, Column's best response is Y, not Z, so if Row played the strategy that leads to the higher payoffs, Column would play Y and Row would receive only 6.

A game can have more than one Nash equilibrium. Look at Game 8.3. The best responses are given in Table 8.3. According to the table, all three of Row's strategies lead to Nash equilibria. When Row plays A, Column's best response is Z, and Row's best response to that is A. A and Z are mutual best responses, so they constitute a Nash equilibrium. B and X are also mutual best responses, as are C and Y, so there are three Nash equilibria.

GAME 8.3

		Column		
		X	Y	Z
Row	A	5, −1	4, 1	10, 2
	B	8, 14	2, 10	9, 9
	C	7, 1	6, 3	8, 2

TABLE 8.3   Best Responses for Game 8.3

Strategy Played by Row	Column's Best Response	Row's Best Response
A	Z	A
B	X	B
C	Y	C

In Game 8.3 it is difficult to predict exactly what will actually happen because there is more than one Nash equilibrium. Any of the Nash equilibria could occur. Still, the analysis provides some information. The game has nine possible outcomes corresponding to the nine different cells of the payoff matrix, and the analysis points to only three of them as solutions. In these three cells the players would be satisfied with their performance and would not want to change from their chosen strategies if they were given the opportunity. Of course, some of the Nash equilibria pay better than others. Row likes best the equilibrium in which Row plays A and Column plays Z, while Column most likes the one in which Row plays B and Column plays X. Our theory does not tell us how to decide between equilibria, but it does tell us that equilibrium strategy combinations are the ones on which to focus.

Application: Assigning Duties in a Team

Now that we have seen how to solve games, the next step is to show that games can be useful. To do this, consider the following problem. A firm has two workers and two tasks that need to be performed. One of the tasks is more valuable to the firm than the other, but rather than paying more to the worker who performs that task, the firm pays both workers the same amount conditional on both tasks being completed. The effort costs are as follows. It costs worker 1 $40 to complete task A and $20 to complete task B. It costs worker 2 $30 to complete task A and $15 to complete task B. If both tasks are completed, the firm pays each worker $35. Each worker can complete only one task. Each can also choose to do nothing at all. What will the workers do?

We can present the information from the above paragraph in a payoff matrix, as in Game 8.4. If both workers perform task A, task B is left uncompleted, and the firm pays them nothing. Even so, worker 1 exerts $40 in effort and worker 2 exerts $30, so they lose those amounts. If both workers perform task B, ignoring task A, they again are paid nothing; worker 1 loses $20 in effort costs, and worker 2 loses $15. If worker 1 performs task A and worker 2 performs task B, the firm pays them both $35. Worker 1's payoff is then $35 – 40 = –$5 and worker 2's payoff is $35 – 15 = $20. If worker 1 performs task B and worker 1 performs task A, worker 1's payoff is $35 – 20 = $15 and worker 2's is $35 – 30 = $5.

If one worker does nothing, neither worker gets paid, and the worker who does nothing gets $0. If one worker completes a task but the other worker does nothing, the worker who completes a task loses the effort costs.

GAME 8.4

Column

		A	B	Nothing
	A	$-40, -30$	$-5, 20$	$-40, 0$
Row	B	$15, 5$	$-20, -15$	$-20, 0$
	Nothing	$0, -30$	$0, -15$	$0, 0$

We want to find the Nash equilibria of the game. There are two of them. If worker 1 performs task B, worker 2's best response is to perform task A, and worker 1's best response to that is to perform task B. Worker 1's performing task B and worker 2's performing task A are mutual best responses, so they constitute a Nash equilibrium. If worker 1 does nothing, worker 2's best response is also to do nothing, and worker 1's best response to that is to do nothing. Thus, there is also a Nash equilibrium in which both workers do nothing.

There is no Nash equilibrium in which worker 1 performs task A. If worker 1 performs task A, worker 2's best response is to perform task B, but worker 1's best response to that is to do nothing. Worker 1's performing task A and worker 2's performing task B are not mutual best responses, so worker 1 cannot perform task A in equilibrium. The reason for this is that by performing task A worker 1 fails to satisfy his participation constraint because doing nothing pays better.

The only equilibrium in which workers work occurs when worker 1 performs task B and worker 2 performs task A. Worker 2 has an absolute advantage in both tasks, being able to perform task A for $10 less than worker 1 could and task B for $5 less than worker 1. Worker 1 has a comparative advantage in task A and performs that task. So the prediction of the game is that worker 2 performs the task that affords a comparative advantage.

Lessons about Simultaneous Games
This section has led to several general lessons.

1. *Nash equilibrium consists of a combination of strategies that are best responses to each other.* We use the concept of Nash equilibrium to solve games, and it is the condition that neither player wants to change his strategy given what his opponent is doing. It is

important to remember that a Nash equilibrium is a combination of *strategies*, not a combination of payoffs. It is entirely possible that two different strategy combinations can lead to the same payoffs, so when solving a game we specify strategies, not payoffs.

2. *The Nash equilibrium may or may not be Pareto efficient.* The Nash equilibrium was Pareto efficient in Game 8.1 but not in Game 8.2. This means that one cannot find the Nash equilibrium by finding the cell in the payoff matrix with the highest payoffs because Nash equilibria may not be Pareto efficient.

3. *There may be more than one Nash equilibrium.* An example is provided by Game 8.3. Because there can be more than one Nash equilibrium, one cannot stop looking after finding a single Nash equilibrium. Instead, one must check all of the possibilities.

SIMULTANEOUS GAMES WITH INFINITELY MANY POSSIBLE STRATEGIES

In Chapter 9 we will analyze a game in which workers compete against each other by exerting effort, and the one who exerts the most effort wins a prize, such as a raise, a bonus, or a promotion. Workers do not just have a few effort levels from which to choose, however. They can choose any amount of effort they want, which means that they have an infinite number of possible strategies. Having so many possible strategies requires us to find a slightly different way of finding Nash equilibria.

To see why this is so, think about how we solved games in the previous section. For each of player 1's strategies, we first found player 2's best response, and then we found player 1's best response to that. We found a Nash equilibrium whenever player 1's best response matched the original strategy. This approach was possible because player 1 had only two or three possible strategies from which to choose, so it did not take too many steps to find the Nash equilibria. When player 1 has an infinite number of strategies, though, using this method would take an infinite number of steps. We need a way to streamline the process.

There are other areas of economics in which variables can take infinite numbers of values. One example is supply and demand analysis. The supply function tells how much output firms produce at each price level, the demand function tells how much consumers want to buy at each price level. The equilibrium price level is the one at which quantity demanded equals quantity supplied. In supply and demand analysis, however, we do not make infinitely long tables of how much firms want to produce and how much consumers want to consume at each price level and then search the table for where the two quantities are equal. Instead, we graph the supply and demand *functions* and look for their intersection. We will use a similar approach here.

A strategy combination is a Nash equilibrium if player 1's strategy is a best response to player 2's and, at the same time, player 2's strategy is a best response to player 1's. We can find the Nash equilibria by identifying **best-response functions**, which report a player's best responses to each of the opponent's possible strategies. We can then graph the best-response functions, and wherever the two players' best-response functions intersect we have a Nash equilibrium.

The best way to see how this works is through an example. The one we use here is a very common problem in economics but is not taken from personnel economics. Instead, it is the problem of identifying how much output is produced by a duopoly and is taken from the field of industrial organization.

Application: Output in a Duopoly

Consider a market with two firms. Firm 1 chooses output q_1 to maximize its profit, and firm 2 simultaneously chooses output q_2 to maximize its profit. Total industry output is $Q = q_1 + q_2$. Market demand is given by the function $Q = 120 - p$, where p is the market price. Both firms can produce as much as they want to at zero cost, an assumption we make in order to simplify the problem. How much does each firm produce?

To answer this question we take the following steps. First, we write each firm's profit as a function of its own and its rival's output. Next we find how much output each firm produces as a function of how much its rival produces. These are the firms' best-response functions. Finally, we use the best-response functions to find the Nash equilibrium.

Because demand is given by $Q = 120 - p$, the market price is given by $p = 120 - Q = 120 - (q_1 + q_2)$. As usual, firm 1's profit is revenue minus cost, or

$$\pi_1 = pq_1 - c(q_1)$$

Because costs are zero, this simplifies to

$$\pi_1 = (120 - q_1 - q_2)q_1$$

which can be multiplied out to get

$$\pi_1 = 120q_1 - q_1^2 - q_1q_2$$

The next step is to find the value of q_1 that maximizes π_1. We can do this in two ways. One is by using calculus. Differentiate π_1 with respect to q_1 and set it equal to zero. This yields

$$120 - 2q_1 - q_2 = 0$$

Now solve the above equation for q_1 to get

$$q_1 = 60 - q_2/2$$

This is firm 1's best-response function, and it identifies the profit-maximizing level of q_1 for each possible value of q_2.

Calculus is only one way to attain the best-response function. The other way is to use monopoly theory, and it is a more graphical approach. The demand curve faced by firm 1 is $q_1 = 120 - q_2 - p$. Rewrite this with p on the left-hand side of the equation so that it is easier to graph:

$$p = 120 - q_2 - q_1$$

Now graph the demand curve for firm 1, as in Figure 8.1. This is a **residual demand curve** because it shows how much demand is left over for firm 1 after firm 2 sells q_2 units. Monopoly theory tells us that the firm's marginal revenue curve can be derived from its demand curve by drawing a line through the same vertical intercept but with twice the slope, as in the figure. Double the slope by doubling the coefficient on q_1, and the equation for the marginal revenue curve is

$$MR_1 = 120 - q_2 - 2q_1$$

The firm maximizes profit by producing where marginal revenue equals marginal cost. Because marginal cost is zero, by assumption, firm 1 maximizes profit by producing the level of q_1 that satisfies

$$120 - q_2 - 2q_1 = 0$$

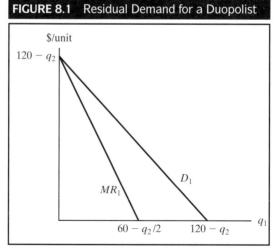

FIGURE 8.1   Residual Demand for a Duopolist

When firm 2 produces q_2, firm 1's residual demand curve is D_1. Its marginal revenue curve, MR_1, has the same intercept but is twice as steep. Firm 1's marginal cost curve coincides with the horizontal axis because its costs are zero, and its profit maximizing output level is where the marginal revenue curve crosses the horizontal axis.

or

$$q_1 = 60 - q_2/2$$

This approach leads us to the same best-response function for firm 1.

We can go through the same steps to find firm 2's best-response function. Firm 2's profit function is

$$\pi_2 = (120 - q_1 - q_2)q_2 = 120q_2 - q_2^2 - q_1q_2$$

which is just like firm 1's profit function but with the 1s and the 2s switched. Firm 2's best-response function is also just like firm 1's but with the 1s and the 2s switched:

$$q_2 = 60 - q_1/2$$

The final step is to find a Nash equilibrium, that is, a pair of values of q_1 and q_2 such that q_1 is firm 1's best response to q_2, which in turn is firm 2's best response to q_1. In other words, we want to solve the system of equations

$$q_1 = 60 - q_2/2$$
$$q_2 = 60 - q_1/2$$

for q_1 and q_2. To do this, substitute the second equation into the first:

$$q_1 = 60 - \frac{60 - q_1/2}{2}$$

and solve it for q_1 to get

$$q_1 = 60 - 30 + q_1/4$$
$$3q_1/4 = 30$$
$$q_1 = 40$$

In the Nash equilibrium, firm 1 produces 40 units of output. Firm 2's output can be found by plugging $q_1 = 40$ into firm 2's best-response function:

$$q_2 = 60 - q_1/2 = 60 - 40/2 = 40$$

In Nash equilibrium, both firms produce 40.

Figure 8.2 shows what we have done graphically. Firm 1's output is measured on the vertical axis and firm 2's is on the horizontal axis. Firm 1's best-response function is given by $q_1 = 60 - q_2/2$, and it is labeled $R_1(q_2)$ in the figure. Firm 2's best-response function is given by $q_2 = 60 - q_1/2$, and it is labeled $R_2(q_1)$ in the figure. Nash equilibrium requires that the output level chosen by firm 1 is a best response to the output level chosen by firm 2, which means that the Nash equilibrium

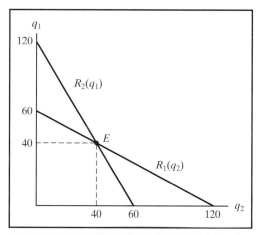

FIGURE 8.2   The Duopolist's Best-Response Curves and Nash Equilibrium

$R_1(q_2)$ is firm 1's best-response curve, showing the optimal response to firm 2's output choice. $R_2(q_1)$ is firm 2's best-response curve, showing the optimal response to firm 1's output choice. They intersect at point E, where both firms are responding optimally to each other's output choices, which makes E a Nash equilibrium.

must lie somewhere on $R_1(q_2)$, firm 1's best-response curve. It also requires that firm 2 best-respond to firm 1, which means that the Nash equilibrium must also lie on $R_2(q_1)$, firm 2's best-response curve. Consequently, the Nash equilibrium is found where the two best-response curves meet, and it is point E in the figure.

SEQUENTIAL GAMES

Consider the following game. A small town has a single auto repair shop, and because it has a monopoly in the town, it charges high prices and earns monopoly profit. Another mechanic is considering moving to the town and opening a competing auto repair shop. If the mechanic does move in, the original repair shop has two choices: either it can cut its prices a little, consistent with being in a duopoly, or it can cut its prices a lot, starting a price war and hoping to drive the newcomer out of business. Let us make the payoffs concrete. If the newcomer stays away from the town, the original firm earns $100,000 and the newcomer earns nothing. If the newcomer opens a new shop and the original firm decides to coexist with it as a duopoly, the original firm earns $60,000 and the newcomer earns $30,000. Finally, if the newcomer opens a new shop and the original firm decides to start a price war, the original firm earns $10,000 and the newcomer loses $20,000. What will happen in the game? In particular, is the threat of a price war enough to keep the newcomer away?

The first step in answering these questions is to find a better way to represent all of the information in the preceding paragraph. For simultaneous games we used a payoff matrix, but payoff matrices miss an important piece of information, namely who moves first and who moves second. In the game we are considering now, the newcomer moves first, deciding whether to open a new shop. The original firm moves second, deciding whether to behave as a duopoly or start a price war. The purpose of the payoff matrix was to show the choices available to the players and the payoffs that ensue from the different strategy combinations. For sequential games we want to present all of this information plus the order of moves.

We can do this with a **game tree**, as shown in Figure 8.3. The straight lines on the tree are called branches, and the points where they connect are called nodes. At the top node the first mover, in this case the newcomer, gets to move. The newcomer can either choose the left branch and stay out of the market or choose the right branch and open a new shop. If the newcomer stays out of the market the game is over because there is nothing left for the original firm to do. If the newcomer opens a shop, however, the original firm gets to make a decision at the node at the end of the first branch on the right. The

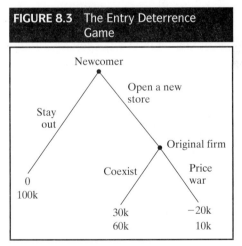

FIGURE 8.3 The Entry Deterrence Game

Newcomer

Open a new store

Stay out

0
100k

Coexist

Original firm

Price war

30k
60k

−20k
10k

A newcomer moves first, deciding whether to open a new store. If the newcomer opens a new store, the original firm can either coexist with him as a duopoly or start a price war. The top payoff at the end of each branch is for the first-mover, in this case the newcomer, and the bottom payoff is for the second-mover, the original firm.

original firm can either choose the left branch and coexist as a duopoly, or it can choose the right branch and start a price war. The payoffs are at the end of each set of branches, with the payoff to the first-mover on top and the payoff to the second-mover below. In this case, the newcomer's payoff is on top, and the original firm's payoff is on the bottom.

Following the branches, we see that by staying out the newcomer gets a payoff of zero and the original firm gets $100,000. If the newcomer opens a new shop and the original firm chooses to coexist as a duopoly, the newcomer makes $30,000 and the original firm makes $60,000. If the newcomer enters and the original firm starts a price war, the newcomer loses $20,000 and the original firm makes $10,000.

We solve sequential games using a concept that is a bit different from Nash equilibrium, and we arrive at it through the process of **backward induction**. Backward induction means that we begin our analysis of the game at the last nodes of the game tree and then work our way back toward the beginning. In Figure 8.3, the last node is the one where the newcomer has already opened a new shop and the original firm must decide whether to coexist or start a price war. If it coexists it earns $60,000, but if it starts a price war it only makes $10,000. Clearly it is better to coexist, so this is what the original firm will do if it is given the choice. Now move back to the node at the beginning, where the newcomer must decide whether to open a new shop or stay out of the market. By staying out of the market the newcomer earns $0. By opening a new shop, from what we have just seen, the newcomer knows that the original firm will choose to coexist, in which case the newcomer makes $30,000. $30,000 is better than $0, so the newcomer will choose to open a new shop, and the original firm will choose to coexist as a duopoly.

It turns out that the original firm cannot keep the newcomer away by threatening a price war. To fully understand why, we must look at the players' strategies. *In a sequential game, strategies are complete contingent plans that tell what move the player will make at every node at which the player could possibly make a decision.* In the simple game shown in Figure 8.3, the newcomer has two possible strategies: open a new shop or stay out. The original firm also has two strategies: coexist if the newcomer opens a new shop or start a price war if the newcomer opens a shop. The equilibrium we found through backward induction has the newcomer choosing the strategy to open a new shop and the original firm choosing the strategy to coexist if the newcomer opens a new shop.

The original firm would like to adopt the strategy of starting a price war if the newcomer opens a new shop. The newcomer's best response to that would be to stay out of the market, and the original firm would earn $100,000. There is a problem with that strategy, however. Once the newcomer opens a new shop, the original firm would not want to follow the price-war strategy because doing so would reduce its payoff by $50,000. The newcomer knows this and, therefore, does not believe the original firm when it threatens to start a price war. In other words, the original firm's threat to start a price war is not credible, and backward induction rules out the use of noncredible threats.

Let us move on to another game. This one has two players, a father and his six-year-old son. The father has two tickets to the circus and would like to take his son. There is a problem, however. The son likes to whine, and the father has threatened to cancel the circus trip if the son whines. The game tree and the payoffs are shown in Figure 8.4. The payoffs reflect the order in which the son and the father prefer the various outcomes. The son's favorite outcome is that he gets to whine and he gets to go to the circus anyway; that outcome is given a 4. His least favorite outcome is that he neither whines nor goes to the circus; that outcome is given a 1. He would rather go to the circus than whine, so his payoff is 3 when he does not whine and goes to the circus and 2 when he whines but does not go to the circus. The father's favorite outcome is that the son behaves and they go to the circus; that outcome gets a 4 for the father. His least favorite outcome is that the son whines and they stay home because then he is stuck at home with a whiny child; that outcome is assigned a payoff of 1. He would rather go to the circus with a whining boy than stay home when his son behaves.

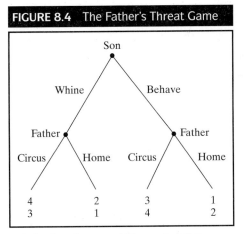

FIGURE 8.4 The Father's Threat Game

A father has threatened his son that if the son whines he will not get to go to the circus. The game tree shows the ensuing possibilities. The son gets to move first, deciding whether to whine. The father must then decide whether to take the son to the circus. The son's payoffs are in the top row, and the father's are in the bottom row. The payoffs reflect the order of preference among the outcomes for the father and son.

What strategies will the two choose? We can find them using backward induction. Begin with the father's decision when the son has already whined. He can either go to the circus for a payoff of 3 or stay home with a payoff of 1, and he would choose to go to the circus if the boy whines. Now look at the father's decision when the son is behaving. He can either go to the circus for a payoff of 4 or stay home for a payoff of 2, and he would rather go to the circus when the child behaves. Thus, the father's strategy is:

Go to the circus if the son whines,

Go to the circus if he behaves.

We can now move to the son's decision at the beginning of the game. If he whines, his father still takes him to the circus, and the son's payoff is 4. If he behaves, his father takes him to the circus, and his payoff is 3. He chooses to whine, and his father still takes him to the circus.

The father wanted to follow the strategy

Stay home if the son whines,

Go to the circus if he behaves.

What is wrong with this strategy? If the father would actually follow this strategy, the son would receive 2 from whining but 3 from behaving, and his best response would be to behave. This is exactly what the father had in mind when he made the threat. But, being an accomplished game theorist, as all children innately are, the son knows that if he whines the father will not follow through with the threat and will still take him to the circus. In other words, the father's threat is non-credible.

In both of the sequential games we have examined so far, the first mover has had an advantage and is able to get the favorite outcome. That is not always the case, as can be seen in the game in Figure 8.5. In the equilibrium of this game, player 2 plays Y if player 1 chooses A, and player 2 plays X if player 1 chooses B. Because of this, if player 1 chooses A the payoff is 1, but if player 1 chooses B the payoff is 3. Player 1 will choose B even though the highest payoff of 4 is only possible from playing A. In this case player 2 threatens to play Y if player 1 plays A, and because that is what player 2 would really do if player 1 actually did play Y, the threat is credible. Player 1 chooses B.

Let us look at one more game, as depicted in Figure 8.6. In this game player 1 moves first, choosing between A and B; then player 2 moves, choosing between L and R; and then player 1 moves again, choosing between X and Y. It is possible to find the equilibrium strategies using

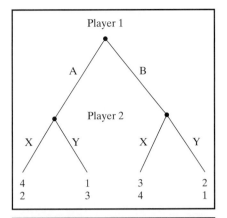

FIGURE 8.5   A Sequential Game
That Player 2 Wins

This is an example of a sequential game in which player 2 gets a higher payoff than player 1 in equilibrium.

backward induction. During the second turn player 1's equilibrium strategy is

X if AL, X if AR, Y if BL, and X if BR

FIGURE 8.6   A More Complicated Sequential Game

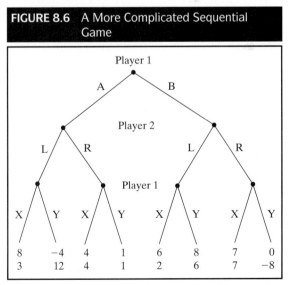

In this game player 1 moves first, choosing either A or B. Player 2 moves second, choosing either L or R. Player 1 then moves again, playing either X or Y.

where X if AL means that player 1 plays X if player 1 first played A and then player 2 played L. Remember that as the first mover, player 1's payoff is on top at the end of each branch. During player 2's turn the equilibrium strategy is

R if A, and R if B

Finally, we move to the beginning of the game, where player 1 plays B. The outcome of the game is that player 1 plays B, player 2 plays R, and player 1 plays X. Player 1's payoff is 7 and player 2's is also 7.

Backward induction is straightforward to use, but it may seem strange that even though player 1 plays B, it is still necessary to specify what player 1 would do after playing A in the first stage. The reason is that we must specify what will happen if player 1 had chosen A in order to see whether playing A or B is the better choice. Remember, a strategy is a complete contingent plan, and it includes specifying what will happen at nodes that are not reached.

Lessons about Sequential Games

Sequential games differ from simultaneous games in that time passes and players have to consider what will happen in the future. Three general rules should be followed when analyzing sequential games.

1. *Sequential games are solved using backward induction.* To solve the games, look at the actions taken by the player moving last. Then work your way back to the beginning of the game, finding the optimal move for each player at each decision node.

2. *In sequential games, strategies are complete contingent plans.* A strategy must say what the player will do at every possible decision node. The best way to think about a strategy is that it is a set of written instructions that the player could hand to someone else who could then serve as a substitute for the player. The strategy handles every possible contingency, even those that the instruction-writer expects not to occur.

   The reason that one needs complete contingent plans is that one needs to be able to check that strategies are equilibria, or best responses to each other. If one does not specify what will happen at every decision node, it will be impossible to tell whether one strategy is better than another.

3. *Threats must be credible.* In sequential games a player can threaten to take a future action that will punish an opponent for making an undesirable choice. In equilibrium, though, the only threats that work are those that are believable. To be credible, a threat must be consistent with the action that the player actually would take at that decision node. If the player making the threat would be

better off by not fulfilling the threat when the time comes, the threat is noncredible.

Backward induction automatically eliminates all noncredible threats. It does this by making each player choose a best response at every decision node, and a player will not choose noncredible threats because they make the player worse off than doing something else.

Homework Problems

1. What is the difference between a strategy in a simultaneous game and a strategy in a sequential game?
2. Find the Nash equilibria of the following games:

		Column		
		X	Y	Z
	A	2, 8	2, 0	2, 2
Row	B	5, 3	3, 4	1, 1
	C	7, 4	0, 8	3, 3

(a)

		Column		
		X	Y	Z
	A	7, 5	4, 2	9, 1
Row	B	6, 2	3, 4	8, 7
	C	1, 6	8, 7	2, 2

(b)

		Column		
		X	Y	Z
	A	8, 8	2, 10	0, 1
Row	B	10, 2	5, 5	0, 1
	C	1, 0	1, 0	1, 1

(c)

3. Construct a payoff matrix for the following game and then find the Nash equilibria.

There are two players, Ann and Bob, and they are trying to meet at the same place. They have not talked to each other about where to meet; they are just hoping to bump into each other. Fortunately, they live in a small town, and the only two possible places to meet are the coffee shop and the bowling alley. Ann likes to bowl, but Bob does not. Bob drinks coffee, but Ann does not. If they both end up at the bowling alley, Ann gets a payoff of 5 and Bob gets a payoff of 3. If they meet at the coffee shop Bob gets a payoff of 5 and Ann gets 3. If Ann goes to the bowling alley and Bob goes to the coffee shop, Ann and Bob both get 2. If Ann goes to the coffee shop and Bob goes to the bowling alley, Ann and Bob both get payoffs of zero.

4. Solve the following games being sure to write down the strategies for the two players.

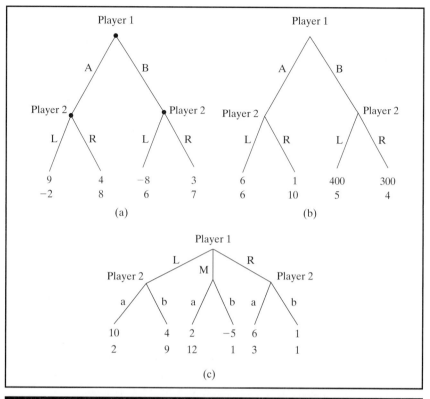

PROBLEM 8.4 Games to Be Analyzed in Problem 4

5. A student who is about to graduate has a job offer with firm A that will provide a net benefit of 7,000. Firm B has also made an offer that will provide him net benefit of 8,000 and will provide firm B with profit of 4,000. Firm B also knows the details of firm A's offer. The student agrees to accept firm B's offer if B sweetens it a little, giving the student net benefit of 9,000 and providing only 3,000 in profit to the firm. The student also threatens to accept firm A's offer if firm B does not sweeten the offer, in which case firm B gets no profit.

   a. Draw a game tree starting with firm B's decision of whether to sweeten the offer or not.
   b. Solve the game.
   c. Is the student's threat to work for firm A credible?

6. Two firms in a duopoly have cost functions given by $C(q) = 60q$, in which case marginal cost is constant and equal to 60. The market demand curve is $Q = 360 - p$. Find the Nash equilibrium output levels.

CHAPTER

9 | TOURNAMENTS

S o far we have only examined compensation schemes in which pay is tied directly to output. While this type of incentive pay is used in many types of jobs, it is far from the only way that workers are motivated to perform. For many workers, especially white collar workers, output is an ill-defined notion because their jobs entail many different tasks, few of which can be measured as output. If output cannot be measured, some other means of motivation must be found. One common method is the tournament, where workers work hard to compete for raises, bonuses, or promotions. In this chapter we analyze tournaments, determining how they motivate workers, what facets of the tournament are important for motivating workers, and whether tournaments provide incentives for undesirable behavior in the same way that piece rates do.

SOME EXAMPLES

Tournaments and contests are common in society and are the basis for all sporting events and TV game shows. They are also used in the workplace to motivate workers. Tournaments and contests are different, but related, forms of competition. For an example of a tournament, think about the NCAA basketball tournament, which starts with 64 teams and goes through six rounds to determine a national champion. The winners in the first round go on to compete in the second round; the winners there proceed to the third round; and so on. A tournament usually has several rounds, or levels, through which one must go to reach the top. A contest, in comparison, has only one round. Thus, each game in the NCAA tournament is a contest. In this chapter we study both tournaments and contests, but we will call them all tournaments. This is acceptable because contests, after all, are just single-round tournaments.

Tournaments also occur in major league baseball, with teams competing during the regular season for a spot in the playoffs and then competing in the playoffs for a spot in the World Series, and finally competing for the championship. For our purposes, however, baseball has a more important tournament. Players compete in high school and college to be drafted by a major league team. After they are drafted they must work their way up through the minor leagues before finally making it to the majors. Thus, a player must compete with others in Class A ball in order to be promoted to a Class AA team, and those players compete with each other to be promoted to a Class AAA team. The players in Class AAA compete with each other for a chance at playing in the major leagues. Minor league salaries tend to be low, with league minimums set at $1,050 per month for Class A players and $2,150 per month for Class AAA players in 2005. Players in the majors make much more, with minimum annual salaries set at $316,000 in 2005.

We can also consider employment in the military as a tournament. An officer enters the army as a second lieutenant making about $2,300 per month in 2005. Officers compete with each other to move up through the ranks, getting pay increases at each stage. So, for example, a major with ten years of experience earns $5,300 per month, but a promotion by one grade to lieutenant colonel would increase pay to $5,600 per month. A full colonel with twelve years of experience earns $6,100 per month, but a promotion by one grade to brigadier general would increase that pay to $8,100 per month. The salary increases tend to become larger as one moves up through the ranks. The number of officers in each rank, however, becomes smaller. For example, in 2004 there were only about 65 percent as many lieutenant colonels as majors, and only about 40 percent as many full colonels as lieutenant colonels.

Many corporations employ the same sort of tournament structure. Executives enter at low ranks with minimal responsibilities, and those who perform well are promoted to the next level. The number of executives becomes smaller and salaries rise substantially as one moves up the ladder. Workers exert effort so that they can move up through the corporate hierarchy and earn those large raises. Many firms also use contests to motivate workers. Whenever you go into a store and see a plaque with the name of the employee of the month, you are looking at the winner of a contest. The prize can range from simple recognition to a cash bonus or some sort of merchandise. Workers compete for the prize by exerting more effort and producing more for the firm.

A MODEL OF A TOURNAMENT

To keep things simple, suppose that only two workers compete for a prize in a tournament. The prize is of size A and can be thought of as a bonus or the raise that comes with a promotion. The supervisor deciding who wins wants to reward the worker who exerts more effort. Accordingly, worker 1 exerts effort e_1, and worker 2 exerts effort e_2.

Effort is costly for the workers, and the cost function is $C(e)$, with $C(0) = MC(0) = 0$, as usual.

The supervisor observes the difference between the two effort levels, $e_1 - e_2$, and wants to reward worker 1 if the difference is positive and wants to reward worker 2 if the difference is negative. But the supervisor does not watch everything the two competitors do and so does not observe $e_1 - e_2$ perfectly. Instead, the supervisor observes the difference with some error and so observes $e_1 - e_2 + \tilde{\varepsilon}$, where $\tilde{\varepsilon}$ is a random noise variable. The supervisor rewards worker 1 if $e_1 - e_2 + \tilde{\varepsilon} > 0$ and worker 2 if $e_1 - e_2 + \tilde{\varepsilon} < 0$.

Because the supervisor does not observe the effort difference perfectly, it is entirely possible that worker 1 exerts more effort than worker 2 but worker 2 is rewarded. This is obviously unfair to worker 1. It is also realistic. Workers often think that they were unjustly passed up for a promotion, although at the same time the supervisor believes the right person received the promotion. The model allows for this by adding noise to the supervisor's observations.

Suppose that worker 1 exerts effort e_1 and that worker 2 exerts effort e_2. Worker 2 wins the tournament if $e_1 - e_2 + \tilde{\varepsilon} < 0$, which reduces to $\tilde{\varepsilon} < e_2 - e_1$. Thus, any draw of $\tilde{\varepsilon}$ below $e_2 - e_1$ makes worker 2 a winner. Worker 1 wins if worker 2 does not, so any draw of $\tilde{\varepsilon}$ above $e_2 - e_1$ makes worker 1 the winner.

Now look at Figure 9.1. It is the probability distribution $P(\varepsilon)$ of the noise variable $\tilde{\varepsilon}$, and it has the following interpretation: The height of the curve at value x is the probability of drawing a value of $\tilde{\varepsilon}$ no higher than x. So, $P(x)$ is the probability that $\tilde{\varepsilon} \leq x$. We can use this function P to determine the probability that each worker wins, given their effort choices. As argued above, worker 2 wins if $\tilde{\varepsilon} < e_2 - e_1$, so worker 2 wins with probability $P(e_2 - e_1)$. Worker 1 wins the rest of the time, so worker 1 wins with probability $1 - P(e_2 - e_1)$.

The marginal probability distribution, also known as a density function, turns out to be crucial to our analysis. As typical with the marginal version of a function, its height is the slope of the original function. Looking at the probability distribution function P in Figure 9.1, we see that it starts out fairly flat, then becomes steeper until it reaches $\varepsilon = 0$; then it becomes flatter again. Accordingly, the marginal probability distribution MP shown in Figure 9.2 is low for the lowest levels of ε, climbs as ε grows until $\varepsilon = 0$, and then falls again.

The marginal probability distribution shown in Figure 9.2 has two key features that will be exploited in our analysis of tournaments. The first is that it is symmetric about the vertical axis. This means that the probability of drawing a value of ε above some number x is the same as the probability of drawing a value below $-x$, so that, on average, the errors cancel out. In other words, the expected value of the error is zero. In this sense, the errors can be interpreted as being fair. The supervisor's observations are not perfect, but at least they do not

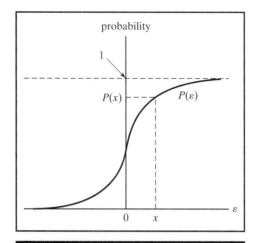

FIGURE 9.1   The Probability Distribution for the Random Noise Variable

$P(\varepsilon)$ is the probability distribution function for the random noise variable $\tilde{\varepsilon}$. Its height at point x is the probability of drawing a value of ε that is no greater than x. Accordingly, it starts off at zero for low values of ε and increases as ε increases, finally reaching a value of one for the highest possible value of ε.

FIGURE 9.2   The Marginal Probability Distribution

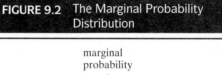
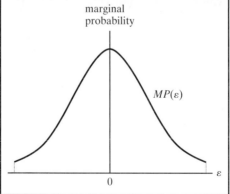

$MP(\varepsilon)$ is the marginal probability of drawing the value ε from the probability distribution $P(\varepsilon)$. Its height is the slope of the probability distribution in Figure 9.1, and it can be interpreted as the increase in probability per unit increase in ε.

unfairly favor one worker or the other. To see why we make this assumption, suppose that $\tilde{\varepsilon}$ was positive more often than not. This would mean that the supervisor would tend to observe more of worker 1's effort than of worker 2's and so would tend to unfairly favor worker 1 in the award decision. But if the supervisor knew that she observed more of worker 1's effort than worker 2's, she could compensate for this in her decision by subtracting the average size of the error from her observation. This would leave an effective average error of zero, so we might as well begin by assuming that the errors average out to zero.

The second key feature of the marginal probability distribution is that the curve peaks when $\varepsilon = 0$ and falls as ε moves away from zero in either direction. This is the familiar bell shape that is common in statistical analysis, and we use it here. Its interpretation is that values near zero are relatively common, and extreme values that are far from zero are relatively rare. Thus, the supervisor is more likely to make errors that are small, in the sense of being close to zero, than to make errors that are large, in the sense of being far from zero.

With these tools in place, we can now go on to analyze how workers respond to the incentives provided by the tournament.

OPTIMAL EFFORT FOR AN INDIVIDUAL WORKER

In this section we look specifically at the effort decision of worker 1, assuming that worker 1 knows exactly how much effort worker 2 will exert. In reality, both workers choose their effort levels without the other knowing what the choice will be, but here we are taking an intermediate step toward addressing the more realistic setting. In the language of game theory, we find worker 1's best response function. The key issues for this section are to determine how worker 1's effort changes when (1) worker 2 exerts more effort, and (2) the size of the prize for winning the tournament changes.

Suppose that worker 2 exerts effort e_2 and that the prize for winning the tournament is A. How much effort should worker 1 exert? As usual, the answer comes from marginal analysis, that is, equating expected marginal benefit and marginal cost. Worker 2's expected benefit from exerting effort is the probability of winning the tournament times the size of the prize. Recall that the probability that worker 1 wins is the probability that the noise variable $\tilde{\varepsilon} < e_2 - e_1$, which we found to be $1 - P(e_2 - e_1)$. Consequently, expected benefit is given by the formula

$$EB(e_1) = [1 - P(e_2 - e_1)] \cdot A$$

The cost is simply the effort cost, $C(e_1)$.

The benefit expression, $[1 - P(e_2 - e_1)] \cdot A$, has two parts, the probability of winning and the size of the prize, but only the probability of winning depends on the amount of effort exerted by worker 1. Also, the probability of winning increases when worker 1 exerts more effort. This can be seen by noting that when e_1 increases, $e_2 - e_1$ decreases, and by Figure 9.1, $P(e_2 - e_1)$ decreases because P is an increasing function. Marginal expected benefit is given by the formula

$$MEB(e_1) = MP(e_2 - e_1) \cdot A$$

The marginal expected benefit of effort is the marginal probability of winning times the size of the prize. The marginal condition is

$$MP(e_2 - e_1) \cdot A = MC(e_1) \qquad \qquad \textbf{(9.1)}$$

The left-hand side of the equation is the marginal expected benefit of effort, which comes from increasing the probability of winning, and the right-hand side is the marginal cost. Worker 1 chooses an effort level that equates the two.

The goal of this section is to determine how the optimal effort level changes when worker 2 exerts more effort and when the prize is made larger. The key to this is equation (9.1), which states that worker 1 exerts effort until the marginal expected benefit of further effort is exactly offset by the marginal cost. If something happens to make the marginal expected benefit rise, then worker 1 can exert more effort before marginal expected benefit equals marginal cost. Because marginal expected benefit is given by

$$MEB = MP(e_2 - e_1) \cdot A$$

marginal expected benefit could increase in two ways. One is to increase the marginal probability, $MP(e_2 - e_1)$, and the other is to increase the size of the award for winning the tournament, A. If either the marginal probability increases or the size of the award increases or both, the worker exerts more effort.

We begin by exploring how worker 1's optimal effort level changes when worker 2 exerts more effort. When e_2 increases, $e_2 - e_1$ also increases. The impact on $MP(e_2 - e_1)$, and consequently on worker 1's marginal expected benefit of effort, depends on the relative values of e_2 and e_1. When $e_2 > e_1$, so that worker 2 is exerting more effort than worker 1, an increase in e_2 moves worker 2 farther ahead. It also means that $e_2 - e_1$ is to the right of zero in Figure 9.3, and the increase in e_2 means a movement farther to the right. As can be seen in the figure, the marginal probability falls as a result of this move, reducing worker 1's marginal expected benefit of effort. As usual, when his marginal expected benefit falls, he reduces his effort level. This yields the result that when worker 2 exerts more effort than worker 1, further increases in e_2 induce decreases in e_1.

Now look at the opposite situation, where $e_2 < e_1$, so that worker 1 is ahead. An increase in e_2 means that worker 2 is catching up.

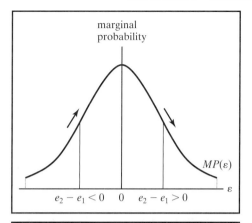

FIGURE 9.3   Worker 1's Response to an Increase in Worker 2's Effort

When worker 2 exerts more effort than worker 1, $e_2 - e_1 > 0$. An increase in e_2 is a movement to the right, which causes a movement down the *MP* curve, as shown by the downward-sloping arrow.

When worker 2 exerts less effort than worker 1, $e_2 - e_1 < 0$, and an increase in e_2 causes a movement up the *MP* curve, as shown by the upward-sloping arrow.

Graphically, it means that $e_2 - e_1$ is to the left of zero in Figure 9.3, and the increase in e_2 translates in a movement to the right. In this portion of the graph, however, *MP* increases with movements to the right, so worker 1's marginal expected benefit increases when worker 2's effort level increases. The increase in worker 1's marginal expected benefit of effort means that he will exert more effort, yielding the result that when worker 2 exerts less effort than worker 1, increases in e_2 induce increases in e_1.

Figure 9.4 summarizes these results in a graph that plots worker 1's optimal effort level against worker 2's chosen effort level. At points above the 45° line, $e_2 < e_1$, so worker 1's optimal effort level increases when worker 2 exerts more effort. At points below the 45° line, $e_2 > e_1$, and worker 1's optimal effort level decreases when worker 2 exerts more effort. The only thing left to explain in the graph is why worker 1 exerts a positive amount of effort when worker 2 exerts no effort at all.

To that end, suppose that $e_2 = 0$. We can narrow worker 1's decision to two basic choices: Either exert $e_1 = 0$ or exert $e_1 > 0$. Choosing $e_1 = 0$ cannot be optimal. If worker 1 chooses $e_1 = 0$, then $e_2 - e_1 = 0$, and *MP* is at its peak in Figure 9.3. Consequently, worker 1's marginal expected benefit of effort is positive when $e_1 = 0$. However,

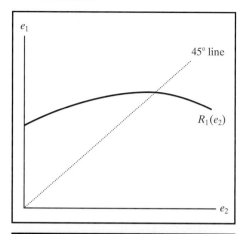

FIGURE 9.4 Worker 1's Best-Response Curve

$R_1(e_2)$ is worker 1's best-response curve, showing his optimal effort level for each effort level chosen by worker 2. It starts off with a positive value of e_1 when $e_2 = 0$, increases until it reaches the 45° line where both workers exert the same amount of effort, and then decreases.

worker 1's marginal cost is zero by the assumption that $MC(0) = 0$. Thus, when e_1 and e_2 are both zero, marginal expected benefit exceeds marginal cost, and worker 1 should exert more effort. This establishes that when worker 2 does nothing, worker 1 should still exert *some* effort.

The curve in Figure 9.4 is worker 1's **best-response curve**. It shows worker 1's optimal effort level for every possible effort level chosen by worker 2, which can be thought of as worker 1's reaction to worker 2's choice of effort level. The curve shows that worker 1 exerts positive effort when worker 2 does nothing; he increases his effort as e_2 rises until the two are equal; and then he decreases his effort.

Worker 2's effort level is just one of the factors that affect worker 1's optimal effort level. The size of the award for winning the tournament also affects worker 1's decision. To see how, recall that marginal expected benefit equals $MP(e_2 - e_1) \cdot A$, so increasing A also increases marginal expected benefit. When MEB rises, effort must also increase to equate it to marginal cost. What is important here is that an increase in A increases MEB for *every* value of e_2 chosen by worker 2. Consequently, an increase in A shifts the entire best-response curve upward, as in Figure 9.5.

Worker 1's optimal effort level also changes when the cost of effort changes. When the marginal cost of effort rises, the worker

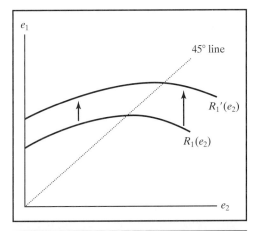

FIGURE 9.5 The Effect of an Increase in the Prize on the Best-Response Curve

When A increases, worker 1 exerts more effort for every possible effort level chosen by worker 2, and worker 1's best-response curve shifts upward from $R_1(e_2)$ to $R_1'(e_2)$. The best-response curve also shifts upward when effort becomes less costly.

reduces effort to equate the marginal expected benefit and the marginal cost. This is true for every possible effort choice made by worker 2, so when worker 1's marginal cost curve rotates upward, his best-response curve falls.

COMPETITION BETWEEN WORKERS

The best-response curve constructed in the preceding section assumes that worker 1 can respond to worker 2's effort choice, implicitly assuming that worker 2 chooses before worker 1. This is not realistic, however. In many cases, workers competing for a promotion are in different divisions of the firm or in different geographic areas, so they would have difficulty observing how hard their competitors are working. Also, many workplace contests pit workers in one location against workers in another, again making observation difficult. Even if the two competitors work together, they may not be able to see everything that the other worker does, and they cannot know how much effort their competitors will exert during the time before the prize is awarded. For all of these reasons, it makes sense to model the competition as if both workers make their effort choices simultaneously, without being able to see how hard the other is working.

In situations like this we look for a Nash equilibrium, as discussed in Chapter 8. In a Nash equilibrium, both workers choose effort levels that are best responses to each others' effort choices. Put another way, worker 1 responds optimally to worker 2's equilibrium effort choice, and worker 2 responds optimally to worker 1's equilibrium effort choice. This is where the best-response curves discussed previously come in. Worker 1's best-response curve shows his optimal effort choice for every possible effort level chosen by worker 2. Worker 2 also has a best-response curve showing his optimal effort choice for every possible effort level chosen by worker 1.

Figure 9.6 shows both workers' best-response curves in the same graph. $R_1(e_2)$ is worker 1's best-response curve, and $R_2(e_1)$ is worker 2's best-response curve. It looks just like worker 1's best-response curve except transposed to account for the fact that the axes are reversed from worker 2's perspective. The two best-response curves intersect at point E, where worker 1 exerts effort level e_1^* and worker 2 exerts effort level e_2^*. Let us see if point E is an equilibrium. There are two things to check. First, given worker 2's choice, is worker 1 behaving optimally? When worker 2 exerts effort level e_2^*, worker 1's optimal response is found on his best-response curve at $R_1(e_2^*)$, which, from the graph, is seen to be e_1^*. So e_1^* is the optimal response to e_2^*. Second, given worker 1's effort choice, is worker 2's effort choice

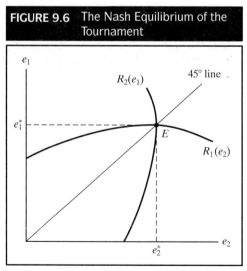

FIGURE 9.6 The Nash Equilibrium of the Tournament

$R_1(e_2)$ is worker 1's best-response curve, showing the optimal response to worker 2's effort choice. $R_2(e_1)$ is worker 2's best-response curve, showing the optimal response to worker 1's effort choice. They intersect at point E, where both workers are responding optimally to each other's effort choices, which makes E a Nash equilibrium.

optimal? Given that worker 1 exerts effort level e_1^*, worker 2's best response is e_2^* because it is on his best-response curve. At point E, both workers are making best responses to the other's effort choice, and E is a Nash equilibrium.

Figure 9.6 shows how the equilibrium effort levels are determined. The employer has control over the parameters of the tournament, however, and can adjust them to obtain the desired amount of effort. One obvious parameter is the size of the prize the winner receives, A. As shown in the preceding section, an increase in A causes worker 1's best-response curve to shift upward. It would also shift worker 2's best-response curve to the right, as in Figure 9.7. The new equilibrium is at point E', and both workers exert more effort when the prize is made larger.

A second factor under the firm's control is how accurately it measures the workers' performance. The firm can spend more resources on monitoring the workers, in which case the supervisor will have a more accurate assessment of which worker exerts more effort. In terms of the model, this increased precision changes the marginal probability distribution by shifting probability away from the tails and toward the center, as shown in Figure 9.8. Essentially, there is a new, taller, thinner bell-shaped marginal probability distribution. This increases the amount of effort a worker exerts when a competitor exerts no effort, and it makes the best-response curve steeper. Essentially, the best-response curves shift outward, just as in Figure 9.7,

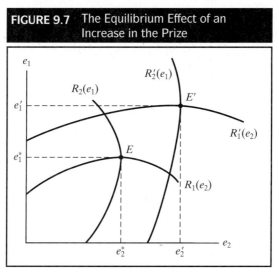

FIGURE 9.7   The Equilibrium Effect of an Increase in the Prize

When the prize for winning the tournament increases, both best-response curves shift outward. This causes both workers to exert more effort in the new equilibrium, E'.

DO LARGER PRIZES REALLY INDUCE MORE EFFORT?

Data on individual performance in promotion tournaments in actual businesses are hard to come by. Data are much easier to obtain for sporting events, and many of them, such as golf, bowling, and various races, have tournament structures. Michael Maloney and Robert McCormick of Clemson University explore whether runners run faster in races with larger prizes. Virtually all competitive runners who regularly finish in the money at these races claim that they run all out, at their physical limits, in every race. This would mean that there would be no prize effect, because runners could not possibly run any faster.

Maloney and McCormick find three reasons that there are faster times in races with higher stakes. The first is that the higher stakes attract faster runners who might otherwise go elsewhere. The second is that the higher stakes attract *more* runners, and so chance alone predicts that the fastest times decrease (i.e., get faster) when the number of runners increases. The third, and the one that is of interest here, is that the individual runners try harder when the prizes are larger, contrary to the runners' own claims.

To uncover this result, Maloney and McCormick examined the results of 115 races in the southeastern United States over a five-year period. In these 115 races, there were 136 individual runners who won monetary prizes at least three times. Maloney and McCormick look at the effect of an increase in the gap between the individual runner's prize in one of these races and the prize for the next-best runner in that same race. According to our tournament model, when the gap gets bigger, the individual runner has a greater incentive to run faster. They find that the bigger prize gaps do induce runners to go faster. In fact, their result holds for both sexes and all age classes, although they find, interestingly, that women are more responsive to the prize incentives than men.

SOURCE: Maloney, M. and R. McCormick, "The Response of Workers to Wages in Tournaments: Evidence from Foot Races," *Journal of Sports Economics* 1 (May 2000), 99–123.

and the workers respond to the increased marginal expected benefit by exerting more effort. This yields the result that when there is less noise in the evaluation system and workers are identical and treated fairly, they exert more effort.

This result has some intuitive appeal. The more noise in the evaluation system, the less likely it is that increased effort will lead to a

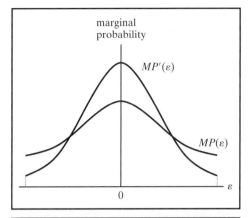

FIGURE 9.8 The Effect of Increased Precision on The Marginal Probability Distribution

When the evaluation process becomes more precise (less noisy), the marginal probability distribution becomes tighter, shifting from $MP(\varepsilon)$ to $MP'(\varepsilon)$.

promotion, and so the less willing the worker is to exert that additional effort. By making the evaluation system more precise, the worker's reward is tied more closely to performance, increasing the incentive to perform.

The firm has two ways to control the amount of effort exerted by the workers in a tournament. First, it can adjust the size of the prize until it induces the workers to exert the optimal amount of effort. Increasing the prize induces workers to exert more effort, and decreasing the prize induces them to exert less. Second, it can adjust how much it monitors the workers. Increased monitoring also leads to increased effort.

A Numerical Example
To better understand the mechanics underlying the tournament model, consider the following numerical example. Two workers compete for a prize worth 800. Their marginal effort cost functions are given by $MC(e) = 12e$. The supervisor does not observe effort perfectly, however, and the marginal probability of the noise variable is given by

$$
MP(\varepsilon) = \begin{cases} \frac{1}{10} + \frac{1}{100}\varepsilon & \varepsilon < 0 \\ & \text{if} \\ \frac{1}{10} - \frac{1}{100}\varepsilon & \varepsilon \geq 0 \end{cases}
$$

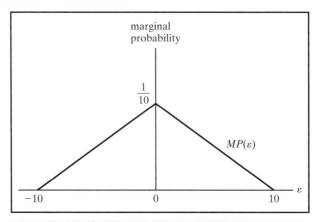

FIGURE 9.9 The Marginal Probability Distribution for the Numerical Example

This figure shows the marginal probability function for the numerical example. The area under the curve is 1, which is consistent with probabilities summing to 1.

This function is graphed in Figure 9.9. To make sure that it is a marginal probability function, compute the area under the curve in the figure. The area should be one. There are two triangles, each with a height of 1/10 and a base of 10. Using the formula for the area of a triangle, each triangle has area 1/2, and so the total area is 1, which is as it should be for a marginal probability function.

From equation (9.1) worker 1's marginal condition is

$$MP(e_2 - e_1) \cdot A = MC(e_1)$$

First look at the case in which $e_1 > e_2$ (so that $e_2 - e_1 < 0$). Substituting the values of the marginal probability and marginal cost functions and the size of the prize and then solving for e_1 as a function of e_2 yields part of worker 1's best-response function:

$$\left[\frac{1}{10} + \frac{1}{100}(e_2 - e_1) \right] \cdot 800 = 12e_1$$
$$80 + 8(e_2 - e_1) = 12e_1$$
$$80 + 8e_2 = 20e_1$$
$$e_1 = 4 + \frac{2e_2}{5}$$

Now repeat the analysis for the case of $e_1 < e_2$ (so that $e_2 - e_1 > 0$):

$$\left[\frac{1}{10} - \frac{1}{100}(e_2 - e_1) \right] \cdot 800 = 12e_1$$
$$80 - 8(e_2 - e_1) = 12e_1$$
$$80 - 8e_2 = 4e_1$$
$$e_1 = 20 - 2e_2$$

The best-response function is

$$R_1(e_2) = \begin{cases} 4 + \frac{2}{5}e_2 & e_2 < e_1 \\ & \text{if} \\ 20 - 2e_2 & e_2 \geq e_1 \end{cases}$$

and it is graphed in Figure 9.10. Because the workers are identical, we can find worker 2's best-response curve in exactly the same way, and the equilibrium is where the two curves intersect, which is also where they cross the 45° line. We can find it algebraically by noticing that along the 45° line the two segments of the best-response curve meet, and therefore

$$4 + \frac{2}{5}e_2 = 20 - 2e_2$$
$$\frac{12e_2}{5} = 16$$
$$e_2 = \frac{20}{3}$$

In the Nash equilibrium both workers exert effort equal to 20/3.

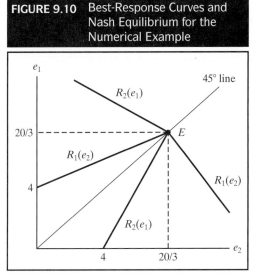

FIGURE 9.10 Best-Response Curves and Nash Equilibrium for the Numerical Example

In the numerical example, the workers exert 4 units of effort if their opponents exert no effort. The best-response functions then slope upward until they cross the 45° line, and then turn backward. The Nash equilibrium is where the two best-response curves intersect, which is where both workers exert 20/3 units of effort.

GENERAL IMPLICATIONS FOR MOTIVATING WORKERS

The last three sections presented a general model of tournaments, not just promotion tournaments. In this section we turn specifically to promotion tournaments and highlight some implications of the model for motivating workers using promotion tournaments.

Pay for Performance?

As we learned in the last section, workers exert more effort when the prize is made larger. In a promotion tournament, the prize is the raise the worker gets when he is promoted. This gives rise to some strange notions of pay for performance.

The strangeness arises because the promotion tournament induces workers to exert a lot of effort before they are promoted, when their pay is low. After the tournament ends, one worker is promoted and is paid more. This means that salaries are set to provide incentives to the workers at the next lower level, not the workers who are actually receiving that salary. Thus, workers' current pay is unrelated to their current activities. When promotion tournaments are used to motivate workers, pay is not based on current performance but on past performance, and workers are motivated by future pay, not by current pay.

Pay Structures in Hierarchies

Many firms, as well as the federal and state governments and the military, have a hierarchy of positions. A worker can move up through the ranks by being promoted to successively higher positions. What does the model say about how the salaries should rise as one moves up through the hierarchy?

In most hierarchies, salaries increase more rapidly the higher up one moves. This is also true of most sports tournaments, as illustrated in the box on the prize structure in golf tournaments. The pattern that getting promoted to the top position carries with it a much higher pay raise than getting promoted to the second-highest position is a sensible way to structure the pay schedule. The reason is that pay for a given rank motivates everyone below that rank. Thus, for example, workers in the second-highest position exert effort trying to win the promotion to the highest position so that they can get the biggest raise. Workers in the third-highest position exert effort in an attempt to win a promotion to the second-highest position, thereby garnering the second-largest raise. But there is an additional reward for being promoted to the second-highest position—the right to compete for a promotion to the highest position. The size of this additional reward, known as the **option value** of the promotion, depends in part on the size of the reward for being promoted to the highest position. In a similar way, the workers in the fourth-highest position exert effort to win a promotion to the third-highest position. The winner gets a raise, plus the option value of being in the third-highest position and being able to compete for the second-highest position, plus the possibility of eventually making it to the highest position. In general, the option value of a promotion is the expected benefit of all further promotions.

The existence of the option value means that the raise that comes with the highest promotion should be the largest of all the raises. The possibility of a promotion to the highest position motivates all workers, while promotions to lower levels only motivate workers who have not yet reached that level. Because the pay raise that accompanies a promotion to the highest level motivates everyone, it should be large for the firm to get the most bang for its buck.

THE PRIZE STRUCTURE IN GOLF TOURNAMENTS

The PGA Championship is one of the four major worldwide golf tournaments. In 2004, prize money for the tournament totaled $6.25 million. The winner received $1.125 million, or 18 percent of the total. This is typical of golf tournaments. The gap between first and second was $450,000, so the second-place winner got only 60 percent of the amount the winner got. This, too, is typical. The third-place winner earned $425,000, which is 63 percent of the second-place winner's prize of $675,000. As one moves down the ranks, the prizes become increasingly larger shares of the next-highest prize, with the sixth-place winner receiving 90 percent of the fifth-place winner's prize and the fifty-fifth–place winner receiving 99 percent of the fifty-fourth–place winner's prize.

The Peter Principle

The **Peter Principle**, first introduced by the sociologist Laurence J. Peter, states that in every hierarchy each employee tends to rise to his or her own level of incompetence.[1] The Peter Principle sounds pessimistic, but it is a necessary byproduct of using a promotion tournament. As long as workers do their jobs well, they continue to be promoted to the next level of the hierarchy. If they reach a level where they cannot perform well, they are not promoted anymore. Thus, workers stop when they reach a level at which they are incompetent—the Peter Principle.

---

[1]Peter, L. J. and R. Hull, *The Peter Principle: Why Things Always Go Wrong* (New York: William Morrow & Co., 1969).

Just as with Murphy's Law (anything that can go wrong will go wrong), the Peter Principle has led to a number of related statements. The book *The Official Rules* lists two corollaries to the Peter Principle.[2] The first states, "Every post tends to be filled by an employee incompetent to execute its duties." The promotion tournament model suggests that this is not strictly true. Some of the workers in a particular job at any given time will be good at the job. However, some will also be bad. The good ones are promoted to the next level, whereas the bad ones remain for the rest of their careers. Thus, every job slowly accumulates workers who are incompetent at that job but were competent at the prior job.

The second corollary states, "Work is accomplished by those employees who have not yet reached their level of incompetence." Employees who have reached their level of incompetence are, well, incompetent, so they are not terribly productive. But they could still do some work if they were properly motivated. The problem, according to the promotion tournament model, is that they are no longer motivated by the promotion tournament. Competent workers always win the promotion tournament, so an incompetent worker's marginal expected benefit from effort is zero. To equate marginal expected benefit and marginal expected cost, the worker will exert no effort. Thus, there are two reasons why workers who have reached their level of incompetence do no work: incompetence and lack of motivation. These mean that any work that is done is accomplished by employees who still have a chance to advance in the hierarchy.

The final Peter-Principle–like statement we mention here comes from Charles Vail, a former vice president of Southern Methodist University. Vail said, "In any human enterprise, work seeks the lowest hierarchical level."[3] This could be because bosses delegate tasks to their underlings. It could also be that workers at the lowest level have the most motivation from a promotion tournament.

Promotions from Within Versus Hiring from Outside

Sometimes firms promote workers from within, and sometimes they hire workers from outside the company. For example, in 2001 American Express promoted Kenneth Chenault to CEO. He had previously worked at American Express for 20 years. In contrast, in 2001 Home Depot named Robert Nardelli to the CEO post. He was new to Home Depot, having worked for General Electric for 30 years.

Hiring from outside has obvious advantages. By expanding the pool from which workers are chosen, a better candidate can be found. But hiring from outside has serious harmful implications for the firm's

---

[2]Dickson, P., *The Official Rules* (New York: Dell Publishing, 1978), 195.
[3]Ibid., p. 236.

promotion tournament. Hiring the top executive from outside removes the motivation for the next lower level of executives because it lowers their marginal expected benefit of effort. If the firm has passed one of them over for an outsider once, it is likely to do so again, and the marginal probability of a promotion is low, no matter how hard the executive tries. Because working hard is unlikely to have much positive impact on future promotion chances, the second-tier executives are unmotivated.

Because of option values, this effect bleeds down to lower levels in the hierarchy as well. Executives farther down in the firm see that the top prize is most likely unattainable, and because the probability of eventually reaching the top level is diminished, the marginal expected benefit from effort is also diminished. Consequently, an outside hire must add a great deal of expertise to the company to make it worthwhile to bear the costs of diminishing the incentive effects of the promotion tournament. Airline companies and most Japanese firms have systematically promoted workers from within and have avoided hiring highly-placed workers from outside, enabling the promotion system to more effectively motivate employees. Whenever an airline hires a pilot, for example, it starts that pilot on the least desirable routes, and the pilot must work upward through the system to obtain better routes and more favorable schedules.

TOURNAMENTS WHEN ONE WORKER HAS AN ADVANTAGE

In the analysis we have done so far, neither worker had an advantage over the other. They both had the same effort cost, so neither could produce output more easily than the other. Also, the supervisor was fair, so neither worker was the favorite. Neither of these assumptions is terribly realistic because supervisors often have favorites whom they are more likely to promote, and workers often have different abilities. In this section we look at how we can model favoritism and ability differences and determine their effects on the equilibrium of the tournament model.

Ability Differences

The way to capture ability differences within the model is to assume that the high-ability worker has lower effort costs than the low-ability worker. This is what we did in Chapter 7 to analyze piece rate compensation schemes when workers have different abilities. The low-effort-cost worker can produce the same amount of output at lower cost than the high-effort-cost worker, which leads the low-effort-cost worker to produce more than the high-effort-cost worker when they face the same incentives.

Assume that worker 1 has lower effort costs than worker 2. Let C_1 denote worker 1's cost function and let C_2 denote worker 2's cost function. We assume that $C_1(e) < C_2(e)$, so that worker 1's cost of exerting e units of effort is lower than worker 2's, and also that $MC_1(e) < MC_2(e)$, so that it costs worker 1 less to exert one more unit of effort than it does worker 2. We also assume each worker knows the other's effort cost function.

To find the impact of worker 1 having lower cost than worker 2, fix the amount of effort exerted by worker 2 and look at worker 1's marginal condition:

$$MP(e_2 - e_1) \cdot A = MC_1(e_1)$$

When worker 1's costs fall, the right-hand side of the marginal condition falls, and now marginal expected benefit is higher than marginal cost. When the marginal expected benefit of an activity exceeds its marginal cost, it is worthwhile to engage in more of that activity, so worker 1's effort increases.

Figure 9.11 shows what happens to the best-response curves. A decrease in effort costs shifts upward the best-response curve of worker 1, because he exerts more effort for every level of effort exerted by worker 2. The point E is the equilibrium when the two workers have the same effort costs, and point E' is the equilibrium

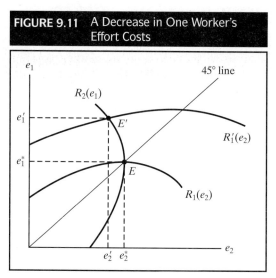

FIGURE 9.11   A Decrease in One Worker's Effort Costs

When worker 1's effort costs fall, his best-response curve shifts upward from $R_1(e_2)$ to $R_1'(e_2)$. Then new equilibrium is E', which gets more effort from worker 1 and less effort from worker 2. Since worker 1 exerts more effort than worker 2, he is more likely to be promoted than worker 2.

when worker 1's effort costs fall. The new equilibrium is above the 45° line, so worker 1 exerts more effort than worker 2. In fact, worker 1 exerts more effort when his cost is low than when his cost is high, and worker 2 exerts *less* effort when 1's cost is low than when 1's cost is high. Because the supervisor is more likely to reward the worker who exerts more effort, the higher-ability worker, in this case worker 1, is more likely to be promoted than the lower-ability worker.

Favoritism

Favoritism occurs when the supervisor selects one worker over the other even though all evidence suggests that the other worker should have been selected. This can be captured in the model by changing the marginal probability curve. The original marginal probability curve was symmetric about the vertical axis, which meant that the supervisor was fair. Let us see what we have to do to it so that the supervisor favors worker 1. Worker 1 wins the prize if $e_1 = e_2 + \tilde{\varepsilon} < 0$. $e_1 - e_2 + v \times$ Worker 1 is more likely to win if $\tilde{\varepsilon}$ is likely to be larger, which would occur if the marginal probability curve shifted to the right, as in Figure 9.12.

To determine how worker 1 reacts to the favoritism, look at his marginal condition:

$$MP_1(e_2 - e_1) \cdot A = MC(e_1)$$

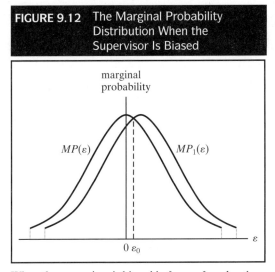

FIGURE 9.12 The Marginal Probability Distribution When the Supervisor Is Biased

When the supervisor is biased in favor of worker 1, the marginal probability of worker 1 winning shifts to the right. Since a high value of ε is good for worker 1, the new marginal probability curve, $MP_1(\varepsilon)$, makes higher values of ε more likely.

If $e_2 - e_1 < \varepsilon_0$, worker 1's marginal probability of winning falls as a result of favoritism, and if $e_2 - e_1 > \varepsilon_0$, worker 1's marginal probability rises. An increase in the marginal probability of winning makes marginal expected benefit exceed marginal cost, and worker 1 exerts more effort. On the other hand, a drop in the marginal probability of winning leads worker 1 to exert less effort.

The new best-response curve is drawn in Figure 9.13. To get it, first draw the line corresponding to the equation $e_1 = e_2 - \varepsilon_0$. At every point on this line, $e_2 - e_1 = \varepsilon_0$, and by Figure 9.12, the marginal probability is unchanged when $e_2 - e_1 = \varepsilon_0$. Because the 45° line graphs the equation $e_1 = e_2$, the new line is parallel to and slightly below the 45° line. Above the new line $e_2 - e_1 < \varepsilon_0$, so worker 1 exerts less effort. Below the new line $e_2 - e_1 > \varepsilon_0$, so worker 1 exerts more effort. The new best-response curve is below the old one for low levels of e_2 and above it for high levels of e_2.

The opposite pattern occurs for worker 2. When the supervisor favors worker 1, she acts against worker 2, so worker 2's marginal probabilities move in the opposite direction of worker 1's. Consequently, worker 2's best-response curve shifts outward for low levels of e_1 and inward for high values of e_1. Figure 9.14 shows the new equilibrium. In the new equilibrium in which the supervisor favors worker 1, both workers end up exerting less effort. Favoritism is costly for the firm because it generates less effort from both workers with the same prize money.

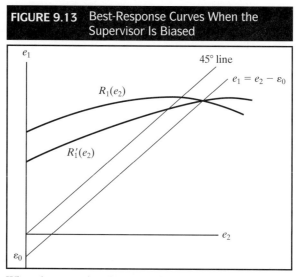

FIGURE 9.13 Best-Response Curves When the Supervisor Is Biased

When the supervisor favors worker 1, the worker's best-response curve shifts so that the worker works less for low levels of e_2 and works more for high levels of e_2.

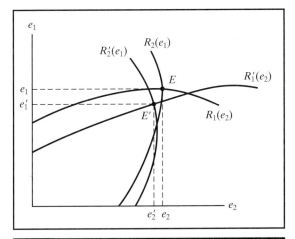

FIGURE 9.14   Equilibrium When the Supervisor Is Biased

When the supervisor is fair, the equilibrium is E. When the supervisor favors worker 1, worker 1's best-response curve shifts so that it is lower for low levels of e_2 and higher for high levels of e_2. Worker 2's best-response curve shifts the opposite way, so that it is higher for low levels of e_1 and lower for high levels of e_1. The new equilibrium is E'', and both workers exert less effort.

The results of this analysis make some sense. If the supervisor favors worker 1, worker 1 no longer needs to work as hard to win the prize. Because the deck is stacked against worker 2, he has to work harder to win the prize, but his incentives are diluted somewhat because he is less likely to win. Consequently, he reduces his effort as well.

INFLUENCE ACTIVITIES

Promotion tournaments are designed to encourage workers to undertake productive activities that have value for the firm. The worker's reward for engaging in these activities is an increased chance of being promoted and getting a raise. One problem with promotion tournaments is that they give workers the incentive to undertake *any* activity that improves their chances of being promoted, whether the activity is valuable for the firm or not. So, for example, a worker trying to be promoted not only has an incentive to work harder, which makes him look better, but also has an incentive to make competitors look bad. The worker further has an incentive to take actions that benefit the supervisor making the promotion decision, whether these actions benefit the firm or not.

Influence activities are activities that improve a worker's probability of promotion without adding to the profitability of the firm. More familiar names for the same concept are corporate politics, industrial politics, and organizational politics. Influence activities can take many forms, but by definition, they are all harmful to the organization because, at the very least, they take time away from productive tasks.

The promotion tournament model can be adapted easily to explain why workers engage in influence activities. Suppose that a worker can either exert costly effort, e, or engage in an influence activity, a, which is also costly. Both activities increase the worker's probability of promotion. We have already seen that the worker should exert effort until the marginal expected benefit of doing so equals the marginal cost. The same goes for influence activities: The worker should engage in influence activities until the marginal expected benefit of doing so equals the marginal cost. Consequently, unless the worker is in an organization that completely ignores influence activities in making promotion decisions, they are a fact of life. Given the number of different forms that influence activities can take, at least some of them are likely to matter in the promotion decision. A few of the many forms that influence activities can take are discussed here.

Sucking Up

Workers have long recognized that one way to get ahead is to ingratiate themselves to the decision-makers who control the promotion, otherwise known as sucking up to the boss. This could entail simple things such as laughing at the boss's jokes or expensive things like taking her to lunch. Everyone has their own stories of (usually others) sucking up to get what they want. For example, Andrew DuBrin's popular-press book *Winning Office Politics* tells of an investment banker whose co-workers "would sit on the edge of their chairs and nod with approval at almost anything a principal said" in order to get on their bosses' good sides. They would also "compete with each other to see who could stay latest at the office. Of course they would all exit quickly as soon as the last partner left the office."[4] These activities are not without costs. Their spouses or partners would complain that they were poor companions because they always missed dates. But to the extent that these activities help the workers get promoted, they are worthwhile, at least to the worker.

Backstabbing

A more problematic influence activity is backstabbing, in which workers undertake activities that make their co-workers look bad.

---

[4]DuBrin, A., *Winning Office Politics: DuBrin's Guide for the 90s* (Upper Saddle River, NJ: Prentice Hall, 1990,), p. 3.

Backstabbing can take many forms, from making sure that supervisors know of a co-worker's failures to undermining a co-worker's relationships with a client, thereby making a deal fall through. This latter example increases the backstabber's probability of a promotion, but it is bad for the firm because it hurts productivity. Yet it is in the best interest of the backstabber, so it will occur.

Withholding Information

Firms rely on information to make decisions. Occasionally workers learn information that makes them look bad but is valuable to the firm because it would help others avoid the same problem. Workers in promotion tournaments have disincentives to provide this type of information because, even though it is valuable to the firm, it could hurt their chances of getting a promotion and a raise if it benefited their opponents more.

Similarly, on occasion workers are in a unique position to pass on information that would make a co-worker look good or information that would enable co-workers to increase their productivity. These workers have a disincentive to pass on such information because doing so could only hurt their chances of promotion.

Misrepresenting Information

Employees can misrepresent information in a number of ways. For example, they can say that they have completed tasks when they really have not, or they can embellish reports to make themselves look better, perhaps by minimizing their own contributions and emphasizing factors beyond their control when a project ends in failure. Accurate information is valuable to the firm because without accurate information the firm cannot decide correctly which projects to continue and which to terminate.

In all of these cases, the influence activities are costly to the firm in a number of ways. (1) Employees waste time pursuing influence activities when it could have been spent exerting productive effort. (2) Backstabbing could lead to reductions in productivity as workers undermine other employees' projects. (3) Information that is important for the firm's decisions is withheld or misrepresented. (4) The wrong worker is promoted. (5) When promotions are related to influence activities rather than productive effort, the workers' marginal expected benefit of productive effort is reduced, and workers do not work as hard in areas that are profitable to the firm.

Homework Problems

Consider a tournament with two workers who both have the same marginal cost function:

$$MC(e) = 8e$$

The award for the winner is 100, and the marginal probability function for the noise variable is given by:

$$MP(\varepsilon) = \begin{cases} \frac{1}{5} + \frac{1}{25}\varepsilon & \varepsilon < 0 \\ & \text{if} \\ \frac{1}{5} - \frac{1}{25}\varepsilon & \varepsilon \geq 0 \end{cases}$$

1. Graph the marginal probability function.
2. Verify that the area under the function is 1.
3. Write worker 1's marginal condition when $e_1 > e_2$.
4. Solve the marginal condition in problem 3 for e_1 to get part of worker 1's reaction function, $R_1(e_2)$.
5. Write worker 1's marginal condition when $e_1 < e_2$.
6. Solve the marginal condition in problem 5 for e_1 to get the rest of worker 1's reaction function, $R_1(e_2)$.
7. Graph the reaction function.
8. Find the equilibrium effort level for the two workers.

CHAPTER

10 | EFFICIENCY WAGES

So far we have considered two ways of motivating workers to perform. The first was to tie current pay directly to current performance through either piece rate compensation schemes or commission schemes. In both of these the worker exerts extra effort in order to earn extra pay. The second way was to tie future pay to current performance through promotion tournaments. In that setting workers exert extra effort in order to receive a promotion and with it an increase in pay. In this chapter we explore a completely different method of motivating workers. By simply paying a high salary or hourly rate can a firm motivate workers to exert extra effort?

In light of Chapters 4 and 5, the answer should be no. According to those chapters, if workers are paid a flat rate per unit of time, they should exert zero effort. Even so, one may question this particular result from Chapters 4 and 5 because even if they are paid a flat rate, workers will still work enough not to be fired. Working so as not to be fired is the whole idea behind this chapter. Basically, if a firm sets its pay high, workers will exert extra effort so that they can keep their jobs and continue to earn the high pay.

The U.S. Bureau of Engraving and Printing, which is responsible for printing all of the currency in the United States, uses an idea like this to keep their employees from stealing. According to the bureau's claims, the reason its employees do not steal is that they are paid much more than they could make elsewhere, so they refrain from stealing in order to not risk their high-paying jobs. This claim has some merit. It may be possible for an employee to steal a small amount of currency but probably not a large amount. The payoffs from doing this would be temporary and relatively small, however, and hardly worth jeopardizing future pay (along with the punishment that comes with getting caught and convicted).

The approach we will take in this chapter is a bit different from our approach in previous chapters. We start with the idea that workers exert extra effort when firms pay them above-normal wages, and we then try to find a model in which this behavior occurs. By finding the model, we isolate the conditions that must be in place for this combination of high pay and high effort, and we can then use these findings to discuss real-world situations.

A MODEL OF EFFICIENCY WAGES

Before we can construct a model of efficiency wages, it is important to make clear precisely what we mean by efficiency wages. The term does not refer to a specific level of pay; instead, it refers to a compensation scheme, or a way of compensating workers. This entails specifying both what the firm pays the workers and what the workers do for their money. We say that a firm and a worker participate in an **efficiency wage scheme** if the firm pays the worker an above-normal wage and the worker exerts extra effort.

To make the model as simple as possible, consider Game 10.1, in which the worker and the firm each have two choices. The worker can choose to exert either the normal effort level or extra effort, and the firm can pay either the normal wage or a high wage; they make their choices simultaneously without knowing what the other will choose. The firm and the worker participate in an efficiency wage scheme if they choose the strategies corresponding to the upper left cell; that is, if the worker chooses extra effort and the firm chooses high wage. The task is to find a game in which the upper left cell is an equilibrium.

GAME 10.1

		Firm	
		High wage	Normal wage
Worker	Extra effort	20, 20	13, 24
	Normal effort	24, 13	15, 15

The payoffs are important. If the firm pays a normal wage and the worker exerts normal effort, both parties receive net benefits of 15 from the employment relationship. The idea is that by exerting normal effort the worker generates surplus that will be shared with the firm. To make the analysis simpler, we assume that the two share this surplus equally. If the firm pays the high wage and the worker exerts extra effort, the amount of surplus available for sharing increases, and they both get payoffs of 20. If, however, the firm only pays the normal wage when the worker exerts extra effort, the firm gets additional profit, for a total of 24, whereas the worker is hurt and gets a payoff of only 13. By paying the normal wage when the worker exerts extra effort, the firm keeps more of the surplus for itself. Similarly, when the firm pays the high wage but the worker exerts only normal effort, the worker gets additional surplus at the expense of the firm.

The central question is, does an equilibrium exist in which the firm pays the high wage and the worker exerts extra effort? This would be an efficiency wage scheme. The answer is no, and the analysis can be found in Table 10.1, which uses Chapter 8's technique for finding Nash equilibria. If the worker exerts extra effort, the firm's best response is to pay the normal wage because that generates profit of 24 whereas paying the high wage generates profit of only 15. High effort and the high wage are not mutual best responses, so the efficiency wage scheme is not a Nash equilibrium. However, if the worker exerts normal effort the firm's best response is to pay the normal wage, and the worker's best response to that is to exert normal effort. The only Nash equilibrium is the one in which the worker exerts normal effort and the firm pays the normal wage.

In order to get efficiency wages, it is necessary to change something about this game. One candidate for change is the payoffs, but that would lack realism because it would require, for example, that the firm would earn more from paying the high wage when the worker exerts extra effort than it would from paying the normal wage when the worker exerts extra effort. Because the wage is just a payment from the firm to the worker, paying more cannot make the firm better off unless the worker changes his behavior at the same time. Therefore, we need to change the game in other ways.

Before doing so, it is worth examining whether Game 10.1 accurately describes what happens in the work environment. In particular, is the game really simultaneous? In a simultaneous game the players need not take their actions at exactly the same instant in time; rather, the key to a simultaneous game is that neither player knows what action the opponent will choose at the time they make their own choices. There are certainly circumstances under which the firm must pay the employee without knowing what the employee has done during the pay period, either because the firm's bureaucracy requires that

TABLE 10.1   Best Responses for Game 10.1

Strategy Played by the Worker	Firm's Best Response	Worker's Best Response
Extra effort	Normal wage	Normal effort
Normal effort	Normal wage	Normal effort

pay requests go in early in the month or because the firm cannot measure the employee's output until after the employee has been paid. Many employees are paid at the end of a pay period for work that has already been done, so that the employees cannot know for certain how much the firm will pay. More importantly, however, the simultaneity assumption is merely a convenience here, and the same results hold if one of the players moves first and the other moves second.

For example, suppose that the worker moves first, deciding whether to exert normal or extra effort. The firm then observes how much effort the worker exerted and decides whether to pay a normal wage or a high wage. In this case the high pay can be considered normal pay plus a bonus. To find the equilibrium of this sequential game, start at the end and work back toward the beginning. When it is time for the firm to make a decision, the firm will choose normal pay and, therefore, no bonus, no matter how much effort the worker exerted because the firm's payoff is higher when it chooses normal pay. Because the worker knows that the firm will choose normal pay in equilibrium, the worker will choose normal effort. Thus, even when moves are sequential instead of simultaneous, there is no equilibrium in which the firm pays efficiency wages.

Repetition

Because the game did not lead to an efficiency wage scheme, let us modify it in a way that will yield an efficiency wage scheme. To find a way to modify the game, think back to the example of the workers at the Bureau of Engraving and Printing. The reason that they do not steal a small amount of currency today is so they can come back to work tomorrow and continue earning a high wage. The game analyzed above had no tomorrow, so the worker had no reason to exert extra effort today in the hope of something good tomorrow. Let us add some tomorrows. More specifically, change the game so that Game 10.1 is repeated T times, where T is some finite number larger than one.

Repeating the game makes it a sequential game, and as discussed in Chapter 8, the appropriate way to analyze a sequential game is to start at the end and work back to the beginning, the process known as backward induction. In this case the end is the last period, in which the worker and the firm make their decisions simultaneously for the last time.

Suppose that Game 10.1 is repeated twice, so that $T = 2$. What choices will the worker and the firm make in period 2? The game in the last period is just like the one-shot game analyzed above because there is no future after period 2. The worker's optimal choice is to exert normal effort no matter what the firm does, and the firm's optimal choice is to pay the normal wage no matter what the worker does. Consequently, in period 2 both players earn 15.

Now go back to period 1. Both players determine that they will earn 15 in period 2, no matter what happens in period 1. Combining the period 2 payoffs with the possible period 1 payoffs yields Game 10.2. Every payoff in Game 10.2 is obtained from adding 15 to the corresponding payoff in Game 10.1. The labels for the player's actions also change because now they specify what the player will do in period 1 *and* in period 2. By first figuring out what will happen in period 2, we can collapse the entire 2-period game to one simultaneous-move game as depicted in Game 10.2.

GAME 10.2

		Firm	
		High wage now, normal wage in period 2	Normal wage now, normal wage in period 2
Worker	Extra effort now, normal effort in period 2	35, 35	28, 39
	Normal effort now, normal effort in period 2	39, 28	30, 30

What is the equilibrium of Game 10.2? Look at Table 10.2, where the terminology "extra, normal" means that the worker exerts extra effort in period 1 and normal effort in period 2. The only row where the first and third columns match is the bottom one, and therefore, the only equilibrium is for the worker to exert normal effort in both periods and the firm to pay the normal wage in both periods. We cannot obtain an efficiency wage scheme by playing the original game twice.

Playing the game a third time does not help. In the third period the worker exerts normal effort and the firm pays the normal wage for exactly the same reason it did at the end of the two-period game. The

TABLE 10.2 Best Responses for Game 10.2		
Strategy Played by the Worker	*Firm's Best Response*	*Worker's Best Response*
Extra, normal	Normal, normal	Normal, normal
Normal, normal	Normal, normal	Normal, normal

game played in the second period of the three-period game is the same as the one shown in Game 10.2, except with period 2 changed to period 3 in the descriptions of the actions; for the same reasons as given above, the worker exerts normal effort in period 2, and the firm pays the normal wage in period 2. Because both players earn 15 in period 2 and 15 in period 3, the entire three-period game can be collapsed to a simultaneous-move game, Game 10.3, which is obtained from Game 10.1 by adding 30 to each payoff and relabeling the actions appropriately.

GAME 10.3

		Firm	
		High wage now, normal wage in remainder	Normal wage now, normal wage in remainder
Worker	Extra effort now, normal effort in remainder	50, 50	43, 54
	Normal effort now, normal effort in remainder	54, 43	45, 45

Once again, the game's only equilibrium has the worker exerting normal effort every period and the firm paying the normal wage every period. As you can probably guess, this is true for any finite number of repetitions. The worker exerts normal effort and the firm pays the normal wage in the last period; they do the same in the next-to-last period; they do the same in the period before that, and so on all the way back to the beginning of the game. It is impossible to obtain an efficiency wage scheme by repeating Game 10.1 a finite number of times. Just having a future is not enough.

Harsh Punishment

An alternative idea that comes from thinking about what happens at the Bureau of Engraving and Printing is that the workers behave themselves so that they will not be fired. What happens if we change the original game so that the firm can fire the workers? Will this be enough to obtain an efficiency wage scheme? Firing a worker can be considered harsh punishment for bad behavior. It is certainly much harsher than just reducing the worker's pay to the normal wage. Maybe the possibility of harsh punishment is enough to induce the worker to exert extra effort. But in the equilibrium of the original game, the firm did not pay the high wage, either, so we should also provide a means for the worker to punish the firm harshly.

Game 10.4 differs from Game 10.1 by adding one more choice for each player. The firm can fire workers. If it does, the fired workers generate no profit for the firm, so the firm's payoff is zero. If workers are fired unexpectedly, however, they do not have time to find alternative employment, and their payoff is -5. Workers can also quit. If they do, they exert no effort but get no pay, so their payoff is zero. The firm, however, is caught unaware, and its payoff is -5. If workers quit and the firm fires them at the same time, both parties get payoffs of zero.

GAME 10.4

Firm

Worker		High wage	Normal wage	Fire
	Extra effort	20, 20	13, 24	−5, 0
	Normal effort	24, 13	15, 15	−5, 0
	Quit	0, −5	0, −5	0, 0

This game has two equilibria that satisfy the mutual best response criterion of Chapter 8, as can be seen in Table 10.3. If the worker exerts normal effort, the firm's best response is to pay the normal wage because 15 is the firm's highest payoff in the middle row. If the firm pays the normal wage, the worker's best response is to exert normal effort because 15 is the highest payoff for the worker in the middle column. Thus, in one equilibrium the worker exerts normal effort and the firm pays the normal wage. In the second equilibrium the worker quits and is fired at the same time. If the worker quits, the firm can either earn 0 or −5, so firing is the best response. If the firm fires the worker, the worker's best response is to quit.

TABLE 10.3   Best Responses for Game 10.4

Strategy Played by the Worker	*Firm's Best Response*	*Worker's Best Response*
Extra effort	Normal wage	Normal effort
Normal effort	Normal wage	Normal effort
Quit	Fire	Quit

Neither of these equilibria generates an efficiency wage scheme. If the worker exerts extra effort, the firm's best response is to pay the normal wage. Likewise, if the firm pays the high wage, the worker's best response is to exert normal effort. The addition of a harsh punishment option by itself is not enough to generate efficiency wages.

Repetition and Harsh Punishment Together

At the Bureau of Engraving and Printing, workers refrain from walking off with small amounts of currency because they are worried about being fired, which keeps them from earning high pay in the future. It seems that harsh punishment and repetition work together to keep them from stealing. We can capture both effects by repeating Game 10.4.

To keep things as simple as possible, let us keep the future short and only play Game 10.4 twice. This is the minimum number of periods for which we have a future. To find an equilibrium of the two-period game, we must specify strategies for the two players and determine whether they have the mutual best response property. Remember, however, that in sequential games strategies are *complete contingent plans*, as discussed in Chapter 8. Think about a strategy this way. Suppose that you are one of the players in the two-period game but you cannot be there to make your moves. Instead, you must write down directions for a friend who is going to make the moves on your behalf. The directions would have to tell your friend what to do in every possible contingency in order to always do exactly what you want. This set of directions would be a strategy.

Consider the following strategy for workers: They exert extra effort in the first period. Their choice in the second period depends on what happened in the first period. If they exerted extra effort in the first period, *and* if the firm paid the high wage in the first period, the workers exert normal effort in the second period. If either the workers failed to exert extra effort in the first period or the firm failed to pay the high wage, the workers quit in the second period.

We need a strategy for the firm, too. The firm pays the high wage in the first period. If it paid the high wage in the first period and if the worker exerted extra effort in the first period, the firm would pay the normal wage in the second period; otherwise, it would fire the worker in the second period.

These strategies are summarized in Table 10.4. Note that the description of the strategies changes a bit in the table. In the first period, the worker is supposed to exert extra effort and the firm is supposed to pay the high wage. If both of these happen, then both the worker and the firm follow the designated strategy in the first period, and there are *no defections* in that period. If one or both of the players fails to follow the designated strategies in the first period, however,

TABLE 10.4   Strategies for Two-Period Version of Game 10.4

Period/Contingency	Worker	Firm
Period 1	Extra effort	High wage
Period 2		
No prior defections	Normal effort	Normal wage
Prior defections	Quit	Fire

one or both of them defects in the first period. There are two possible contingencies, then, for which the second-period strategies must specify an action: the contingency in which there are no defections in the first period and the contingency in which there is a defection in the first period. If there were no defections in the prior period, the worker is supposed to exert normal effort and the firm is supposed to pay the normal wage. If there was a prior defection, the worker is supposed to quit and the firm is supposed to fire the worker.

We need to see if these are equilibrium strategies; that is, we need to see if they have the mutual best response property using the process of backward induction. Begin in period 2, which is the last period. If there were no prior defections, the worker is supposed to exert normal effort and the firm is supposed to pay the normal wage. Looking at Game 10.4, we see that these are best responses to each other. If there were prior defections, the worker is supposed to quit and the firm is supposed to fire the worker. Again from Game 10.4, these are best responses to each other. In fact, these are the two equilibria we found in the one-shot version of the game. The strategies are mutual best responses in period 2.

Now consider period 1. The worker is supposed to exert extra effort. Assuming that the firm follows the designated strategy, by exerting extra effort in period 1, the worker earns 20 in period 1, and because there would be no defections in period 1, goes on to earn an additional 15 in period 2, for a total of 35. On the other hand, by exerting normal effort in period 1, still assuming that the firm follows the designated strategy and pays the high wage in period 1, the worker earns 24 in that period. But because this constitutes a defection, the worker earns zero in period 2, for a total of 24. Thus, the worker can either exert extra effort and earn a total of 35 over the two periods or exert normal effort and earn a total of 24 over the two periods. Obviously, it is better to exert extra effort and earn 35.

The firm's situation in period 1 is almost exactly the same. Assuming that the worker follows the designated strategy, the firm can pay the high wage in period 1 and earn 20 in that period and another 15 in period 2, or it can pay the normal wage in period 1 and earn 24 in that period but nothing in period 2. Paying the high wage yields the higher total payoff, so the firm pays the high wage in period 1. We have now established that the designated strategies are best responses to each other, and they constitute an equilibrium of the two-period game.

Look at what happens in the first period. The worker exerts extra effort and the firm pays the high wage. This is an efficiency wage scheme. Why do they do this? Let us consider the reasoning for the worker, keeping in mind that the reasoning for the firm is essentially the same. The worker exerts extra effort in the first period because doing so generates higher payoffs in the future period than exerting normal effort does. By exerting extra effort in the first period, the worker can continue to get the normal pay in the second period. By instead exerting normal effort in the first period, the worker gets fired and receives no payoff in the last period. The existence of a future plays an important role because the incentive for working hard now is continued pay in the future. Harsh punishment pays an important role, too, because the threat of being fired and earning nothing in the future is what keeps the worker from defecting and exerting normal effort in the first period.

One might wonder why the strategies did not specify extra effort and high pay for the second period if there were no prior defections. The reason is that these are not best responses to each other. If the firm is going to pay the high wage in the last period, the worker's best response is to exert normal effort. Likewise, if the worker is going to exert extra effort in the last period, the firm's best response is to pay the normal wage. Because these are not mutual best responses, we cannot have an equilibrium with extra effort and high pay in the last period. Efficiency wage schemes break down at the end of the game.

GENERAL LESSONS

The lessons from the preceding section are simple and require little elaboration. Efficiency wage schemes entail the firm paying a higher-than-normal wage and the worker exerting higher-than-normal effort, and it is possible for such schemes to arise in equilibrium. Two crucial factors must be in place for efficiency wage schemes to occur, however. First, there must be a future, so that defections from the efficiency wage scheme can be punished. Second, the punishment must be harsh, so that it deters defections from the efficiency wage scheme. As we saw, threatening a worker with a reduction in pay from the high wage to the normal wage was not enough to induce the efficiency wage scheme in the repeated version of the original game. Harsh punishment was needed to keep the worker from exerting normal effort and the firm from paying the normal wage in the beginning of the game.

Efficiency wage schemes can be thought of as a carrot-and-stick method of motivation. High future wages act as the carrot the firm uses to reward extra effort, while firing is the stick used to punish reductions in effort. At the same time, the worker uses the possibility of extra future effort as the carrot that rewards the firm for paying the high wage, while quitting is the stick used to punish the firm for wage reductions. Thus, our ability to construct a model in which efficiency wage schemes arise means that, in general, systems of future rewards and punishments can be used to motivate extra effort.

RESTRICTIONS ON THE FIRM'S BEHAVIOR

The firm's equilibrium strategy summarized in Table 10.4 allows for efficiency wage schemes, but it requires the firm to take some actions that may be difficult or illegal, depending on the industry and the laws under which the firm operates. In particular, according to its strategy the firm is supposed to fire the worker if the worker fails to exert high effort in the first period, but in many cases it is difficult to fire an employee. For an immediate example, your professors may have tenure, which makes firing them difficult. It is also difficult to fire state employees who have been in the same job for a sufficiently long time. In addition, the strategy requires the firm to reduce the worker's pay from the high wage in period 1 to the normal wage in period 2. Laws or other rules may state that the firm cannot reduce a worker's pay unless the worker agrees to the reduction, as when the airlines negotiate for salary reductions with unionized employees. How do these restrictions in wage reductions and firing affect a firm's ability to use an efficiency wage scheme to motivate its employees?

Restrictions on Wage Reductions

Suppose that the firm is unable to reduce a worker's wage. This means that once the firm has paid the high wage in period 1 it is no longer able to pay the normal wage in period 2 as the strategy in Table 10.4 requires. This creates two possibilities for a firm that has already paid the high wage: Either it can pay the high wage in period 2, or it can fire the worker in period 2. Does either of these allow for an efficiency wage scheme?

First suppose that the firm adopts a strategy in which it pays the high wage in period 2, as shown in Table 10.5. The worker, who faces no restriction on reducing effort, still exerts the normal level of effort in period 2. We must check to see if these strategies are mutual best responses according to backward induction. For the usual reasons, the worker quitting and the firm firing the worker in the same period are an equilibrium, so we need not check the contingency in which there were prior defections. Accordingly, suppose that there were no defections in

TABLE 10.5 Strategies when the Firm Cannot Reduce Wages in Period 2

Period/Contingency	Worker	Firm
Period 1	Extra effort	High wage
Period 2		
No prior defections	Normal effort	High wage
Prior defections	Quit	Fire

period 1. If the firm pays the high wage in period 2, the worker's optimal response is to exert normal effort because 24 is the highest payoff the worker can get in period 2. If the worker exerts normal effort in period 2, the firm can either pay the high wage or fire the worker because paying the normal wage is against the law. From Game 10.4, paying the high wage yields the firm a profit of 13, whereas firing the worker yields a profit of zero, so paying the high wage is a best response. The two second-period strategies are mutual best responses and compatible with an equilibrium.

Now look at the first period. Assuming the firm follows the proposed strategy, by exerting extra effort in period 1 the worker earns 20 in period 1 and 24 in period 2, for a total of 44. By defecting and exerting normal effort in period 1, the worker earns 24 in period 1 but nothing in period 2. Clearly it is better for the worker to follow the proposed strategy in period 1. Turning attention to the firm, under the assumption that the worker follows the proposed strategy, paying the high wage in period 1 generates 20 in profit for the firm in period 1 and an additional 13 in period 2, for a total of 33. If the firm defects and pays the normal wage in period 1, it earns 24 in period 1 but nothing in period 2 because the worker quits after the defection. Paying the high wage in period 2 is obviously better. We still get an efficiency wage scheme in the first period.

The other possible way to change the firm's strategy from that in Table 10.4 is to have the firm fire the worker in the second period because it cannot pay the normal wage. If workers know they are going to be fired, their best option is to quit at the same time, which yields the strategies in Table 10.6.

TABLE 10.6 Strategies when the Firm Fires the Worker in Period 2 Because it Cannot Reduce the Worker's Pay

Period/Contingency	Worker	Firm
Period 1	Extra effort	High wage
Period 2		
No prior defections	Quit	Fire
Prior defections	Quit	Fire

In contrast to the strategies in Table 10.5, these strategies do not constitute an equilibrium. To see why, consider the worker's first-period decision. Assuming that the firm follows the assigned strategy, by exerting extra effort the worker earns 20 in period 1 and nothing in period 2, but by exerting normal effort the worker earns 24 in the first period and nothing in the second. Clearly this defection is profitable, and the worker's strategy is not a best response to the firm's strategy. The firm does much better obtaining an efficiency wage scheme if it pays the high wage in the last period than if it fires the worker in the last period.

Restrictions on Firing

Now suppose that the firm cannot fire the workers. This changes the game in a fundamental way, removing the firm's only method of harsh punishment. The intuition we gained from the model of efficiency wages in the first section of this chapter suggests that it will be impossible to sustain an efficiency wage scheme in this setting. Let us make sure that this is true.

Game 10.4 is changed to Game 10.5, in which the column corresponding to the firm firing the worker is deleted from the game. Note that the worker will never quit in this situation because no matter what the firm does, the worker is better off exerting normal effort than quitting. Because quitting is never played, the game is essentially the same as Game 10.1, and we found in the chapter's first section that repeating that game led to the worker's exerting normal effort and the firm's paying the normal wage every period. Our intuition holds: Efficiency wage schemes are impossible when one party loses its ability to punish harshly.

GAME 10.5

		Firm	
		High wage	Normal wage
	Extra effort	20, 20	13, 24
Worker	Normal effort	24, 13	15, 15
	Quit	0, −5	0, −5

We have found that an inability to reduce wages does not preclude the use of an efficiency wage scheme to motivate workers, but an inability to fire workers does. Both of these restrictions were placed on the firm's choice set: When the firm cannot reduce wages, the middle column of Game 10.4 is removed from the last period, and when the firm cannot fire its workers the last column of the game is removed.

Unemployment Insurance

Although it does not change the set of actions available in the game, another policy does change the payoffs to the worker, and it can also have detrimental effects on the ability to use efficiency wages. Suppose that workers have unemployment insurance that will provide them with an income if they find themselves without work for any reason. In many countries, the government requires employers to provide unemployment insurance, and in other countries the government provides the insurance itself. In some countries, such as Sweden, the unemployment benefits can be quite lucrative. We analyze the effects of such lucrative unemployment benefits here.

The payoffs in the game tables are the worker's share of the surplus generated by the employment relationship. To get this surplus, the worker exerts costly effort and receives a paycheck from the firm. If the paycheck is greater than the cost of the effort exerted, he receives a positive net benefit, and the payoff in the table is positive. If the worker does not work, then under normal circumstances the worker exerts no effort and receives no pay, for a net benefit of zero. With unemployment insurance, however, the worker exerts no effort and still receives some pay. The net benefit enjoyed by the worker could be anything, and it could even be larger than the benefit from the efficiency wage scheme if the unemployment insurance payments are large enough and effort is sufficiently costly. This would make workers want to lose their jobs, and then efficiency wages obviously cannot work.

Efficiency wage schemes can still break down if the worker's net benefit when unemployed is below the net benefit received when earning the normal wage and exerting normal effort, as long as the net benefit when unemployed is still relatively high. In Game 10.4 the worker receives a payoff of 15 from exerting normal effort and receiving the normal wage. Suppose that, whether because of quitting or being fired, an unemployed worker receives enough unemployment insurance to generate a net benefit of 12. The payoff table changes to that in Game 10.6.

GAME 10.6

Firm

	High wage	Normal wage	Fire
Extra effort	20, 20	13, 24	12, 0
Worker Normal effort	24, 13	15, 15	12, 0
Quit	12, −5	12, −5	12, 0

The strategies in Table 10.4 no longer constitute an equilibrium. Consider the first period. Assuming that the firm follows the assigned strategy, by exerting extra effort the worker earns 20 in period 1 and 15 in period 2, for a total of 35. By defecting and exerting normal effort, the worker earns 24 in period 1 but then is fired and receives unemployment benefits in period 2 for an additional 12. Thus, the worker gets 35 from exerting extra effort but 36 from exerting normal effort. Because unemployment pays so well, firing the worker is not harsh enough punishment, and the efficiency wage scheme breaks down.

Homework Problems

1. What is an efficiency wage scheme?
2. What are the two key ingredients for achieving an efficiency wage scheme?

    The remaining problems are based on the following game:

Firm

	High wage	Normal wage	Fire
Extra effort	10, 10	3, 15	−2, 0
Worker Normal effort	15, 3	4, 4	−2, 0
Quit	0, −2	0, −2	0, 0

3. Suppose that the game is played 3 times. Are the strategies below consistent with an equilibrium? Why or why not?

Period/Contingency	Worker	Firm
Period 1	Extra effort	High wage
Period 2		
No prior defections	Extra effort	High wage
Prior defections	Quit	Fire
Period 3		
No prior defections	Normal effort	Normal wage
Prior defections	Quit	Fire

4. Suppose that the game is played 3 times. Are the strategies below consistent with an equilibrium? Why or why not?

Period/Contingency	Worker	Firm
Period 1	Extra effort	High wage
Period 2		
No prior defections	Normal effort	Normal wage
Prior defections	Quit	Fire
Period 3		
No prior defections	Normal effort	Normal wage
Prior defections	Quit	Fire

11

TEAM INCENTIVES

M
any students have been exposed to team compensation through group projects in their classes. In a typical group assignment, students are either assigned to a group by the professor or they are allowed to choose their own groups. Then they must research a topic, write a paper, and present it to the class, with everyone in the group getting the same grade for the project. For many students, this turns out to be a bad experience. Usually they think that they did more work than the other members of the group, so that their hard work helped people who did not deserve it. Some students even go so far as avoiding classes that have group assignments.

In spite of these bad experiences, many firms use team incentives to compensate their employees. The most common team incentive is profit sharing, where all of the employees are rewarded when the firm's profit goals are met. Also, in many instances firms reward smaller units on the basis of their performance. In this chapter we analyze how, and how well, team compensation works.

WHY TEAMS?

Why do firms choose to compensate workers based on team performance instead of individual performance? They have several reasons. These include complementarities, identification of contributions, knowledge transfer, and fairness.

Complementarities

One reason for considering teams as opposed to individuals is that the members of the team can produce more when they work together than they can when they work individually. If this is the case, the firm should encourage them to work together rather than pursue individual activities that are rewarded separately. This is best achieved by rewarding the workers as a team.

This begs the question of why workers might accomplish more together than separately. Consider the following examples. A person with an interesting public life might not have any skills in writing or storytelling, whereas an author with these skills might not have any worthwhile stories to write. Neither could write a bestseller alone. Together, however, they could write an autobiography that sells more copies than both the books they would have written separately.

Success in hockey requires teammates working together. One of the National Hockey League's minor leagues used to have an all-star game in which the previous year's champion would play the all-stars from the rest of the league. It is unlikely that the previous year's champion would have half of the league's best players, especially considering that in minor league hockey the best players get to move up to the next level. So even though the all-star team had more talent on average than the previous year's champion, the previous year's champion would typically win the all-star game.

These two examples establish that complementarities exist and can be important, but they do not work that well for explaining why a firm might want to consider its employees as members of teams instead of as individuals. In a corporate setting complementarities arise for three main reasons. The first is that a task or project might simply be too big for one person to accomplish effectively. Think about moving a couch. While one person can move a couch, given enough time and ingenuity, two people together can move it much more easily. The second reason, which is related, is specialization. By placing employees in teams, the firm can allow each employee to specialize in one subset of the production process. Through specialization employees can become more adept at their own tasks, thereby reducing the time it takes to complete the task and reducing production costs. These benefits of specialization are exploited in assembly line production. Of course, in an assembly line, the rate at which one employee can complete an assigned task depends on how fast the other workers complete theirs, and the entire production line really is a team.

The third reason is that sometimes workers develop a relationship in which they work really well together. For example, two advertising executives might bounce ideas off each other, with each one improving upon the ideas of the other, until the final product is much better than anything one of the individuals could have come up with alone. All three of these reasons describe situations in which workers are able to accomplish more as part of a team than they could as individuals.

Identification of Contributions

In many cases it is nearly impossible to determine what a single worker has accomplished independently. The best example here is management. In many firms one group of workers does the actual production and another group of workers manages that first group. These managerial tasks include making assignments for workers, filling out paperwork, and reporting to upper management. The members of the management group do not actually produce anything themselves, but without them the workers they manage would not be so productive. What is the value of the members of the management group? Because these workers' contributions cannot be identified easily, it makes sense to reward them based on the performance of the workers they supervise.

The example of the two advertising executives also illustrates a situation in which the contributions of individual workers are difficult to identify. If the two executives come up with the advertising campaign together, then how can the firm tell how much one contributed and how much the other contributed? In the absence of this information, the two must be rewarded as a team.

Knowledge Transfer

When workers are placed in teams, they can learn from each other. For example, when new workers join a firm, they might be teamed with more experienced workers for a period of time while they learn their jobs. If the more experienced worker takes her training duties seriously, she produces less during the training period. If she is rewarded individually based on output, however, she would have an incentive to neglect her training duties. Consequently, treating the trainer and the trainee as a team can lead to more knowledge transfer.

Knowledge transfer does not just take place in a training situation, however. A team might bring together workers with different areas of expertise, and through team interactions they share their expertise with the other members of the team. This knowledge transfer can make everyone on the team more valuable to the firm, even after the team project ends.

Fairness

When workers perform well, the entire firm benefits and profit increases. This increased profit goes to the owners of the firm. Some workers might find it discouraging that the owners reap the benefit of the workers' effort instead of the workers retaining that benefit themselves. If worker morale falls, the workers become less productive or leave the firm, and profit declines.

To combat this harmful effect of high profits, the owners of the firm might choose to share the profit with the workers who earned it for them. This creates a team consisting of the workers and the owners and provides part of the rationale behind profit sharing plans.

THREE APPROACHES TO ANALYZING TEAMS

In this section we want to treat team incentives analytically. To do this we take three separate approaches. First, we construct a game that captures all of the important aspects of team incentives. Second, we look at the effort in a team environment as providing a public good. Finally, we examine the behavior of a worker mathematically. All three approaches give us the same answer: Team incentives are ineffective for inducing effort from workers.

A Game-Theoretic Approach

The goal of this subsection is to construct a game that captures all of the important aspects of the behavior of workers in teams. To keep things simple, assume that each worker must choose between exerting one unit of effort or two units of effort. Further, suppose that each unit of effort costs the worker who exerts it $20 but costs the other worker nothing. Each unit of effort generates $30 for the firm to use to pay the workers. Because the workers are in a team, all pay is split equally between the two workers.

This generates the payoffs in Game 11.1. If both workers exert one unit of effort, they generate a total of $60 in pay. The firm splits this $60 between the two workers, so they both get $30. The unit of effort costs $20, so each worker earns a net benefit of $10. Similarly, if both workers exert two units of effort, total pay is $120 and each worker gets $60. Effort costs $40 for each worker, so both workers earn net benefit of $20.

If worker A, who is represented by the row player, exerts 2 units of effort but worker B exerts only 1 unit, total effort is 3 units and total pay is $90. The firm splits this between the two workers, and each worker is paid $45. Worker A exerted $40 of effort to be paid $45, for a net benefit of $5. Worker B exerted only $20 of effort to be paid $45, for a net benefit of $25. Clearly worker B benefits from A's extra effort. The payoffs when worker B exerts 2 units of effort and worker A exerts only 1 can be calculated in the same way.

<table>
<tr><td colspan="5" align="center">GAME 11.1</td></tr>
<tr><td></td><td></td><td colspan="2" align="center">Worker B</td></tr>
<tr><td></td><td></td><td align="center">1 unit of effort</td><td align="center">2 units of effort</td></tr>
<tr><td rowspan="2">Worker A</td><td>1 unit of effort</td><td align="center">10, 10</td><td align="center">25, 5</td></tr>
<tr><td>2 units of effort</td><td align="center">5, 25</td><td align="center">20, 20</td></tr>
</table>

This game has only one Nash equilibrium, and in that equilibrium both workers exert the minimal effort. No matter how much effort worker B exerts, worker A gets higher net benefit from exerting one unit of effort than from exerting two units of effort. Similarly, no matter what A does, B gets higher net benefit from exerting one unit of effort. Consequently, in equilibrium both workers exert one unit of effort. They would both be strictly better off if they both exerted two units of effort instead of one, but the equilibrium of the game prescribes exerting one unit of effort.

The reason for workers exerting as little effort as possible should be clear. For every $20 in effort exerted, the worker is paid an additional $15 (that is, $30 in total pay split between the two workers). Because the marginal benefit of effort is less than the marginal cost, the worker should exert as little effort as possible. In Game 11.1, that is one unit of effort.

The problem here is that individual workers bear the cost of their own effort, but everyone shares the benefits. If the team has more workers, these benefits are even more diluted. Thus, the general lesson from this section is that, because they dilute benefits, team incentives tend to lead to minimal amounts of team effort.

A Public Goods Approach

When economists use the term *public good*, they have something very specific in mind. A good is a **public good** if it satisfies the two criteria of being nonexclusionary and nonrival in consumption. Let us take these two criteria one at a time.

A good is **nonexclusionary** if there is no way to keep someone from consuming it. A radio broadcast over the airwaves is nonexclusionary because anyone in the area with a radio can tune in, and there is no way to keep any single person from tuning in. National defense is also nonexclusionary because the government cannot protect my neighbor's house from a missile attack without protecting mine as well. Cars, on the other hand, are exclusionary because there is a way to keep people from consuming a particular car. By not giving someone the key, that person is excluded from using the car.

A good is **nonrival in consumption** if the existence of someone consuming the good does not preclude someone else from consuming it, too. A radio broadcast is nonrival in consumption because one person tuning in does not suck the radio waves out of the atmosphere. The signal strength is not diminished in any way and anyone else can tune in to the same station. In contrast, an apple is rival in consumption. When one person eats the apple, no one else can.

When a firm pays team members equally based on team output, the pay generated by worker effort is a public good. It is nonexclusionary because the worker exerting the effort cannot keep any coworkers from receiving its benefits. It is nonrival in consumption because, when the pay is divided equally among the team members, the decision of any worker to take or turn down the pay does not affect how much any other member is paid. If any members turn down their share, the firm keeps it.

In general, public goods are not paid for directly by the people who consume them. For example, most radio broadcasts are paid for by advertisers, not by listeners. National defense is paid for by the federal government, which in turn receives its money from taxpayers, but nobody makes a direct contribution to the government for national defense. Consumers have a good reason not to pay for public goods – they do not have to. Because the good is nonexclusionary, people can consume it whether they helped pay for it or not. Because it is nonrival in consumption, a noncontributor's consumption does not affect a contributor's consumption, so contributors have no reason to care who else consumes the good. Essentially, the good is free to the consumers, and their benefit from consuming it is the same whether they contribute to paying its expense or not.

In a team production environment, the public good is the pay that comes from a member's effort, and the members can contribute to the public good by exerting costly effort. However, because people tend not to contribute to public goods, one would expect that team members would exert little effort toward projects that benefit the team.

A term that arises from economists' studies of public good provision is **free-riding**. When contributing to public goods, individuals tend to free ride by making minimal contributions themselves and then enjoying the benefits of the contributions made by others. In a team production setting, individual workers do not do much work but reap the benefits of any effort exerted by their fellow team members. This is free-riding.

Free-riding can be seen easily in a public good contribution game. Suppose that there are two players, each of whom starts with $10. Each player can either contribute $10 to the pot or contribute nothing. The amount in the pot is multiplied by 1.5 and then split between the two players. This leads to Game 11.2.

GAME 11.2

		Column	
		Contribute $10	Contribute $0
Row	Contribute $10	15, 15	7.50, 17.50
	Contribute $0	17.50, 7.50	10, 10

The formula for ascertaining the payoffs is as follows. Suppose that the row player contributes R and the column player contributes C. The row player's payoff is then

$$(10 - R) + 1.5(R + C)/2$$

The $(10 - R)$ term accounts for how much of the $10 the row player has after the contribution. The pot is $(R + C)$, which is multiplied by 1.5 and then split, so that the row player's share of the pot is $1.5(R + C)/2$. For example, if the row player contributes $10 and the column player contributes $0, the row player's payoff is $(10 - 10) + 1.5(10 + 0)/2 = 7.50$. The column player's payoffs can be calculated in the same way after switching the Rs and the Cs in the formula.

The Nash equilibrium of Game 11.2 has both players contributing $0. No matter what the column player does, the row player is better off contributing $0. The reason becomes clear from the formula. Rearranging the formula so that there is just one R yields

$$10 - 0.25R + .75C$$

Every dollar he contributes reduces the row player's payoff by 25¢, so the contribution should be made as small as possible. This is exactly what we found in the first approach to the problem.

A Mathematical Approach

The mathematical analysis we will use here is similar to the one we used to analyze piece rates in Chapter 5. Suppose that a worker is part of an n-worker team. The worker's pay consists of three components. First, the worker receives a salary component denoted by s. Second, the worker receives a share of the income generated by the other members of the team. The income generated by the other team members is denoted T, and the worker's share is one nth of that, or T/n. Finally, the worker generates income for the team by exerting effort, and that amount of income is denoted by $I(e)$. The worker keeps a share of this equal to $I(e)/n$. Effort is costly, and the cost of effort is denoted by $C(e)$. The worker's net benefit, then, is given by

$$NB(e) = s + T/n + I(e)/n - C(e)$$

To find out how much effort the worker will exert, assuming that his participation constraint is satisfied, look at the marginal condition. Only two terms on the right-hand side of the above expression depend on effort, so the other two terms are absent from the marginal condition. The marginal condition is:

$$MI(e)/n = MC(e)$$

The term on the left is the worker's share of the income generated from one more unit of effort, and the term on the right is the cost of one more unit of effort. The marginal condition states that these two are equal at the optimum.

The key feature of the marginal condition that we will discuss here is that the left-hand side, which is the marginal benefit of effort, falls when the size of the team rises. Mathematically, when n rises,

$MI(e)/n$ falls for any value of e. The reason for this is that any benefits from the worker exerting effort must be shared with all of the team-mates, so the bigger the team, the smaller the worker's share. The right-hand side, which is the marginal cost of effort, does not change when the team gets bigger. So, when the team grows, the marginal benefits shrink, and the worker exerts less effort.

SPLITTING THE BILL IN A RESTAURANT

Consider two different ways for a group of unrelated people to deal with the payment at the end of a meal at a restaurant. One way is for the group to ask for separate checks, so that every member of the group pays for their own meal. A second way is to get one check and split the amount evenly among everyone at the table. Splitting the check leads to a situation that is the reverse of the team production problem. In team production one worker bears all of the costs but shares the benefits with the team-mates. In the restaurant problem, each person receives all the benefits of his own meal but shares the costs with everyone else.

Three economists studied how people behaved in the two payment methods – separate checks or splitting the bill. They found that people order higher-priced meals when they are split-ting the bill, which is consistent with what the theory predicts. When they get separate checks the individual orders a meal to set $MB = MC$, and if they split the bill the individual orders a meal to set $MB = MC/n$, where n is the number of people at the table. Because $MC/n < MC$ when $n \geq 2$, the individual orders a more expensive meal when the table is splitting the bill equally. This is inefficient because every-one orders larger meals and ends up spending more than they would if they were paying separately.

SOURCE: Gneezy, Uri, Ernan Haruvy, and Hadas Yafe, "The Inefficiency of Splitting the Bill," *Economic Journal* 114 (April 2004), pp. 281–303.

GENERAL LESSONS

The first two sections of this chapter offer three general lessons. Workers working together may have productive advantages, but pay-ing them as a team inhibits incentives, and this effect gets worse as the team grows. In particular, the larger the team is, the more diluted the incentives are.

It appears that a firm could get more bang for its buck by paying workers individually because then incentives are not diluted at all. But as argued in this chapter's section "Why Teams?" teamwork may make workers more productive than they would be individually. Thus, the firm faces a tradeoff between the increased productivity from teamwork, which arises from complementarities and other effects, and the diluted incentives from team compensation.

WHEN CAN TEAM COMPENSATION WORK?

There are three keys to successful team compensation. First, there must be a valid reason for using team compensation. This means that there must be some productivity advantage to teams, as discussed previously. The best reason to encourage teams is when there are complementarities between the workers. The second key is a small group. Incentives are diluted more in large groups than in small ones, so keeping teams small gives the incentives more impact. When teams are very large, team incentives become virtually nonexistent. Both of these keys involve both the firm and the team. The firm must benefit from the team members working together, and the team must benefit from the firm paying them. The third key concerns interactions of members within the team. Look back at Game 11.1. It looks a lot like Game 10.1. In Game 11.1 the best outcome for the team is when both workers exert two units of effort. The equilibrium of the game has both workers exerting only one unit of effort, however.

In Chapter 10, an efficiency wage scheme arises when workers exert extra effort and the firm pays an above-normal wage. It was impossible for an efficiency wage scheme to arise from Game 10.1. In order to get efficiency wages, it was necessary to augment the game to give both players harsh punishment strategies and to repeat the game so that the future would matter. Because Game 10.1 and Game 11.1 are so similar, perhaps we can use comparable methods to achieve higher team production in Game 11.1.

The employer is passive in Game 11.1; the game involves only the workers. Using the lessons from Chapter 10, the workers can cooperate by exerting more effort and earning higher payoffs if the game is augmented to allow for harsh punishment and if the augmented game is repeated. Because we worked through the mechanics of the game in Chapter 10, we will not do so again here. Instead, we will focus attention on how harsh punishment could be added and whether repetition is sensible in this setting.

When a team is small enough and the members are located sufficiently close together, they can be aware of what their fellow members are doing. If one member works especially hard, the other members will know it, and conversely, if one member slacks off the other members will know it. In such cases the team will know when a member should be punished for deviating from the cooperative, high-effort outcome in which all members are better off (corresponding to both workers exerting two units of effort in Game 11.1). The question is, when they know that a member is slacking, can the rest of the team punish that member for it? This depends on whether the team can make the slacker's life sufficiently unpleasant that exerting the extra effort is more desirable than facing the punishment. One way to make the slacker's life unpleasant is to refuse to help him with his individual tasks when he needs it, so that he has to work harder on those individual tasks. A more common method is to ostracize the slacker, that is, to shun him socially. If the slacker is stuck with a fixed set of coworkers and spends most of his day with that set of coworkers, then ostracism can be a very harsh form of punishment. This can also be thought of as peer pressure: Workers exert extra effort on behalf of the team in order to avoid the wrath of their peers.

Obtaining the efficient outcome also requires repetition so that team members exert high effort now in order to continue receiving high payoffs in the future. For this to work, teams must stay intact for extended periods of time. If management reshuffles teams often, the possibility of a profitable future relationship is diminished and members will not find it worthwhile to exert extra effort. Only when teams are stable over time can cooperative team effort arise.

PROFIT-SHARING AND GAIN-SHARING

Many companies have profit-sharing plans. All three of the major U.S. auto makers have had profit-sharing plans in place for decades. In 2000, before the economic downturn, Daimler-Chrysler employees received an average of $8,100 each in profit-sharing payments, and Ford employees received an average of $8,000 each. In a typical profit-sharing plan, the company sets a target for profits. If that target is met, a portion of the profit is shared with the employees, with individual employees' payments based on their salary or wages. Gain-sharing programs are similar to profit-sharing programs but are based on different targets. So, for example, a gain-sharing program could be based on a revenue target or a cost-reduction target, and if the target is reached the employees share in the gains.

Proponents of profit-sharing plans typically offer several reasons for adopting them, including getting employees to work together and helping employees to focus on the profitability of the firm. But do profit-sharing plans really provide incentives? Think about Daimler-Chrysler. The company has about 86,000 employees eligible for profit-sharing. This means that if an employee takes an action that generates $1,000 additional profit for the company, that employee's share is, on average, 1¢. This does not provide much of an incentive, which should not be surprising based on the fact that for team incentives to work, the team should be small.

Why, then, do companies use profit-sharing plans? There are probably three good reasons. The first has to do with fairness and morale. High profits benefit the owners of the firm and, if they have stock-based incentives, the upper management of the firm. Without profit-sharing, the workers get nothing when profit is high. This could cause resentment, which in turn could reduce morale, thereby reducing profitability. To maintain morale and sustain profitability, the firm might want to share high profits with its workers. The second reason involves recruiting new workers. If workers find profit-sharing plans attractive, firms that offer them might be able to get better workers, which would increase profitability. The third reason is closely related. If workers find profit-sharing plans attractive, firms that offer them can pay lower wages, which also increases profitability. Thus, there are at least three reasons why profit-sharing plans can increase profitability, but none of them has anything to do with team incentives.

Homework Problems

1. Give an example (different from those in the text) of a good that is nonrival in consumption and a good that is nonexclusionary.

2. Suppose that two workers are paid as a team, and that the total payment to the two for different total effort levels is given by the following table:

Total Effort	Total Pay (To Be Split)
0	500
10	800
20	1,040
30	1,240
40	1,400

The firm splits pay evenly between the workers regardless of how hard they have worked. Each worker has the choice of exerting either 0 units of effort, 10 units of effort, or 20 units of effort. It costs a worker nothing to exert no effort, 200 to exert 10 units of effort, and 360 to exert 20 units of effort.

Construct a payoff matrix that shows the payoffs to the team members for the different combinations of effort levels.

3. Find the Nash equilibrium of the game in Problem 2, and state its implications for team incentives.

4. A firm earns net revenue of $110 for each unit of effort that is exerted by its workers. The firm rewards the workers as a team, paying every worker some amount per unit of team effort. The firm has

four workers, all of whom share the same effort costs given by the following table.

Effort Level	Effort Cost
0	0
1	40
2	100
3	180
4	280
5	400
6	540
7	700
8	880

a. What is the optimal effort level for each worker?
b. If the firm pays $100 per unit of effort to the team, how much effort will each worker produce?
c. How much would the firm have to pay to the team for each unit of effort to induce the optimal amount of effort from each worker?

12 | COMPARISON OF INCENTIVE SCHEMES

S o far in this book we have looked at four ways to motivate workers: piece rates, tournaments, efficiency wages, and team incentives. Each of the schemes was introduced individually to determine how they were able to induce workers to exert the right amount of effort. Now it is time to compare them.

There are several good reasons for doing so. The most basic reason is to find out if there are circumstances under which it makes more sense to use one of the incentive schemes than the others. In particular, under what circumstances is it even possible to use a specific compensation scheme, and how does the scheme impact the firm's profit? These questions are of major concern to the employers but not so much to the employees. The workers care more about which scheme gives them the highest net benefit, so we will also look at that issue. A third issue is cooperation between workers. Team incentives seem to be geared toward cooperation, but what about the others? Finally, each of the incentive schemes has its problems, and we can compare those, as well.

GETTING WORKERS TO WORK

When firms design a compensation scheme, the primary goal is to design one that enables them to maximize profit. They do this by inducing the workers to exert the optimal amount of effort and by paying them as little as they have to in order to get them to produce the optimal amount of effort. At the very least, then, a compensation scheme must induce workers to exert effort. However, the firm should also be able to fine-tune the compensation package so that it also induces workers to exert the *right* amount of effort. In this section we review how the different compensation schemes induce workers to work and how the firm can fine-tune them to get the right amount of work.

In a piece rate compensation scheme the firm sets the piece rate, which is a payment to the worker for each unit of output produced. Workers respond to the piece rate by producing the level of output at which their marginal effort cost is equal to the piece rate. This is the worker's marginal condition. By increasing the piece rate the firm can induce the worker to exert more effort, and the piece rate can be set optimally to maximize the firm's profit.

When the firm uses a tournament to motivate its workers, the workers exert effort in an attempt to win the prize. Because the firm awards the prize to the worker who exerts the most effort, workers can improve their chances of winning by exerting more effort. The marginal condition states that the worker exerts effort until the marginal cost of effort equals the marginal probability of winning times the size of the prize, which is the expected marginal benefit of effort. The firm can induce workers to increase their effort by increasing the size of the prize because that increases the expected marginal benefit of effort. When the prize is set correctly, the firm induces workers to exert the optimal amount of effort.

Efficiency wage schemes are different from the other two schemes because as they were modeled in Chapter 10 they did not involve a marginal condition. Instead, the efficiency wage scheme arises as part of the equilibrium of a game between the firm and the worker. Workers exert high effort so they can continue to earn high wages in the future, and the firm pays high wages so that it can continue to earn high profits from the workers exerting high effort in the future. The firm can influence the amount of effort the workers exert by adjusting the standard that distinguishes high effort from normal effort. The higher the standard that workers must meet, the more effort they exert as part of the efficiency wage scheme.

Finally, team incentives are just like a piece rate scheme, except that now workers are rewarded as part of a team instead of individually. If a worker is a part of a team, any output that individual worker produces increases the payment to every member of the team. The workers' marginal condition states that they exert effort until the marginal cost of effort equals their share of the team's payment per unit of effort. But because the worker only gets a share of the total team payment for a unit of effort, the firm's payment for effort is diluted, and workers exert less effort than they would if they were paid individually.

WHEN CAN THE DIFFERENT SCHEMES BE USED?

The different incentive schemes require different information for the employer to implement them. Workers are paid on the basis of some action, and therefore, to implement the incentive scheme the firm must measure those actions. This is most obvious with piece rate schemes. In a piece rate scheme workers are paid for each unit of output, so the firm must measure each employee's output. Sometimes this is straightforward. For example, at Safelite Glass Corporation windshield installers are paid a piece rate of $22 per installation. To implement this scheme Safelite just has to keep track of how many windshields each worker installs. For other employers, measuring each employee's output is more difficult. How would you pay a prison guard using a piece rate? What output would pay be based upon? It would not be the number of prisoners guarded, because that number would tend to stay the same, and it is beyond the guard's control anyway. It would not be the number of prisoners the guard has to punish for misbehavior, either, because the prison wants the inmates to behave, not misbehave. For prison guards, and many other occupations, there is no good notion of output that could be used as the basis of a piece rate incentive scheme.

A piece rate scheme is most plausible when the employee has one well-defined task that the employer can measure. Salespeople are often paid by commission which, as we saw in Chapter 5, is essentially a piece rate. Piece rates can also be used in manufacturing jobs where the worker is supposed to perform one task, and because many manufacturing plants are automated, it is easy to keep track of what each worker does.

Tournaments require much less information than piece rate schemes, especially promotion tournaments. All a supervisor needs to do to decide whom to promote is decide which employee is better than all of the others. The supervisor does not even need to make a complete ranking of all of the employees but just decide which one is best. A prison supervisor could determine which of the guards is best and most deserving of a promotion and name that guard the winner even without being able to measure (or define) the guard's output.

Promotion schemes have the added advantage that the supervisor does not have to define one single task for which the employee will be rewarded. If the firm values several tasks the supervisor can promote the worker who does best at all of the tasks rather than a worker who does well on one task but ignores the others.

In efficiency wage schemes, the information requirement is easier than in piece rate schemes but harder than in promotion schemes. In an efficiency wage scheme workers are supposed to exert extra effort instead of normal effort, and the firm pays the workers the high wage as long as they exert extra effort but fires them if they exert normal effort instead. To implement this scheme, the firm must set a standard that marks the line between extra effort and normal effort. The worker then works to meet or exceed this standard. To implement the efficiency wage scheme, the firm must measure performance well enough to determine whether or not the worker meets the standard.

As with promotion schemes, this allows the firm to use multidimensional criteria to evaluate the worker's performance. For example, many parents pay babysitters using an efficiency wage scheme. They pay the sitters a high wage so that the sitters will be willing to sit again in the future. The sitters exert high effort by being available, being punctual, cleaning up, and so on. If the sitter fails to do something that the parents expect, such as failing to pick up the toys or failing to get the children to bed before the parents come home, the parents can try to find a new sitter next time. Sitters are not paid separately for each task but are paid an efficiency wage with the expectation that they will fulfill all of the parents' requests.

Team incentives are much like piece rate schemes, and in order to implement them the firm must be able to measure the team's performance. Often firms get around this difficulty by treating the entire firm, or perhaps an entire division of the firm, as a team. Firm performance is measured quarterly anyway, so profit-sharing plans can be based on how quarterly profit compares to a target level. Workers are rewarded if profit exceeds the target.

With the exception of profit-sharing, tournaments are the easiest of the four schemes to implement. In a tournament the firm only needs to identify the winner, whereas with efficiency wages the firm must compare performance to a standard; with team incentive schemes the firm must be able to measure team output; and in piece rate schemes the firm must be able to measure individual output. Because output is either difficult or impossible to measure for many types of workers, piece rate schemes and team incentives based on the output of small groups of workers are simply not feasible in many instances. Profit-sharing, tournaments, and efficiency wages are feasible in most circumstances.

Other considerations might inhibit a firm from using one of these last three schemes, however. Tournaments do not motivate workers well when effort comparisons between workers are subject to a large amount of random noise or when supervisors are biased, so tournaments should be avoided when supervisors cannot make an unbiased, reasonably accurate judgment of who should win. Profit-sharing can only occur when the firm earns a profit, and many firms regularly suffer losses. Furthermore, many workers are employed in the government or not-for-profit sectors, so they have no profits to share. Finally, efficiency wage schemes depend on the credibility of the firm's threat to fire a worker who underperforms. For this threat to be credible, there must be a stock of replacement workers to take the fired worker's place.

WHO GETS THE SURPLUS?

The reason why workers and firms enter into an employment relationship is that the relationship generates surplus that the two parties can share. When there is a surplus, the firm can afford to pay workers enough to compensate them for their time and effort and still have enough left over to make a profit from the relationship. If there is no surplus, neither party gains from the relationship unless the other party loses, and the losing party would refuse to enter into the relationship. Thus, whenever a worker and firm voluntarily join forces they generate a surplus, and both parties want as much of that surplus as possible.

Workers have two types of costs. One is their effort cost and the other is their opportunity cost, which is the net benefit they would receive from working at the next best alternative employer. Using the notation from earlier chapters, the workers' costs are $C + u_0$, where C is the effort cost and u_0 is the net benefit they would earn at the next best alternative employer. When workers exert effort they generate net revenue for the firm of NR. The surplus is the difference between net revenue and the workers' costs, or

$$\text{Surplus} = NR - (C + u_0)$$

The worker's and the firm's shares of the surplus are determined by how much the firm pays the worker. Letting W denote the worker's pay, the shares are:

$$\text{Firm's share} = NR - W$$
$$\text{Worker's share} = W - (C + u_0)$$

If W is close to NR, the firm's share of the surplus is small and the worker's share is large. If W is close to $C + u_0$, the worker's share is small and the firm's share is large.

The different compensation schemes lead to different ways of sharing the surplus. So far, we have only discussed how the surplus is shared for a piece rate scheme. In Chapter 5 we saw that when the firm sets the piece rate and the salary component optimally in order to maximize profit, the firm gets all of the surplus and the worker gets none of it. We need to see if the other incentive schemes also allow the firm to capture all of the surplus.

Team incentives are the same as piece rate schemes except that the piece rates are paid to the entire team instead of a single individual. Because of the similarity, the firm is also able to capture all of the surplus when it pays the team a piece rate.

With efficiency wages it must be the case that the worker and the firm share the surplus so that both get strictly positive surplus. This should be clear from looking at the games in Chapter 10. In the efficiency wage scheme the worker exerts extra effort, and the firm pays an above-market wage. The alternative is that the worker exerts the normal amount of effort and the firm pays the market wage. In the games both the worker and the firm earn strictly higher payoffs in the efficiency wage scheme than in the normal effort/normal wage scheme.

Efficiency wages must generate strictly positive surplus for both parties. To see why, recall that if workers quit they get zero surplus.

Exerting extra effort must be strictly more attractive to them than quitting, and so they must earn strictly positive surplus from the efficiency wage scheme. The same reasoning works for the firm. If the firm gets none of the surplus it can fire the worker and not be any worse off. To entice the firm to pay the high wage, the firm must get some of the surplus. In efficiency wage schemes, then, both the worker and the firm get positive shares of the surplus.

In tournaments, pay depends on whether the worker wins the prize. Thus, the formulas for the firm's and the worker's *expected* shares of the surplus must use *expected* pay EW instead of W. Because the employment relationship is voluntary, the firm's expected surplus must be positive and so must the worker's. Consequently, just as with the piece rate and team incentives, the firm and the worker share the expected surplus. The big difference is that in a tournament only one of the workers gets the prize and the other workers do not. Essentially, the winner takes surplus away from the losers, so the winner's share of the total surplus is definitely positive but the losers' shares might be negative. All of the workers are willing to exert effort because their expected share of the surplus is positive, but after the tournament ends only the winner receives an actual positive share.

Tournaments are different from all of the other incentive schemes in terms of sharing the surplus. The firm gets a positive share of the surplus in all four schemes, but only in tournaments can a worker end up with a negative share. Efficiency wages guarantee the worker a positive share, whereas piece rates and team incentives can leave the worker with a zero share.

A COMPARISON OF PROBLEMS

As we saw in Chapters 5 and 6, many things can go wrong when the firm uses a piece rate system to motivate employees. If the system is set up improperly, it can motivate the wrong behavior, as with the problem of Sears auto mechanics being paid by the repair job, or it can lead to employees focusing on one part of the job and ignoring the others, as with the problem of telephone operators focusing on speed at the expense of accuracy. There can be other problems, as well.

When workers are paid by a piece rate, their income depends directly on their own output. Any time spent helping out coworkers is time that could have been spent producing more output, so piece rate systems provide a disincentive for worker cooperation. This does not mean that workers will never scheme together to manipulate the system, however. The optimal piece rate is determined in part by the workers' effort costs, which the firm has to infer from how workers respond to the piece rate. If workers collude and cut back their output, the firm will think that effort costs are higher than they really are.

Based on this information, the firm sets a higher piece rate to compensate for the higher effort costs. By colluding and cutting back output, workers end up not working very hard but being paid more than they were before, which increases their share of the surplus and decreases the firm's share.

Even though team compensation is very similar to a piece rate system, these last two issues—lack of cooperation and collusion to manipulate incentives—are not as problematic in a team setting. First, teams are often formed for the express purpose of fostering cooperation, so lack of cooperation is not a problem. Second, collusion to manipulate the incentive scheme works best if the people doing the colluding know each other well and each can see what the other is doing. Teams might not fit these requirements. For example, suppose that a team is the sales staff at a particular store for a national chain, and their pay is a salary plus a percentage of the total sales made by that store. These sales clerks would not know sales clerks from all of the other stores around the country, and they would have a very hard time finding out how those other stores are performing. In that case, the workers at one store might not find it worthwhile to cut back their sales in the hope of getting their commission rates raised because they would not know if the clerks at the other stores were also cutting back their own sales. Attempts at collusion to manipulate the incentive structure would probably fail, and collusion is not the problem for teams that it is for piece rates.

Team incentive plans still have the other two problems of piece rate schemes. If the plan is designed poorly, it motivates the wrong behavior. Likewise, if the plan does not reward all valuable activities equally, team members only perform those that pay the highest. More importantly, however, team incentive plans have one problem that piece rate schemes do not—free-riding. As discussed in Chapter 11, incentives are diluted in teams, and it is in the best interest of team members to do as little work as possible, collecting their pay from the effort made by the rest of the team.

Tournaments have one problem in common with the other two incentive schemes and two new ones. The old problem is lack of cooperation. If one worker helps another it improves the second worker's chance of winning, so there is a direct disincentive to cooperate with other workers. One of the new problems is the incentive for influence activities, which are activities that improve a worker's chance of winning without generating any benefit for the firm. The tournament provides workers with the incentive to do anything that increases the probability of winning, and this includes influence activities.

The second new problem is unique to tournaments, especially promotion tournaments. The firm gives the best worker a promotion and a new title. The new title is then a clear signal to anyone who cares that this worker was better than all of his colleagues. Other firms might value this information because they can use it to identify and then steal the best employees. Thus, when a firm uses promotion tournaments to motivate its workers, it also sets its best workers up for raiding by other firms.

The final incentive scheme to be considered is efficiency wages. Efficiency wages operate by comparing a worker's performance to a standard and, if that standard is met, paying the worker a high wage. This opens the door for collusion to manipulate the standard. If all workers act like effort is more costly than it really is, the firm could respond by reducing the standard, which would allow the workers to be paid highly for doing less work. The other problems suffered by efficiency wage schemes are similar to those suffered by piece rate schemes. Worker A will not help worker B unless worker A is already passing the standard and additional output of his own will not matter to his pay, so efficiency wage schemes do not foster cooperation. Also, if the standard is poorly designed so that it either rewards the wrong behavior or fails to reward some valuable behavior, workers will not behave in a way that is optimal for the firm.

Table 12.1 summarizes the chapter thus far.

CHOOSING THE RIGHT INCENTIVE SCHEME

The different incentive schemes have their own strengths and weaknesses. Which one should be used depends on the circumstances. Consequently, the only way to talk about the issue is through a series of examples.

Technical Support Operators

Many firms, especially computer and software-related firms, employ technical support operators to answer calls from customers and help them with problems with their products. Which incentive scheme would work best for motivating these employees?

Piece rates might be problematic. It would be a simple matter to pay the operator per call, but that would provide the incentive to end calls quickly, possibly before the problem is solved. Team incentives are unlikely because there are no real team advantages in this setting. That leaves tournaments and efficiency wages. If supervisors know who the best employees are, a promotion tournament could work, as long as promotion opportunities came along sufficiently often to motivate the workers. Promotion tournaments cause problems with cooperation, but that is not an issue for this type of work. Two difficulties caused by promotion tournaments that matter here, however, are the subsequent influence activities and the problem caused by workers who know that they will never win the tournament and are, therefore, not motivated by the tournament.

TABLE 12.1 Comparison of Different Incentive Pay Systems

Criterion	Piece Rates	Tournaments	Efficiency Wages	Teams
Why workers work	To increase output, which increases pay	To increase the probability of winning the prize	To keep their jobs so that they can continue earning high pay in the future	To increase team output, which increases team pay
What firms must be able to measure	Each individual worker's output	The best worker	Workers' attainment of a standard	Each team's output
Incorrect incentives	An incorrectly designed system can motivate the wrong kinds of activities; workers ignore activities that are not rewarded	Influence activities	No problem	Same as piece rates
Cooperation among workers	Disincentive	Disincentive	No effect	Incentive
Collusion to manipulate the incentive scheme	Collude to get piece rate raised	Disincentive for collusion	Collude to get standard lowered	Difficult to collude across teams

Efficiency wages might be the best alternative. In an efficiency wage scheme the firm pays the operators an above-market wage but requires them to exceed a performance standard. Any operator falling below the performance standard would be fired, and the high pay makes operators want to keep their jobs. The performance standard can incorporate everything that matters to the firm, including setting limits on how much time is spent not answering calls and standards regarding how well the operator solves customers' problems.

College Football Coaching Staffs

Every college football team has a large coaching staff. The top person is the head coach, followed by the offensive and defensive coordinators, followed by the position coaches. What incentive scheme should a college use for everyone but the head coach?

Piece rates are possible, but impractical. The linebacker's coach could be paid per tackle, but that would provide an incentive to make lots of tackles, which only occurs if the other team's offense stays on the field. The quarterback's coach could be paid per completion, and the running back's coach could be paid per rushing yard, but then how much they were paid would depend on which plays were called, over which they have no control.

Team incentives are also possible. The entire coaching staff could be paid per win. This would give all the coaches the incentive to work together so they would win more games, but college football teams only play eleven or so games per year, so an additional win or loss would mean a substantial variation in each coach's pay. Their income would be extremely risky, and the college would end up paying them a lot more to bear this risk. Also, there are possible collusion problems. If the team has a bad year and expects another one next year, to ensure that the coaches' wages are competitive with salaries at other schools, the pay per win would have to be very high the next year. This would give the coaching staff the incentive to have a bad season in order to vastly increase their pay the next season.

Efficiency wages could work here. The college could pay coaches an above-market wage and, if the team does poorly, fire them. This works best for schools with the very best teams. Schools with lower-ranked teams need not incur the expense because their coaching staffs are motivated by tournaments. The best coaches at lower-ranked schools have the opportunity to move up to a higher-ranked, higher-paying school. Because the lower-ranked schools do not have to pay for the prizes when a coach moves to a higher-ranked program, the tournament structure runs itself very cheaply.

Dental Hygienists

Dental hygienists clean patients' teeth. After the hygienist is done with a patient, the dentist comes in and examines the patient's teeth.

Because of this, it is possible to pay hygienists using a piece rate. The dentist checks the quality of the job when it is done, so the hygienist cannot ignore quality and only concentrate on speed. But, if one hygienist is faster than another, the dentist can schedule more patients for the faster one, so speed will be rewarded.

Team compensation and promotion tournaments make no sense in this setting. There are no team advantages in this type of work, and there is no job for successful hygienists to be promoted to. They cannot be promoted to dentist, because that requires a degree from dental school and a license. Efficiency wages could also work so that hygienists perform well to avoid being fired.

Homework Problems

1. Which incentive scheme tends to give the most surplus to the workers?
2. What is the difference between cooperation between workers and collusion among workers?
3. In your opinion, which incentive scheme is the most appropriate for motivating police officers in the homicide division? Explain your reasoning.
4. In your opinion, which incentive scheme is the most appropriate for motivating emergency room nurses? Explain your reasoning.
5. In your opinion, which incentive scheme is the most appropriate for motivating a receptionist at a dentist's office? Explain your reasoning.

13 EXECUTIVE COMPENSATION

E very year *Forbes* magazine provides information about the compensation packages of the 500 highest paid corporate executives in America. In 2003 the top 100 corporate executives averaged $18.5 million in total compensation. This pay came in various combinations of salary, bonuses, incentive clauses, shares of stock, and stock options. Chief executive officers make about 500 times more than the production workers at their companies, and this multiplier has been growing over time. These facts raise two obvious questions that will be the focus of this chapter. First, why are CEOs paid the way they are, especially in regard to stock and stock options? Second, why are they paid so much?

A FEW EXAMPLES

We begin this chapter with a few examples from the 2003 *Forbes* list of the 500 highest paid corporate executives. All of the examples come from prominent companies, and all of the executives are highly paid, but not all in the same way.

James E. Cayne has been the CEO of Bear Stearns, a financial services company, for ten years. His cash compensation for the fiscal year ending in November 2003 was $33.9 million. Of this, $200,000 was salary and $11 million was a bonus. The remaining $22.7 million was long-term compensation. Cayne owned $500 million of the company's stock, and he had no stock options.

Vance D. Cofmann has been the chairman of the board of Lockheed Martin, an aerospace and defense company, since 1998 and the CEO since 1997. His cash compensation for the fiscal year ending December 2003 was $13.8 million, of which $1.7 million was salary and $3.3 million was a bonus. He owned $17 million in stock and had $14 million in stock options.

John W. Thompson has been the chairman of the board and CEO of Symantec, a software company, for four years. In the fiscal year ending in March 2003, his cash compensation was $2.9 million, which was low for this group of CEOs. His salary was $750,000 and he received a $2 million bonus. He owned $10 million in stock and had $80 million in stock options. He exercised $11.9 million in options that year.

Robert J. Ulrich has been chairman of the board and CEO of Target, the retailer, for nine years. In the fiscal year ending in February 2003 his cash compensation was $7.0 million, including $1.4 million in salary and a $4.6 million bonus. He owned $33.6 million in company stock and $84.3 million in stock options. He exercised $12.2 million in options that year.

Finally, Jeffrey P. Bezos is the founder and head of Amazon.com. His total compensation reported in 2003 was $81,840, all of it salary. He had no stock options. Of course, he owned $2.8 *billion* in Amazon.com stock.

There is a pattern here that can inform our discussion: CEO salaries tend to be a relatively small portion of their total compensation. Most of their pay comes from bonuses, stock ownership, and stock options. How pay is divided among these three varies from corporation to corporation.

ALIGNING THE CEO'S AND THE OWNERS' INTERESTS

The first step in discussing how CEOs should be paid is determining what behavior should be rewarded. CEOs are different from production workers because they do not actually produce anything. Instead, they make decisions that determine the future course of the firm. To give the incentive to make the right choices, the pay should reward a CEO for good decisions.

The CEO is paid by the owners of the firm, or by the board of directors, which represents the owners. The owners are the stockholders. So when we talk about a decision being good or bad, we mean that it is good or bad from the perspective of the stockholders. What do the stockholders care about? They care about the value, or price, of their stock. Decisions that make the stock price rise are good from their perspective, whereas decisions that make the stock price fall are bad.

Because the owners of the firm care about the stock price, it makes sense to make the CEO's pay depend on the price of a share. One way to do this is through a system that pays a piece rate or commission for each $1 change in the price of the company's stock. Suppose that the board wants to increase the CEO's pay by x every time the share price increases by $1 and decrease it by x every time the share price falls by $1. This turns out to be very easy to do. Just give the CEO x shares of the company's stock with the restriction that it cannot be sold. Then every time the stock price rises by $1 the CEO's wealth increases by x; conversely, the CEO's wealth falls by x every time the share price falls by $1. As we saw in the preceding section, CEOs own a large amount of their firm's stock. For example, James Cayne, the CEO of Bear Stearns, owns 5.8 million shares of Bear Stearns stock, so he makes $5.8 million every time the share price rises by $1. However, he also loses $5.8 million every time the share price falls by $1.

By now we have raised several issues. First, because a CEO's income is determined largely by fluctuations in the price of a single stock, that income is very risky and may even be negative some years. In spite of this, the CEO's *wealth*, or accumulated assets, remains positive. Continuing to use James Cayne as an example, before any price changes he owns $500 million in Bear Stearns stock. If the share price falls by $10 he will still own $500 − 58 = $442 million in stock, and he will still be a very wealthy individual. Even so, his income fluctuates wildly.

The second issue is that the firm must give the CEO stock in order to align his interests with those of the shareholders. Compensating the CEO in this way is very expensive. To get Cayne those 5.8 million shares so that his income would change by $5.8 million every time the share price changes by $1, Bear Stearns had to give him $500 million in stock. They may not have given it all at once, and Cayne may have purchased some of the shares on his own, but to give him a high-powered incentive to improve the stock price, Bear Stearns had to give him a substantial amount of money.

The third issue arises from the fact that often CEOs are awarded stock in order to align their incentives with those of the shareholders, but they are restricted from selling those shares. This means that any income is just on paper, and it is not as real as cash. Does that reduce the incentives in any way? The answer is probably not. First, the CEOs can certainly borrow against their stockholdings. Second, many CEOs attain that position near the end of their careers, and they would be able to sell the shares after retirement. The fact that the income is only on paper is also advantageous to the CEO, who does not have to pay taxes on the gains or losses until he or she actually sells the shares.

Stocks Versus Stock Options

A stock option is the right to buy a share of the stock for a prespecified price during a designated time period. The prespecified price is called the **exercise price**, and an option of this form (the right to buy a share of stock) is commonly known as a **call option**. The opposite kind of option is a **put option**; it is the right to *sell* a share of stock for a prespecified price during a designated time period. We will only look at call options. To see how a call option works, suppose that the CEO of a company has the right to buy one million shares of stock for an exercise price of $40. If the current stock price is $45, the CEO can exercise those options and buy one million shares for $40 dollars each and then sell the shares on the open market for $45 each. The CEO makes a profit of $5 per share, for a total of $5 million. Thus, call options allow the CEO to make a profit when the actual share price is higher than the exercise price.

What if the stock price falls below the exercise price? For example, suppose that the stock currently sells for $35 per share. It no longer makes sense for the CEO to exercise those options because doing so would entail buying shares of stock for $40 each, which is $5 more than they would cost on the open market. Thus, when the current share price is below the exercise price, there is no value to exercising options.

To illustrate the difference between owning stock and having an option to buy the stock, suppose that the current stock price is $40 per share, and compare a CEO who owns one million shares to a CEO who has options to buy a million shares at an exercise price of $40. If the stock price rises by $1 per share, the CEO with stock gains $1 million. Under the same circumstances, the CEO with the options can exercise them to buy a million shares at $40 each and then sell them for $41 each, earning a profit of $1 million. Thus, the gain is the same whether the CEO owns stock initially worth $40 per share or owns options to buy the stock at a $40 per share exercise price.

Now look at what happens if, instead of rising by $1, the share price falls by $1 from $40 to $39. The CEO who owns stock now has $39 million in stock instead of the original $40 million, so the drop in the share price causes a loss of $1 million. The CEO with the options, however, would choose not to exercise them because the share price is lower than the exercise price. So, the CEO with the call options loses nothing.

One of the primary differences between stock and stock options is that stock options limit the downside risk faced by the owner. When the CEO owned the stock valued at $40 per share, an increase in the stock price led to a gain, but a decrease in the price led to a loss. When the CEO owned options with a $40 exercise price, an increase in the stock price led to a gain but a decrease in the price did not lead to a loss. Thus, stock options still provide a CEO with the incentive to take actions that make the share price rise, but they prevent the CEO's income from becoming negative.

The degree to which the downside risk is limited depends on where the exercise price is relative to the current stock price. Suppose again that the current stock price is $40 but that the CEO has options to buy one million shares at an exercise price of $38. By exercising these options the CEO would be able to earn a $2 per share profit, for a total of $2 million. But if the share price falls by $1 from $40 to $39, exercising the options would only result in a $1 per share profit, and the CEO's wealth would fall by $1 million relative to what it was before the price drop. If the share price fell by another dollar to $38, the CEO's wealth would fall by another $1 million. From there, however, the CEO cannot suffer any additional losses. If the share price falls to $37, the CEO would choose not to exercise the options. The most the CEO can lose is $2 million. In general, the most the CEO can lose is the difference between the current share price and the exercise price multiplied by the number of shares available through options.

One of the issues identified in the previous section concerning giving the CEO shares of stock to align his interests with those of the shareholders was that giving him stock makes his income very risky. Giving the CEO options instead reduces the risk, specifically the downside risk, so options provide a solution to this problem. A second issue raised earlier is the expense involved in giving the CEO stock. Do options reduce this expense?

Suppose that the firm wants to construct the compensation package so that the CEO makes $1 million every time the share price rises by one dollar. Further assume that the current share price is $40. If the firm wants to achieve its compensation goal by awarding the CEO a million shares of stock, the firm would ultimately pay the CEO $40 million. Now look at what happens if the firm instead achieves its compensation goal by awarding the CEO a million stock options with an exercise price of $40. Because the CEO has no reason to exercise the options, the firm pays nothing at the time it awards the options. It only has to make a payment to the CEO if the stock price actually rises.

To see why, suppose that the stock price rises by $2 and the CEO decides to cash out by exercising the options. The current stock price is $42, but the firm has to sell the stock to the CEO for $40 per share. This means that the firm loses $2 per option that the CEO exercises, for a total of $2 million. At the same time, the CEO makes $2 million by buying a million shares for $40 each and then selling them for $42 each. Essentially, then, when the CEO exercises that option the firm pays $2 million. Thus, when the firm uses options to align the CEO's interests with the shareholders', the firm only makes a payment to the CEO when the options are exercised, and then only in an amount equal to the CEO's profit on the transaction. Options are much cheaper for the firm than shares of stock.

Giving the CEO options solves both of the problems presented by giving stock. It makes the CEO's income less risky, and it is cheaper for the firm. It would seem, then, that awarding options is definitely better for the firm than awarding stock, but we have not yet considered all of the issues. Remember that the reason for awarding stock in the first place was to get the CEO to make decisions that would increase the firm's share price. In some instances, awarding options can lead the CEO to make decisions that hurt the share price instead of improving it.

Once again suppose that the current share price is $40 and this time the CEO has options to buy a million shares for $45 each. The options are currently "out of the money," and unless the share price rises above $45, exercising the options has no value. A vice president comes to the CEO with a proposal for a new project, garlic cola. The vice president reasons that because flavored colas are all the rage garlic cola could be the next big thing. If the project succeeds, the share price will rise to $48. If it fails, however, the share price will fall to $30. The vice president assesses the probability that garlic cola succeeds at 20 percent.

What will the CEO do, green light the garlic cola project or shut it down? The shareholders would hope that the CEO would shut it down. To find the expected impact of the garlic cola project, look at the expected value of the share price if the project goes forward:

$$\text{Expected share price} = (0.2)(\$48) + (0.8)(\$30) = \$33.60.$$

If the garlic cola project goes forward the expected share price will drop by $6.40, from $40.00 to $33.60.

Now look at the CEO's incentives. If the garlic cola project succeeds, the share price rises to $48. The CEO's options have an exercise price of $45, so the options are worth $3 million. If it fails the options are out of the money. But if the CEO does nothing, the options are still out of the money. The only way to get a payoff from the options is to green light the garlic cola project and hope it succeeds. From the CEO's perspective, the expected payoff from the garlic cola project is

$$\text{CEO's expected payoff} = (0.2)(\$3,000,000) = \$600,000$$

Because of the options, it is in the CEO's best interest to adopt the garlic cola project even though it is not in the best interests of the shareholders.

Stock options do not perfectly align the CEO's and the shareholders' interests. The reason is that the CEO's losses are limited by the difference between the current price and the exercise price, while the shareholders can lose their entire investment in the company. In the above example, the CEO approved a project that had considerable downside risk for the shareholders but none for the CEO, because the exercise price was higher than the prevailing share price.

The higher the option's exercise price, the less downside risk the CEO faces. Conversely, the lower the exercise price, the more downside risk the CEO faces, and the more closely the CEO's interests are aligned with the shareholders'. But the lower the exercise price, the more the firm must spend when the CEO exercises the options. Because the lower exercise price makes the CEO's income riskier, the more the firm must pay the CEO to compensate for that risk. At the limit, when the exercise price is zero the option is identical to a share of stock.

Obviously the firm faces some important tradeoffs when constructing the CEO's compensation package. The compensation packages for the five CEOs profiled earlier showed that firms use a mixture of stock and options. In 1999, 94 percent of the companies listed in the S&P 500 granted stock options to their top executives, so a large majority of the firms choose options either instead of or in addition to stock in the CEO's compensation plans. Of those choosing options, 94 percent set the exercise price equal to the prevailing share price on the day the options were granted. Thus, almost all of the options left the CEO heavily shielded from downside risk. The options were also a substantial part of the compensation package, accounting for 47 percent of total CEO pay.

INSULATING CEOs FROM BROAD MARKET SWINGS

When compensated using options or stock, a CEO's income can fluctuate for two reasons. First, when the firm performs better or worse its stock price goes up or down, and this in turn affects pay. In fact, these fluctuations are what make the compensation package work because the CEO's pay changes in the same direction as the value of the shareholders' stock. The second type of fluctuation is caused by the stock market. Stock prices often move together because of general economic conditions or because of important national or international events. For example, in several instances the Dow Jones Industrial Average fell by 400 points or more in a single day, and virtually all stocks posted substantial losses on those days. Needless to say, individual CEOs have little control over such events, but their pay fell drastically because of those events. This source of income risk, because it is outside of the CEO's control, does neither the firm nor the CEO any good, and in fact, CEOs dislike this sort of risk.

When individuals dislike risk, they must be compensated for bearing income risk. Otherwise, they would take a job somewhere else where the pay is subject to less risk. We saw this in Chapter 6 regarding piece rates. CEOs are risk averse just like (nearly) everyone else, so if their pay is risky, it must also be higher on average to compensate them for bearing the income risk. In fact, it has been estimated that, on average, CEO pay is 40 percent higher than it would be if this risk could be avoided.

Downward movements in the stock market are not the only problem. When the stock market does well, all CEOs are paid more. This leads to the often unpalatable circumstance in which a firm can do very poorly and be forced to lay off workers, but because of the strength of the market, the CEO is paid more than ever before.

Firms do not take steps to insulate their CEOs from market-wide fluctuations, although they could. To illustrate how, first note that when CEOs own a substantial amount of firm stock, their pay is positively related to the performance of the stock market as a whole. To balance this, their pay should have another component that is negatively related to the performance of the market. A way to do this would be to make their pay go down when the stock prices of competing firms go up. Such a scheme would accomplish two things. First, if stocks rise as a whole, the firm's stock and its competitors' stocks rise together. The CEOs' pay would rise because of the increase in their own stock's price, but it would decrease because of the increase in their competitors' stock prices. If the pay scheme was designed correctly, the increase and decrease would cancel each other, and the CEOs' pay would be insulated from the broad market increase.

The same thing would happen if the market went down. The firm's stock price would fall, but so would the competitors' stock prices. The drop in the firm's price would cause the CEOs' pay to fall, but the drop in the competitors' prices would cause the CEOs' pay to rise. If the two cancel each other, the CEOs are insulated from broad market downturns.

Making pay depend negatively on the price of the *competitors'* stock does something extra, however. Sometimes events occur that help or hurt all of the firms in a particular industry. For example, a war helps all defense industry firms, and oil companies are helped when OPEC cuts production so that oil prices rise. Defense industry CEOs do not typically start wars, however, and oil company executives have little influence over OPEC ministers. Following the September 11 attacks, the airline industry suffered a major drop in the number of passengers, and their CEOs should not be punished for an event that was beyond their control. When something happens that affects the entire industry, it causes both the firm's stock price and its competitors' stock prices to change in the same direction. If the CEOs' pay depends negatively on the competitors' stock prices, they are insulated from the stock fluctuations resulting from an industry-specific event over which they have no control.

Finally, this scheme makes the CEOs compete more seriously with the other firms in the industry. If the CEOs do something positive for their firm that makes their competitors' stock prices fall, such as taking away market share, they are rewarded for that. Similarly, if a competitor takes away market share, they are punished.

DO CEOs BENEFIT FROM LAYING OFF WORKERS?

A 2002 *Business Week* article touched off a public outcry when it reported that raises for the CEOs at the fifty companies with the most layoffs the previous year averaged 44 percent, while average CEO pay rose only 6 percent over the same period. It would seem that CEOs benefit at the expense of their workers. Does this really happen?

Kevin F. Hallock of the University of Illinois studied this problem. Using data on the 550 largest firms from 1987 to 1995, he found that firms that laid off workers the previous year do pay their CEOs more and give larger raises. However, after controlling for firm size and 781 other firm characteristics, he found that CEO raises actually decline slightly following layoffs.

How do we reconcile the *Business Week* report with Hallock's findings? The 50 firms with the most layoffs also tend to be large firms because large firms have more workers to lay off. Large firms also tend to pay their CEOs more. Thus, the raises reported in the *Business Week* report may be better explained by factors other than layoffs.

SOURCE: Hallock, Kevin F., "Layoffs, Top Executive Pay, and Firm Performance," *American Economic Review* 88 (September 1998), pp. 711–723.

WHY ARE CEOs PAID SO MUCH?

This chapter set out to address two questions. The first was why CEOs are paid the way they are, specifically using shares of stock and stock options. We have determined that both of these can be used to align the CEO's and the shareholders' interests and that the two assets have different strengths and weaknesses that lead some firms to choose more of one and some to choose more of the other. Shares of stock are very expensive for the firm and make the CEO's income risky. Options reduce both the expense and the risk, but they can lead CEOs to take on risky projects that are not in the best interest of the firms.

The second question for this chapter is why CEOs are paid so much. There are several reasons. First, in order to align their interests with those of the shareholders, the CEO must have enough of a stake in the firm that changes in share prices significantly impact the CEO's wealth. Because CEOs tend to be wealthy and successful business people, this stake has to be large, which means that the firm has to give them a large amount of stock or a large number of options. That said, the amounts typically given to the CEOs at the largest U.S. firms tend to be much larger than needed to align their incentives with those of the stockholders.

The second reason that CEOs are paid so much is that the pay schemes make their incomes risky, and they must be compensated for bearing that risk. Studies have estimated that average CEO pay for Fortune 500 companies is 40 percent higher than it would be if all of the compensation came in the form of cash. In other words, CEOs get a 40 percent premium for bearing risk.

Third, every year *Forbes* identifies the 500 highest-paid corporate executives, and the names at the top change from year to year. The ones with the highest incomes for that year are those who exercised their stock options and cashed in on the prior successful performance of the company. These earnings were accumulated over time on paper, but the CEO realized them all at once. Thus, the incomes of the highest-paid CEOs tend to be exaggerated. On the other hand, the people at the bottom of the list are those who did not exercise their options, so their compensation may be understated.

Fourth, the CEOs are at the top of the corporate ladder, and if the firm uses promotion tournaments to motivate workers, the CEO's pay motivates everyone else in the firm. Remember from Chapter 9 that because of the option value of a promotion, pay increases should get larger the higher up the promotion ladder a person goes. The CEO's high salary motivates people one level down to work hard in an effort to become CEO and earn that high salary. The people in the next lower level work hard in part so that they can move up a level and then compete for the high-paying CEO position. This works far down the corporate ladder, and if CEO pay is sufficiently high, everyone works hard for the chance, however remote, to move all the way up the ladder and become CEO.

Finally, CEO pay is high because of labor market competition for CEOs. It is a simple matter to find out who runs a corporation, how that corporation has performed during that individual's tenure as CEO, and how much that individual is paid. So it is a simple matter to determine whether a CEO is worth stealing. To keep their CEOs from being raided by other firms, corporations inflate their CEO's pay and make them too expensive to raid.

The labor market for CEOs is much like the labor market for baseball players, and players' compensation packages are also very large. Every player has a publicly available performance record, just like CEOs. Teams can find out how much a player is being paid, often because it is reported in the media, just as firms can find out how much other CEOs are paid. A player's salary can rise either because his current team raises his salary in order to preempt a bidding war or because other teams enter into a bidding war for his salary. A CEO's salary can be high either because her current firm pays her a large amount to keep other firms from hiring her, or because another firm outbids her current firm.

Homework Problems

1. What tradeoffs does a firm face when trying to decide whether to award its CEO stock or stock options?
2. Explain why a stock option to buy one share of stock at an exercise price of $0 is exactly the same as a share of stock.
3. An executive has 200 stock options with an exercise price of $25. The executive owns no stock in the company. The current share price is $30. The executive can choose whether or not to undertake a project that has a 60 percent chance of increasing the stock price by 7 and a 40 percent chance of decreasing it by 14.

   a. What is the expected change in the share price?
   b. What is the expected change in the value of the executive's options?
   c. Are the interests of the shareholders and the executive aligned in this case?

4. An executive has 500,000 stock options with an exercise price of $10. The executive owns no stock in the company. The current share price is $14. The executive can choose whether or not to undertake a project that has a 20 percent chance of increasing the stock price by $8, a 40 percent chance of decreasing it by $1, and a 40 percent chance of decreasing it by $7.

   a. What is the expected change in the share price?
   b. What is the expected change in the value of the executive's options?
   c. Are the interests of the shareholders and the executive aligned in this case?

14 PERFORMANCE EVALUATION

T he primary lesson of Chapter 4 was that if a firm wants its employees to perform, it must tie pay to performance. In succeeding chapters we went on to investigate piece rates, tournaments, efficiency wages, and team compensation as ways to tie pay to performance. To pay for performance, however, it is necessary to measure performance. When the firm uses efficiency wages and tournaments, pay is not based strictly on output, so managers have some discretion when evaluating performance. This chapter looks at the process by which managers evaluate the performance of their employees.

A TALE OF TWO FIRMS

In the 1970s two researchers, one at Harvard and one at the Massachusetts Institute of Technology, were given access to personnel records for virtually all of the managers at two large manufacturing companies.[1] These records contained information about employees' positions, pay, performance evaluations, and history with the company along with demographic information. Company A provided records for 4,788 managers, and Company B provided records for 2,841. Company A asked supervisors to place their workers into one of four categories: outstanding, good, acceptable, and not acceptable. Company B's rating system had six categories with the following instructions to supervisors:

> Now that you have completed your analysis of his strengths and opportunities for improvement, check the box opposite the paragraph that most nearly describes your evaluation of his overall performance:
>
> • EXCELLENT: Consistently exceeds expected performance in accomplishing objectives and position requirements.

---

[1]Medoff, James T. and Katharine G. Abraham, "Experience, Performance, and Earnings," *Quarterly Journal of Economics* 95 (December 1980), 703–736.

- SUPERIOR: Exceeds expectations and demonstrates high level performance in accomplishing objectives and position requirements.
- GOOD: Accomplishes objectives and position requirements as originally anticipated and in a manner resulting in expected performance.
- SATISFACTORY: Acceptable performance of position requirements with indication of ability for improvement.
- MINIMUM ACCEPTABLE: Probationary performance level for employees in same position for more than twelve months, requiring consultation with the employee and a specified plan for improvement within a designated period of time.
- UNACCEPTABLE: Unsatisfactory. Does not perform at an acceptable level of accomplishment.

Table 14.1 shows the results of the two companies' ratings forms. The first column lists the category; the second lists the percentage of employees rated in that category; and the third column shows the average pay differential between employees in the stated category and employees in the lowest category in which people were actually rated.

Two important patterns emerge from Table 14.1. First, almost everyone is rated in the top half of the ranking categories. At Company A, 94.5 percent of managers are rated either outstanding or good, and at Company B, 98.8 percent of managers are rated in the top three categories. What is more, none of the 2,841 managers at Company B was rated either minimum acceptable or unacceptable.

TABLE 14.1   Performance Ratings at Two Large Companies

Performance Rating	*Percentage of Employees Receiving Rating*	*Percentage Salary Premium Relative to Lowest Nonempty Rating*
Company A (4,788 managers)		
Outstanding	20.2	7.8
Good	74.3	5.3
Acceptable	5.3	1.4
Not acceptable	0.2	—
Company B (2,841 managers)		
Excellent	3.8	6.2
Superior	58.4	3.6
Good	36.6	1.8
Satisfactory	1.2	—
Minimum acceptable	0	—
Unacceptable	0	—

The second pattern is that higher ratings have little effect on pay. At Company A managers receiving the top rating of outstanding earned only 7.8 percent more on average than managers receiving the bottom rating of not acceptable. At Company B no one received the bottom two ratings, but a manager rated excellent earned only 6.2 percent more on average than a manager rated satisfactory, the lowest rating any manager received.

This raises several questions that we will address in this chapter. Why are the ratings so high? Why do ratings not have much impact on pay? Is there a better way to evaluate performance?

THE SUPERVISOR'S PROBLEM

The task a supervisor faces when evaluating an employee's performance is determining what rating to give the employee. Another way to phrase the problem is how high a rating to give the employee. Because this is a how much question, the answer relies on marginal analysis. To explore the determinants of the optimal rating level for the supervisor, we must analyze the costs and benefits of the different rating levels.

From the firm's perspective, this is a simple problem. The supervisor should assign the rating that most closely reflects the employee's performance, and the employee's pay should then be tied to this performance rating. From the supervisor's perspective, however, it is not nearly so simple. The supervisor faces costs and benefits that differ from the firm's.

Look at costs first. From the supervisor's point of view, the biggest cost associated with a bad rating is psychic. Giving a bad rating makes the supervisor feel guilty, and it also makes her worry about how the employee will react. A second cost is the supervisor's time cost if the employee meets with her to complain about the bad rating. The worse the rating, the higher the costs. Giving a rating that is too high may also have associated psychic costs, because the supervisor may feel guilty about shirking her responsibility to give a lower rating.

A cost curve is constructed in Figure 14.1. The horizontal axis shows the rating, with a higher rating being better from the employee's perspective. The vertical axis shows the supervisor's cost. The rating that most closely reflects the employee's performance is denoted r_0. The cost curve is constructed from two component curves. The first curve, labeled C_1, measures the cost from feeling guilty about giving a low rating and the costs associated with dealing with an unhappy or angry employee. It falls throughout the range because higher ratings make the employee happier. The second curve, labeled C_2, measures the cost from feeling guilty about giving the employee an inaccurate rating. That cost is zero when the rating is r_0, and it rises to both sides of r_0. The overall cost curve, labeled C, is the vertical sum of the two curves. Note that the minimum point of the cost curve C is to the right

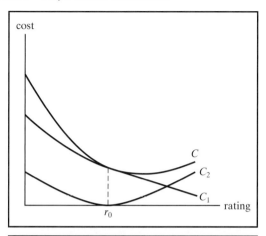

cost

C

C_2

C_1

rating

r_0

FIGURE 14.1 The Supervisor's Cost Function

An accurate rating of the employee would be r_0. The curve C_1 is the cost of giving the employee a low rating, and these costs arise because of employee complaints and the supervisor's feelings of guilt. The curve C_2 is the cost from giving the employee an inaccurate rating. This cost is zero when the rating is r_0. The curve C is the vertical sum of the two component curves, and it reaches a minimum to the right of r_0.

of the most accurate rating, r_0, so that if the supervisor were only interested in minimizing costs, she would give the employee a higher rating than he deserves.

A benefit curve is constructed in Figure 14.2. The horizontal axis is the same as before, with movements to the right corresponding to higher ratings that the employee likes better, and the vertical axis measures the benefit to the supervisor. The benefit curve is upward sloping throughout. There are two reasons for this. First, the supervisor might be evaluated by her own supervisor on the basis of how well her employees do. Giving her own employees high ratings helps her get a high rating herself. Second, the supervisor has to compete for her budget with the other supervisors. Having poorly performing employees hurts her in this budget competition, so she benefits from giving high ratings to her employees.

Figure 14.2 also shows the cost and benefit curves together. The optimal rating is the point at which the benefit curve is farthest above the cost curve; it is denoted r^*. It is no accident that $r^* > r_0$, so that the supervisor gives the employee a higher rating than he deserves. The supervisor's costs are high and her benefits are low when she gives a low rating, while her costs are low and her benefits are high when she

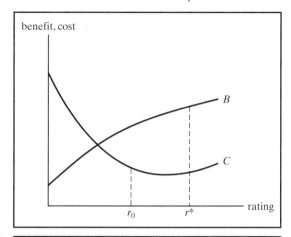

FIGURE 14.2 The Supervisor's Problem

The supervisor benefits from giving an employee a higher rating because better employees reflect well on the supervisor.

The supervisor chooses the rating where the benefit curve is the farthest above the cost curve, which is at point r^*. Because $r^* > r_0$, the supervisor gives the employee a higher rating than he deserves.

gives a high rating. Of course she is going to give a high rating. We get **rating inflation**; all employees receive higher ratings than they deserve.

The high ratings in Table 14.1 reflect the supervisor's psychic and time costs of giving bad ratings and the budgetary and reflected benefits of giving high ratings. One more reason why ratings might be high has nothing to do with the supervisor's decision. Poor performers may not survive very long at the management level, so it may be that all of the managers who survive the weeding-out process are good. All of these reasons together explain why all of the ratings are in the top half.

It is useful to draw the marginal benefit/marginal cost diagram that corresponds to Figure 14.2. The cost curve derived in Figure 14.1 is unusual in that it is downward sloping for much of the range. Because the marginal cost curve measures the slope of the cost curve, the marginal cost curve is negative when the cost curve is downward-sloping. The marginal cost curve is also upward-sloping because the cost curve becomes steeper (or less negatively steep) as the ratings grow. The resulting curve is shown in Figure 14.3. The benefit curve flattens as the rating grows, so the marginal benefit curve is downward-sloping.

The optimal rating r^* is found where the marginal cost and marginal benefit curves cross. The diagram shows clearly why r^* must be greater than r_0, the most accurate rating. At r_0, the marginal cost curve is negative. Because the evaluator gets some positive benefit from

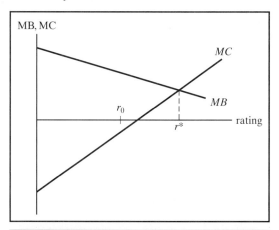

FIGURE 14.3 Marginal Analysis for the Supervisor's Problem

The marginal cost curve starts off negative because the cost curve is downward-sloping. It becomes positive somewhere past r_0. The optimal point is at r^*, where *MB* and *MC* cross.

increasing the rating, the marginal benefit is positive. The two curves cannot possibly cross where the MC curve is negative. The MC curve does not become positive until the rating is well above r_0, and rating inflation results.

HOW MANY RATING CATEGORIES SHOULD THERE BE?

It is common for firms to use performance evaluation systems with either three, four, or five rating categories. Each system has its own advantages and disadvantages. Supervisors find it easier to categorize workers into one of three categories than to categorize them into one of five categories, but a five-category system provides more information than a three-category system.

There is a subtler issue, however. In a three-category system, the middle category is likely to correspond to expected performance. In a five-category system, the middle category is likely to be thought of as a grade of C, whereas everybody expects an A or a B. So the middle category is held in much lower regard in a five-category system than in a three-category system. A four-category system does not have a middle category, which tends to push more people into the top half.

THE WORKER'S PROBLEM

The supervisor benefits from giving workers high ratings because those high ratings both reflect well on her own performance and help her in budget competitions. The supervisor's costs associated with ratings are determined by how far that rating is from what the worker really deserves, by how guilty she feels about the rating, and by how costly it is to deal with the worker's complaints. The worker has no effect on the supervisor's benefits, but he can affect the costs.

The worker can affect the supervisor's costs in three ways. First, he can work harder so that he deserves a higher rating. Second, he can take actions to make the supervisor feel guiltier about a bad rating. Third, he can complain more. All three of these have the same effect on the marginal cost curve in Figure 14.4.

Working harder increases r_0, the rating the worker deserves. This shifts the MC curve to the right, as in Figure 14.4. The reason is that the guilt the supervisor experiences from giving too high a rating is determined by the difference between the rating actually given and the one that is deserved. When the deserved rating increases, shifting the MC curve to the right by that change preserves the difference between the actual and deserved ratings. For example, suppose that the supervisor's marginal cost is 20 if the difference between the actual and deserved

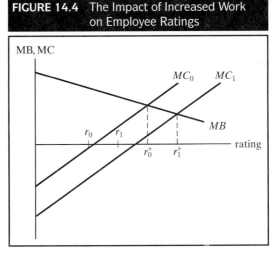

FIGURE 14.4   The Impact of Increased Work on Employee Ratings

When the employee works harder, the deserved rating increases from r_0 to r_1 and the marginal cost curve shifts rightward from MC_0 to MC_1. The supervisor then gives a higher rating, r_1^*, instead of r_0^*.

When the worker takes actions that make the supervisor feel guiltier or complains more, the marginal cost curve shifts downward and the supervisor gives the worker a higher rating.

ratings is 0.5, and her marginal cost is 30 if the difference between the actual and deserved ratings is 1.0. If the worker deserves a rating of 4 and the supervisor gives him a rating of 5, the difference between the actual and deserved ratings is 1.0, and the supervisor's marginal cost is 30. If the worker exerts more effort and his deserved rating rises to 4.5, then when the supervisor gives him a rating of 5 the difference between the actual and deserved ratings falls to 0.5, and the supervisor's marginal cost falls to 20. If the supervisor gives him a rating of 5.5, the supervisor's marginal cost returns to 30. So, if the deserved rating increases by some amount, and the actual rating increases by that same amount, the supervisor's marginal cost stays the same. This is the idea behind shifting the MC curve to the right.

In the figure, when the deserved rating rises from r_0 to r_1, the supervisor's marginal cost curve shifts right from MC_0 to MC_1, which leads the supervisor to give the worker a higher rating. This is as it should be. Better performance should yield a higher performance evaluation, and the analysis shows that it does.

Working harder is not the only way to get a higher rating, however. The worker can affect how guilty the supervisor feels. For example, he can keep the supervisor apprised of all of his upcoming expenses, such as telling the supervisor about badly needed braces for the kids or about impending college expenses. These increased feelings of guilt make it less costly for the supervisor to give the worker a higher rating, and the marginal cost curve shifts downward. We get exactly the case pictured in Figure 14.4, and making the supervisor feel guiltier leads to higher ratings.

Finally, the worker can complain about bad performance ratings. If the supervisor knows that the worker will complain, she can expect bad ratings to be more costly for her. This again makes it less costly for the supervisor to give the worker a higher rating, and again the marginal cost curve falls. Complaining pays off in the form of higher performance ratings.

This analysis helps to explain why employees with high ratings are not paid much more than employees with low ratings. First, rating inflation compacts the ratings into the top half, which does not provide much of a basis for pay differences. Second, ratings reflect not only the worker's performance but also his tendency to complain. Because of this ratings are not accurate reflections of performance, and we learned in earlier chapters that when performance cannot be measured accurately only a small part of pay should be based on performance.

FORCED RATING DISTRIBUTIONS

Many companies use a performance rating system like those described above but with one extra requirement: Supervisors must place a certain percentage of their employees in each rating category. The underlying idea is that worker performance should naturally approximate a bell-shaped curve, so the supervisor should turn in a set of ratings that matches this natural tendency. In a five-category system, then, the supervisor might be forced to place 10 percent in the top category, 25 percent in the second category, 30 percent in the third, 25 percent in the fourth, and 10 percent in the bottom category. Some companies actually do much more than this. They rank all employees company-wide and use this ranking to fire the bottom employees.

These systems are easy to understand with a comparison to grading in a class. A forced rating system would require a professor to award As to 10 percent of the class, Bs to 25 percent of the class, Cs to 30 percent, Ds to 25 percent, and Fs to 10 percent. Students, of course, would not like this, especially because future employers are unlikely to view Cs, Ds, and Fs as good grades. Why, then, would a department require its professors to use such a system? One reason would be to encourage students at the bottom to seek a different major. A better reason would be to get students to work harder so that they can earn those comparatively rare As and Bs.

Firms that use forced rating distributions do so in the belief that they will encourage workers to become more productive. Let us see whether the theory backs up this belief. From the supervisor's point of view, the biggest difference between a normal rating system and a forced rating system is that in the forced rating system giving a high rating carries an opportunity cost. If the supervisor gives some worker a higher rating than he deserves, she must give some other worker a lower rating than deserved to make up for it. This changes the shape of the supervisor's cost curves.

The cost curve generated by a forced rating system is no different for ratings below the deserved ranking, but it is steeper for ratings above the deserved rating, as shown by Figure 14.5. The higher cost reflects the increased opportunity cost of giving the high rating to the worker who deserves rating r_0. With the normal rating system, giving the high rating to this worker carries no opportunity cost because no constraint is placed on the ratings given to other workers. With the forced system, however, giving this worker a high rating means giving a low rating to someone more deserving; the supervisor would experience guilt about that and would also have to deal with hard-to-defend complaints from the other worker.

The marginal cost curve for a supervisor in a forced rating system is shown in Figure 14.6. Because the cost curve switches from being downward-sloping at ratings below r_0 to being upward-sloping at ratings above r_0, the marginal cost curve switches from being below zero to being above zero at r_0. The optimal rating, then, is r_0, and the forced rating system provides an incentive for the supervisor to rate the worker accurately.

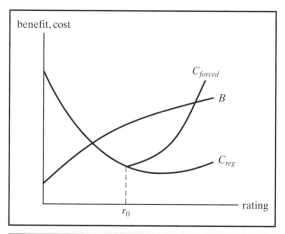

FIGURE 14.5 Cost and Benefit Curves for a Forced Rating System

Under a normal rating system, the supervisor's cost function is given by C_{reg}, and under a forced rating system, the supervisor's cost function is given by C_{forced}. The two coincide when the rating is below the deserved rating r_0, but the costs are higher under the forced rating system when the rating is above r_0.

Complaining or making the supervisor feel guilty are not as effective under a forced rating system. The reason is that if the supervisor decides to give someone a higher rating than deserved, for whatever reason, she must give someone else a lower rating than deserved, leading to more complaints and more guilty feelings. The most effective way for a worker to get a higher rating, then, is to work harder and deserve a higher rating. This justifies companies' rationale for using the forced rating system: it provides an incentive for workers to work harder.

Why, then, do not all firms used the forced rating system? Probably because neither the workers nor the supervisors like it. Workers do not like it for the same reasons students would not like taking a class where 10 percent of the students had to fail. This might affect worker morale and increase turnover, both of which are costly for the firm. Supervisors do not like it because it is hard on them to make close calls on all of the employees who are close to the borderline. A more subtle reason may be even more important. In 2000, the Ford Motor Company instituted a forced rating system that led to two class-action lawsuits alleging discrimination on the basis of age, gender, and race. Employees often disagree with their ratings, and members of protected classes can claim that their low ratings were the result of discrimination. Because ratings are necessarily subjective, it is difficult for a company to defend against these claims. In 2002, Ford settled the

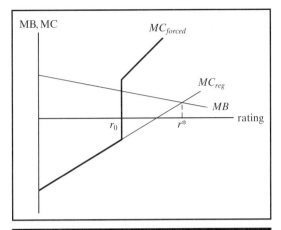

FIGURE 14.6 Marginal Analysis for a Forced Rating System

The marginal cost curve is identical under both rating systems when $r < r_0$. Above r_0 the forced ranking system has positive marginal cost because the cost curve is upward-sloping. Consequently, at r_0 the marginal cost curve jumps from being negative to being positive.

The optimal rating under the regular system is r^*. Under the forced rating system, the optimal rating is r_0, the deserved rating, because that is where the marginal benefit and marginal cost curves intersect.

suits for $10.5 million and dropped the forced rating system. Ford is not alone in this predicament; Conoco, Goodyear, and Microsoft have also faced suits based on forced rating systems.

GENERAL LESSONS

Performance evaluations are apt to display rating inflation, the tendency for ratings to be higher than the workers deserve. There is one simple and basic cause for this. The supervisor giving the ratings bears the costs of giving low ratings, and the costs of giving bad ratings are higher than the costs of giving good ratings. Because there are no benefits to giving bad ratings, a simple cost-benefit analysis shows that supervisors give employees higher ratings than they deserve.

Homework Problems

1. List the supervisor's costs of giving a worker a lower rating than deserved.
2. List the supervisor's costs of giving a worker a higher rating than deserved.

3. List the supervisor's benefits from increasing a worker's rating.
4. Suppose that of two equally productive workers worker 1 complains and worker 2 does not. Show graphically which worker receives a higher performance rating.
5. Draw a graph similar to that in Figure 14.1 showing the cost curve of a manager whose only concern is not giving a worker a rating that is higher than deserved.

CHAPTER

15 ADVERSE SELECTION

Up to this point, this book has been about motivating workers to exert effort. We now turn our attention to a different topic—identifying and hiring workers. We begin with the problem of identifying workers. For many jobs and many firms, the hiring process consists of an application, a short interview, and perhaps contacting references. This process does not reveal much about whether the prospective employee will be particularly adept in the job and environment under consideration. As demonstrated in this chapter, this lack of information can cause serious problems.

TRYING TO HIRE THE BEST WORKERS

Suppose that there are two types of workers, high-productivity and low-productivity. A high-productivity worker generates $25,000 in net revenue for the firm, and a low-productivity worker generates only $18,000 in net revenue. The next best alternative employer for both workers pays $20,000. How should the firm go about hiring a worker?

The firm can attract high-productivity workers by offering them more than $20,000. As long as the pay is less than $25,000, hiring the high-productivity worker is profitable. It is not profitable, however, to hire a low-productivity worker, because the firm would have to pay at least $20,000 to beat out the other employer, and low-productivity workers only generate $18,000 in net revenue. Thus, the firm would lose at least $2,000 if it paid enough to attract a low-productivity worker.

The firm's hiring strategy is clear. If it can tell apart the two types of workers, it will offer a little more than $20,000 to high-productivity workers and nothing to low-productivity workers. The high-productivity workers will accept the job, and the firm will earn almost $5,000 in profit from each worker hired. For example, the firm could offer a high-productivity worker $20,100, which the worker would prefer over the alternative employer, and the firm would earn $4,900 in profit.

This is all fine, except that in many instances the firm cannot tell apart the two types of workers. Suppose that 25 percent of all workers are high-productivity and 75 percent are low-productivity, and the firm cannot tell apart the two types. Hiring a worker, then, is like flipping a pair of coins and getting a high-productivity worker if they both land heads and a low-productivity worker if either coin lands tails. What should the firm do?

Let us try some alternatives to see if they work. Begin with the contract offered when the firm could tell apart the two types. The firm offers workers $20,100, but because it cannot tell apart the two types, it has to offer $20,100 to everyone. The high-productivity workers prefer this to the alternative employer, who pays only $20,000, so they apply for the job. The low-productivity workers also prefer it to the alternative employer, so they apply for the job, too. Because both types apply for the job, the firm has a 25 percent chance of getting a high-productivity worker. The profit from being lucky enough to hire a high-productivity worker is $25,000 − $20,100 = $4,900, whereas the profit from hiring a low-productivity worker is $18,000 − $20,100 = −$2,100. The firm's expected profit is (.25)($4,900) + (.75)(−$2,100) = −$350. The firm loses money hiring workers at this pay level.

Offering more pay does not help. If the firm offers $21,000 instead of $20,100, both types of workers still find the job attractive, so both types apply. This time the firm earns only $4,000 in profit from the high-productivity workers, and loses $3,000 from the low-productivity workers. Its profit is (.25)($4,000) + (.75)(−$3,000) = −$1,250. Offering more pay results in a bigger loss for the firm.

What if the firm offers something lower, like $19,500? Because both types of workers can earn $20,000 working for the alternative employer, neither type finds the job attractive, and neither type applies. The firm hires no workers because no one applies for the job, and its expected profit from hiring workers is $0. This will happen for any pay level less than $20,000.

The only alternative left is for the firm to offer $20,001. This is slightly better than the $20,000 the workers can earn somewhere else, so both types apply for the job. The firm makes $4,999 off high-productivity workers but loses $2,001 on low-productivity workers. Its expected profit is (.25)($4,999) + (.75)(−$2,001) = −$251. The firm again loses money.

No matter what the firm does, it cannot profit from hiring a new worker. Even though a high-productivity worker generates up to $5,000 in profit, any offer that gets high-productivity workers to apply gets low-productivity workers to apply, too. There are enough low-productivity workers in the market to make the firm's expected profit negative, and the best thing for the firm to do is not hire anybody.

This example illustrates a concept known as **adverse selection**, in which the bad types behave the same way as the good types in an attempt to be selected. In the process, they not only ruin the market for themselves but for the good types as well. One can think of a situation with adverse selection as the bad driving the good out of the market. It is clearly a cause of inefficiency. Potential gains from trade exist: The firm is willing to pay up to $25,000 for a high-productivity worker, and a high-productivity worker is willing to accept as little as $20,000. However, the two are unable to exploit these gains from trade because of the presence of low-productivity types whom the firm cannot distinguish from the high-productivity types.

ADVERSE SELECTION AND HIRING AIRPORT SECURITY SCREENERS

Following the September 11, 2001, terrorist attacks, Congress mandated the hiring of 55,000 airport security personnel to screen passengers and baggage. They also mandated that the hiring and training be done quickly. The Transportation Security Administration waded through 1.7 million applications in a ten-month period.

Not surprisingly, some unqualified people managed to be hired. By May 2003, the TSA had fired 1,208 screeners for "suitability issues." These issues included providing false information on job applications, failing drug tests, or having criminal records, including 85 with felony convictions.

WHEN DOES ADVERSE SELECTION OCCUR?

The preceding section provided an example of adverse selection, that is, a situation in which the presence of bad types ruined the market for good types. In this section we use a more general setting to determine the conditions under which adverse selection occurs.

There are two types of workers. High-productivity workers generate net revenue NR_H for the firm, and low-productivity workers generate net revenue NR_L, with $NR_H > NR_L$. This inequality implies that the high-productivity workers really do have higher productivity than the low-productivity workers because they generate more net revenue for the firm than the low-productivity workers. A fraction, p, of the workers are high-productivity, which means that the fraction $1 - p$ of the workers are low-productivity. If the workers do not get a job with the firm in question, they work at another firm, which pays them w_0. As with the example in the preceding section, both types of workers get the same pay from the alternative employer. One justification for this is that the skills that make one group more productive than the other at this firm may not be useful at the other firm, so that all workers are equally productive at the other firm.

The firm cannot distinguish between the two types of workers. Consequently, it has to offer the same wage, w, to all workers. We want to know if there is a value of w that is profitable, that is, if the expected profit from paying a worker w is greater than zero.

To address this issue, the first step is to determine who will apply for the job when the firm offers w. If $w < w_0$, both types of workers are better off working for the alternative employer and being paid w_0 instead of w. So no one applies for the job, no one is hired, and the firm's expected profit is zero. Because we are looking for expected profits above zero, this low wage will not work.

Now suppose that $w \geq w_0$. Both types of workers now apply for the job because both types can earn more working for the firm than they can from the alternative employer. The firm earns profit $NR_H - w$ from the high-productivity workers and profit $NR_L - w$ from the low-productivity workers. The firm's expected profit is

$$E\pi = p(NR_H - w) + (1 - p)(NR_L - w)$$

We can rearrange this expression to

$$E\pi = [pNR_H + (1 - p)NR_L] - w$$

The term in square brackets is the expected net revenue generated by the workers. According to the equation, expected profit is expected net revenue less labor costs, which makes perfect sense.

We are looking for situations in which the firm earns positive expected profit, that is, where

$$E\pi = [pNR_H + (1 - p)NR_L] - w > 0$$

Rearranging, this becomes

$$[pNR_H + (1 - p)NR_L] > w$$

In order to attract workers, the firm must pay at least as much as the alternative employer, which implies that $w \geq w_0$. Adding this inequality to the above expression yields

$$[pNR_H + (1 - p)NR_L] > w \geq w_0. \tag{15.1}$$

The above expression says that for the firm to earn positive profit, the expected net revenue must exceed the wage paid by the alternative employer. If the firm cannot distinguish between the two types of employees but both types apply, then hiring means getting a high-productivity worker with probability p and a low-productivity worker with probability $1 - p$. The expected net revenue earned is p times the net revenue generated by a high-productivity worker and $1 - p$ times the net revenue generated by a low-productivity worker. Expected profit is expected net revenue minus the amount paid to the worker. Because the firm must pay at least w_0 to attract an applicant, expected profit can be no greater than expected net revenue minus w_0. Because this is the most profit the firm can possibly make if it is going to earn positive profit, the *most* it can earn must also be positive. It follows that expected net revenue must be greater than w_0, the amount paid by the alternative employer.

Adverse selection occurs when it is impossible for the firm to earn positive profit. Because the only way for it to earn positive profit is by actually hiring a worker, if it is impossible to earn positive profit there is no incentive for the firm to hire a worker. Consequently, the market for the skills of high-productivity workers disappears. This is adverse selection.

This identifies two conditions that must hold for adverse selection to be a problem:

1. *The firm cannot know the workers' types.* This is asymmetric information. For adverse selection to be a problem, it must be the case that the employer cannot tell apart the different types of workers but the workers know their own types. When the employer cannot tell the high-productivity workers from the low-productivity ones, the low-productivity types can apply for the same jobs as the high-productivity types.

2. *Expected net revenue must be below the wage paid by the alternative employer.* As shown by expression (15.1), if expected net revenue is above the wage paid by the alternative employer, the firm can earn positive profit by hiring a random worker. Adverse selection is a problem when there is no market for the skills of the high-productivity workers. If expression (15.1) holds, there is a market for their skills, so for adverse selection to be a problem, expression (15.1) cannot hold.

CAN BASEBALL TEAMS IDENTIFY HIGH-PRODUCTIVITY PLAYERS?

The occurrence of adverse selection in the hiring process rests on the inability of employers to distinguish between high- and low-productivity workers. How reasonable is this assumption? It is difficult to find data on this issue. One place where data are abundant, however, is in baseball.

Baseball players are drafted and then assigned to a minor league team. Before they can get to the majors, they must progress through the minor league system. Also, baseball is a game of statistics, so teams should have an abundance of information about prospects before they are drafted.

(continued)

If the statistical information were not enough, baseball teams have platoons of scouts who watch prospects play before they are drafted.

With all of this information, if ever there was an employer who should be able to identify high-productivity employees before hiring them, it should be baseball teams. How well can they discern talent? According to Kirk Robinson of TheBaseballPage.com, over 80 percent of the players drafted never make it to the majors. Furthermore, over a third of the players drafted in the *top ten* never play a full season in the majors. Baseball teams hire a lot of low-productivity players.

SOLVING THE ADVERSE SELECTION PROBLEM

There are ways for the firm to solve the adverse selection problem. The problem arises in part because workers have information about their own types that the firm does not have. The fact that the workers know their own types turns out to be the solution. All the firm has to do is arrange things so that high-productivity workers want to work there but low-productivity workers do not. Then only the high-productivity workers apply for jobs, and the low-productivity workers choose to work at the alternative employer. Because there is now a market for the skills of the high-productivity workers, the adverse selection problem is avoided.

This type of solution to the adverse selection problem is called **self-selection**. Basically, the workers self-select in a way that takes care of the problem. High-productivity workers elect to apply for a job with the firm, but low-productivity workers elect not to apply. The workers' actions reveal their types to the firm. Because all information is revealed, information is no longer asymmetric, and adverse selection is no longer a problem.

How does the firm entice the high-productivity workers to apply and keep the low-productivity workers away, thereby revealing their information and solving the adverse selection problem? It does it through the compensation plan. If the compensation plan is constructed correctly, high-productivity workers make more there than at the alternative employer, while low-productivity workers make less. The high-productivity types then find it worthwhile to apply, but the low-productivity types do not. We now describe two compensation plans that induce self-selection to solve the adverse selection problem.

Piece Rates

When the firm uses a piece rate to compensate employees, high-productivity workers are paid more than low-productivity workers.

This occurs for the simple reason that productivity refers to how much output a worker can produce, and a piece rate system pays workers based on output. Because high-productivity workers produce more output than low-productivity workers, they are paid more than low-productivity workers.

Suppose that high-productivity workers can produce x_H units of output and low-productivity workers can produce x_L units. Each unit of output generates net revenue of NR for the firm. The workers can earn w_0 working for the alternative employer. The firm pays the workers using the piece rate b, so that a worker who produces output x gets total compensation bx. Is there a piece rate that will induce self-selection?

The answer to this question becomes obvious once the question is rephrased. Is there a value of b that allows high-productivity workers to earn more than w_0 but forces low-productivity workers to earn less than w_0? If high-productivity workers earn more than they can get at the alternative employer, they will choose to apply, and if low-productivity workers cannot make as much as they would at the alternative employer, they will choose not to apply.

High-productivity workers choose to apply if

$$bx_H > w_0$$

The left-hand side of the expression is the amount that high-productivity workers earn at this firm by producing x_H units and being paid b per unit produced. The right-hand side is the amount they earn at the alternative employer. The expression states that high-productivity workers make more at the firm than at the alternative employer.

Low-productivity workers choose not to apply if

$$bx_L < w_0$$

The left-hand side of this expression is the amount low-productivity workers earn at the firm, and the right-hand side is the amount they earn at the alternative employer. The expression states that they make more at the alternative employer.

Combining and rearranging these two expressions yields the following condition for self-selection:

$$\frac{w_0}{x_H} < b < \frac{w_0}{x_L} \tag{15.2}$$

To induce self-selection, the piece rate b must be high enough to attract the high-productivity workers (the first inequality) but low enough to keep away the low-productivity workers (the second inequality).

The only remaining issue is whether a piece rate in the range identified by expression (15.2) is profitable for the firm. The firm earns net revenue NR from each unit produced, so if a high-productivity worker produces x_H units, the firm's net revenue is $NR \cdot x_H$. This is the most the firm is willing to pay a high-productivity worker. The least the firm can pay high-productivity workers and still attract them away from the alternative employer is w_0. Consequently, it is profitable for the firm to attract a high-productivity worker if $NR \cdot x_H > w_0$, that is, if the most the firm is willing to pay the worker is greater than the least it has to pay the worker to make the job attractive.

To illustrate this, consider the following example. Suppose that a high-productivity worker can produce 12 units per hour and a low-productivity worker can only produce 8. Each unit generates $6 net revenue for the firm. The alternative employer pays $24 per hour. Can the firm use a piece rate to induce self-selection? The answer is yes, because a high-productivity worker generates $6 \cdot 12 = \$72$ per hour in net revenue, and the alternative employer pays only $24 per hour. What range of piece rates will induce self-selection? A high-productivity worker earns $12b$ per hour, and this must be greater than $24 per hour, so b must be at least $2 per unit. Low-productivity workers earn $8b$ per hour, and to keep them from applying this must be less than the $24 they could earn from the alternative employer, so b must be smaller than $3 per unit. Net revenue is $6 per unit, so b must also be smaller than $6 per unit, but if $b < \$3$ then it must also be true that $b < \$6$. The range of piece rates that induce self-selection is $\$2 < b < \$3$.

Probationary Contracts

A second way that the firm can induce workers to self-select is through probationary contracts. A typical probationary contract works as follows. When workers are hired, they must first go through a probationary period of specified length. If they pass the probationary period, they are allowed to continue working and are given a raise. If they do not pass the probationary period, they are fired and must find employment elsewhere.

We begin with an example. Suppose that a firm is hiring workers who will stay with the firm for a total of three years if they pass the probation period. High productivity workers generate $5,500 per month in net revenue for the firm, and low-productivity workers generate $3,200 in net revenue per month. Three-fourths of all workers are low-productivity. The probationary period lasts three months. During that time the new workers earn $3,500 per month. If they pass the probationary period, they earn $5,000 per month for the remainder of the three years. If they go to work for the alternative employer instead, they earn $4,200 per month. High-productivity workers almost always pass the probationary phase, and low-productivity workers almost never do, but sometimes the firm makes mistakes in classifying the workers. More specifically, high-productivity workers are correctly identified, pass probation, and continue with the firm with probability 0.95, and low-productivity workers are correctly identified and fired with probability 0.95. In other words, the firm correctly classifies workers 95 percent of the time and makes mistakes 5 percent of the time. Thus, there is a 5 percent chance that a low-productivity worker will be able to continue with the firm and a 5 percent chance that a high-productivity worker will be fired.

We want to know whether high-productivity workers prefer this contract to working for the alternative employer and whether low-productivity workers prefer the alternative employer. If both of those conditions are met, the contract induces the workers to self-select and solves the adverse selection problem. Begin with the decision faced by high-productivity workers. If they work for the alternative employer, they get $4,200 per month for 36 months, or $151,200. If, instead, they work for the firm in question, they earn $3,500 per month for the 3-month probationary period, and then with probability 0.95 they earn $5,000 per month for the remaining 33 months and with probability 0.05 they are fired and so go to the alternative employer for the remaining 33 months. Their total expected pay is:

$$3(\$3,500) + 33(0.95 \cdot \$5,000 + 0.05 \cdot \$4,200) = \$174,180$$

High-productivity workers find the probationary contract worthwhile because the expected pay of $174,180 exceeds the $151,200 they could earn from the alternative employer.

Low-productivity workers also make $151,200 at the alternative employer. If they choose to work for the firm in question, they are paid $3,500 per month for the first three months, and then with probability 0.95 they are correctly identified as low-productivity workers and fired, in which case they work for the alternative employer for the remaining 33 months. But there is a 5 percent chance that they will be mistakenly identified as high-productivity workers and can remain with the firm making $5,000 per month for the remaining 33 months. Their expected pay is

$$3(\$3,500) + 33(0.95 \cdot \$4,200 + 0.05 \cdot \$5,000) = \$150,420$$

Because their expected pay is less than it would be with the alternative firm, the low-productivity workers do not apply for a job at this firm. The probationary contract induces self-selection, and only high-productivity workers take jobs at the firm.

This raises two subtle questions. The purpose of the probationary contract is to distinguish between the high- and low-productivity workers so that the firm can get rid of the latter. When the probationary contract is designed properly, however, only high-productivity workers take the job. Because there are no low-productivity workers to fire, the only ones who are fired are the unlucky 5 percent of the high-productivity workers who are incorrectly labeled as low-productivity. If the firm knows that the probationary contract is designed correctly so that no low-productivity workers apply, why does it still fire these unlucky high-productivity workers?

The answer is that it has to. If the firm assumes that any worker labeled as low-productivity must really be a high-productivity worker, no one is fired. Then the low-productivity workers will find the job attractive because they now have a 100 percent chance of passing the probationary period. The probationary contract would no longer serve its purpose, and workers would not be induced to self-select.

Because some of the high-productivity workers are fired, the probationary contract is not efficient. It does not always exploit all potential gains from trade. Five percent of the high-productivity workers are incorrectly labeled as low-productivity, and these workers are fired even though it would be beneficial to the firm to hire them.

The second subtle question concerns the firm's net revenue and the probationary wage. During the probationary period all workers are paid $3,500 per month, but low-productivity workers generate only $3,200 per month in net revenue. Why is the probationary wage so high? Does the firm not lose money on the low-productivity workers? The answer is that the amount of net revenue generated by low-productivity workers does not matter to the firm, because no low-productivity workers take the job. Although it is true that the firm would lose money during the probationary period if it did hire a low-productivity worker, a properly designed probationary contract keeps that from happening.

Whether a probationary contract successfully induces self-selection depends on all of the parameters of the contract. For example, if the firm had paid a probationary wage of $3,800 per month instead of $3,500 per month, low-productivity workers would have found the job worth taking. The extra $300 per month for the first three months raises expected pay by $900, making the low-productivity expected pay $151,320, which is greater than the $151,200 paid by the alternative employer. Similarly, if the probationary period were shorter, low-productivity workers would find the job acceptable. Cutting the probationary period in half to 1.5 months (with the $3,500 probationary wage) we find that the expected pay for low-productivity workers is

$$1.5(\$3,500) + 34.5(0.95 \cdot \$4,200 + 0.05 \cdot \$5,000) = \$151,530$$

which is more than they could make from the alternative firm. Finally, if the classification of workers by type becomes less accurate, low-productivity workers have a better chance of passing probation, making the job more attractive than working for the alternative employer. If the probability of being incorrectly labeled as high-productivity rises to 10 percent (with the 3-month probationary period), the worker's expected pay is

$$3(\$3,500) + 33(0.90 \cdot \$4,200 + 0.10 \cdot \$5,000) = \$151,740$$

For it to induce self-selection and solve the adverse selection problem, a probationary contract must be designed carefully.

The military uses a system similar to a probationary wage system to ensure that it gets recruits with the right levels of fitness and dedication. Instead of paying low wages at the beginning, however, it sends recruits to basic training or boot camp. People who would like to join the military for the training and benefits it provides but who are not sufficiently healthy or dedicated will stay out of the military because they know they cannot handle boot camp. By having the harsh basic training, the armed services ensure that they do not get the wrong types of recruits.

ADVERSE SELECTION IN OTHER AREAS OF ECONOMICS

Adverse selection problems arise in many places besides the employment relationship. This section describes three additional areas where adverse selection occurs. The last of the three will be important in Chapter 20.

Used Cars

When people have owned a car for a long time and then decide to sell it, they know more about the condition of the car than the potential buyer does. They know its repair and accident histories and also whether the car needs any current repairs. In many cases it is possible to hide problems with a temporary fix so that the potential buyer cannot find any defects until it is too late. Thus, the seller has information about the quality of the car that the buyer lacks, and this asymmetry leads to an adverse selection problem.

Consider a concrete example. Used cars come in two types—good and bad. Half of all used cars are good, and half are bad. A good used car is worth $10,000 to the original owner, but a bad used car is worth only $5,000. This is the seller's side of the market. Buyers value a good car at $12,000 but a bad car at $6,000. Clearly there are gains from trade for both types of cars, so the efficient outcome would involve both types of cars selling. However, only the seller knows whether the car is a good one or a bad one, and the buyer cannot tell the difference until after the sale when it is too late.

What would happen if the buyer offered $11,000 for a good car? Owners of good cars would try to sell their cars, because the $11,000 offer is higher than the $10,000 the car is worth to the original owner, but so would owners of bad cars because the $11,000 offer is higher than the $5,000 a bad car is worth to the original owner. The expected value of a car bought for $11,000, then, is $(1/2)(\$12,000) + (1/2)(\$6,000) = \$9,000$, which is less than the $11,000 the buyer pays for it. The buyer has an expected loss of $2,000 when offering $11,000 for a car.

In fact, *any* offer greater than $10,000 will attract sellers of both types of cars, and because buyers cannot tell apart the two types of cars, the expected value of the car they buy is $9,000, and they suffer an expected loss. Consequently, no buyer will offer more than $10,000 for a car. The only alternative is for buyers to offer $10,000 or less for a car. But in this case the owners of good cars refuse to sell their cars, and the only cars on the market are bad used cars. Consequently, buyers will not offer more than $6,000 for a car, and only bad used cars are sold.

This is a clear example of adverse selection. Because buyers cannot tell good cars from bad until it is too late, there is no market for good used cars. Bad used cars drive good ones out of the market.

Car Repairs

Unless you have experience in auto mechanics, when something goes wrong with your car you must take it to a mechanic to diagnose and fix the problem. When you do, however, the mechanic has information that you do not have, and this can lead to adverse selection. Suppose that your car has a problem that could be either minor or major. A minor problem can be fixed with a repair that is inexpensive and not very profitable for the mechanic, and a major problem requires a repair that is both expensive and profitable. The major repair also takes care of the minor problem, so the mechanic can recommend either repair to take care of the problem.

From what we have learned about adverse selection so far, we would expect the bad to drive the good out of the market. Here, bad refers to recommending major repairs for minor problems, and good corresponds to minor repairs for minor problems. Because the customer cannot tell whether the car needs major or minor repairs, the mechanic has no reason to recommend a minor repair, and does only major, high-profit repairs.

Health Insurance

For years politicians in both parties have complained about the large portion of the population that does not have health insurance. Most of the affected people are poor or work for small businesses, and children are disproportionately affected. Why does this health insurance crisis exist? A major reason is adverse selection.

When people purchase health insurance policies, they do so because there is some chance that they will have a health problem, in which case they will receive benefit payments from the health insurance company. Not all people are the same, however, and some have higher expected benefit payments than others. The higher expected benefit payments could come because the person is more likely to have a health problem than other people are, or it could be that the person is likely to have a more expensive health problem than others. A problem arises because the people buying the insurance know more about how healthy they are than the company selling the insurance.

Suppose an insurance company offers a policy for qualifying buyers that costs $6,000 per year. This is an expensive insurance policy, and there are two groups of people who would be willing to buy it. One group contains people whose expected benefit payments are less than $6,000 but who are sufficiently risk averse that they would be willing to pay more than $6,000 for the policy. The insurance company expects to make money from people in this low-risk group. The second group contains people whose expected benefit payments exceed $6,000, and the insurance company expects to lose money from this high-risk group.

This is adverse selection. Even though gains from trade are possible with the first group, the high-risk buyers ruin the market for the low-risk buyers. Insurance companies are unwilling to sell individual policies for prices that the buyers find worthwhile because if the buyer finds it worthwhile the insurance company probably will not.

One way to solve this problem is through pooling. Keep in mind that the adverse selection problem arises because individual buyers have information about their health status that the insurer does not possess. Suppose that a company with 1,000 employees wants to buy insurance for all of them. Presumably the company selected its employees for qualifications that had nothing to do with health risks, so these 1,000 employees have about the same average health risk as the working-age population as a whole. The insurer has information about the average health risks of the working-age population as a whole and can, therefore, determine a profitable price for the insurance. Because no information asymmetries can be exploited, the adverse selection problem disappears, and a market for health insurance can exist.

Homework Problems

1. Explain the difference between adverse selection and self-selection.
2. Explain the difference between adverse selection and moral hazard, as defined in Chapter 7.
3. There are two types of workers. High-productivity workers can produce 25 units per hour, and low productivity workers can only produce 20. High-productivity workers can get jobs elsewhere with a wage of $18 per hour, and low-productivity workers can get jobs elsewhere with a wage of $15 per hour. Find the range of piece rates

that will lead workers to self-select and solve the adverse selection problem.

4. A firm wants to hire workers for one year. There are two types of workers, skilled and unskilled. Skilled workers produce 2,000 units per month, and unskilled workers produce 1,500 units per month. Each unit of output generates $1 in net revenue for the firm. There are alternative sources of employment for the two types of workers. Skilled workers can earn $1,800 per month and unskilled workers can earn $1,500 per month in their alternative jobs. The firm cannot tell whether workers are skilled or unskilled until they have been employed for one month. After one month workers' types are correctly identified with probability 0.95, so there is a 5 percent chance that an unskilled worker is incorrectly identified as being skilled and a 5 percent chance that a skilled worker is incorrectly identified as being unskilled. Construct a probationary contract that induces self-selection and generates positive expected profit for the firm.

5. A probationary contract specifies that a worker is paid $2,110 per month for the first m months. After m months the worker is either fired or gets a raise to $2,500 per month for $(10 - m)$ months. A low-productivity worker has a 90 percent chance of being fired at the end of the probationary period. If low-productivity workers can earn $2,200 per month somewhere else, how many (whole) months must the probationary period last to keep them from applying?

CHAPTER

16 SIGNALING

As explained in the previous chapter, adverse selection problems eliminate the market for the skills of high-productivity workers. Employers can benefit from hiring high-productivity workers, however, and firms can take actions through the design of their compensation schemes to solve the adverse selection problem. However, the high-productivity workers also benefit from the solution to the adverse selection problem because they can be paid more if their skills are identified. This chapter explores what high-productivity workers can do to distinguish themselves from low-productivity workers.

GETTING AN EDUCATION

One of the ways high-productivity workers can distinguish themselves is through education. Before discussing how the two different types of workers decide on different levels of education, however, it is instructive to analyze the problem of a single worker deciding whether to get an education.

Consider the problem of someone deciding whether to go back to school to earn an MBA degree. He currently has a job that pays $35,000 per year, but he would have to give it up if he goes back to school. Tuition, fees, books, and other expenses amount to $25,000 per year, and it takes two years to earn an MBA. He has been told that he can expect to make $55,000 per year after he earns a degree. The benefits from school come in the form of higher salary after he finishes, but all of the costs come up front. The longer he works, the more benefits he enjoys. How long must he work for the MBA to be worthwhile; that is, how long must he work before the benefits make up for the up-front costs?

This question is answered using Table 16.1. The first column of the table shows the year. The second column shows the individual's income from continuing at his current job, assuming no raises. The third column shows the income from getting an MBA, again assuming no raises after he gets a job. The first two entries are negative, reflecting both the

TABLE 16.1   Costs and Benefits of Education

Year	Keeps Current Job	Gets MBA, then Works	Net Benefit of MBA	Cumulative Net Benefit of MBA
1	35,000	–25,000	–60,000	–60,000
2	35,000	–25,000	–60,000	–120,000
3	35,000	55,000	20,000	–100,000
4	35,000	55,000	20,000	–80,000
5	35,000	55,000	20,000	–60,000
6	35,000	55,000	20,000	–40,000
7	35,000	55,000	20,000	–20,000
8	35,000	55,000	20,000	0
9	35,000	55,000	20,000	20,000
10	35,000	55,000	20,000	40,000

tuition payments he must make and the fact that he must quit his current job if he wants to go back to school. The fourth column shows the net benefit of the MBA, which is the difference between his income with an MBA and his income without one. The final column is the cumulative net benefit from earning an MBA. The first year he must give up his $35,000 job and pay $25,000 in tuition, for a net benefit of –$60,000. The second year he also foregoes the income from his $35,000 job, and he again pays $25,000 in tuition. His net benefit from the second year is –$60,000. Add this to the net benefit from the first year to get the cumulative net benefit of –$120,000. In the third year, he gets a job that pays $55,000 per year. This is $20,000 more than he would have earned if he had remained in his old job, so $20,000 is added to the cumulative net benefit. Every year after that an additional $20,000 is added to his cumulative net benefit.

At the end of year 8, the worker's cumulative net benefit is zero. This means that after 6 years of work the extra $20,000 per year in salary has made up for the two years of tuition payments and foregone earnings. If he works into year 9 (his seventh year of work), his cumulative net benefit is positive, and getting an MBA is worthwhile. If he works less than 6 years, however, he would be better off staying with his old job. According to the table, to make getting an MBA worthwhile, he must plan to work past year 8.

This analysis raises an important issue that is worth elaboration. The worker's net benefit in a given year is the amount that he earns with an MBA minus the amount he earns without an MBA. Because we subtract the $35,000 he makes in his current job to compute net benefit, we are treating the $35,000 as a cost. In fact, the $35,000 per year is the *opportunity cost* associated with getting an MBA. An opportunity cost is the value of a resource in its next best alternative use, and the resource in question is his time. If he goes to school and then gets a job, he does not have time to work at his old job. The next best alternative use of his time is staying in his old job, which is worth $35,000 per year.

It is easy to see why this $35,000 per year opportunity cost arises in the years when the individual is in school because he cannot work when he goes to school. It is less straightforward why the opportunity cost arises in the years after he finishes school. The reason is that when he takes the MBA-level job he cannot also work at the pre-MBA-level job, so he must give up the $35,000 per year salary. Consequently, he foregoes $35,000 per year every year.

One factor that affects how long someone must work to make additional education worthwhile is the gap between the salary he would make with the additional education and the salary he would make without it. If the salary gap widens, it takes less time working to make education worthwhile. In Table 16.1 the gap is $55,000 – $35,000 = $20,000. If the pay for the holder of an MBA rises to $65,000, the salary gap widens to $30,000. With that gap, the $120,000 cost of the education is paid off after only 4 years of work.

Discounting the Future

The calculations in Table 16.1 make an assumption about how the worker feels about the future. In particular, he does not discount the future at all, so that $1,000 received ten years from now is worth exactly the same as $1,000 received right now. This is probably not an accurate portrayal of the world, and people tend to discount the future much more than this. For almost everyone the value of $1,000 ten years from now is much less than $1,000 today. Even if the $1,000 ten years from now were adjusted for inflation, almost everyone would still want the money today. People are impatient, wanting the consumption that $1,000 brings right away and not wanting to wait ten years to get that consumption.

Impatience can be captured using a discount factor. Let r denote the discount rate, which is generally a number greater than zero, similar to an interest rate. Then the value of the amount x received one year in the future is

$$\frac{x}{1+r}$$

and the value of the amount x received t years in the future is

$$\frac{x}{(1+r)^t}$$

The farther the income is in the future, the greater the exponent t is, and the less valuable that income is now. Increasing the discount rate, r, also makes the denominator larger, so the higher the discount rate, the lower the current value of future income.

TABLE 16.2 Costs and Benefits of Education with a 5 Percent Discount Rate

Year	Net Benefit	Discounted Net Benefit	Cumulative Discounted Net Benefit
1	–60,000	–60,000	–60,000
2	–60,000	–57,143	–117,143
3	20,000	18,141	–99,002
4	20,000	17,277	–81,725
5	20,000	16,454	-65,271
6	20,000	15,671	–49,600
7	20,000	14,924	–34,676
8	20,000	14,214	–20,462
9	20,000	13,537	–6,925
10	20,000	12,892	5,967
11	20,000	12,278	18,245
12	20,000	11,694	29,939
13	20,000	11,137	41,076
14	20,000	10,606	51,682
15	20,000	10,101	61,783

Discount rates reflect impatience, with higher discount rates corresponding to higher degrees of impatience. Table 16.2 computes cumulative net benefits assuming that the discount rate is 5 percent, as compared with the discount rate of 0 percent used in Table 16.1. Because the tuition costs of education come at the beginning, where they are not discounted much, and the benefits come later, where they are discounted more heavily, discounting reduces the cumulative net benefit of an MBA. The higher the discount rate, the longer the individual must work to make an MBA worthwhile. When the discount rate is 0 percent, he must work through year 8, as shown in Table 16.1, but when the discount rate is 5 percent he must work through year 10. It is not shown in the table, but when the discount rate is 10 percent, he must work through year 13, and when it is 15 percent he must work through year 27 to make getting an MBA worthwhile.

General Lessons About Obtaining an Education

In our simplified framework, the only reason for getting an education is to get a higher-paying job. In this case, it is only worthwhile to get an education if the person works long enough at the higher-paying job to make up for the costs of education. These costs are of two types: the actual monetary cost of school, including tuition, fees, books, and other expenses, and the opportunity cost of school, which is the foregone earnings from a lower-paying job that does not require as much education.

The bigger the gap between the higher salary and the lower salary, the less time it takes to recoup the costs of education and the more worthwhile an education is. The more patient the individual is, or, put differently, the lower the individual's discount rate, the less time it takes to recoup the costs of education.

Some Real-World Numbers

Data exist both on the size of the gap between the salary levels with and without an education and on the discount rate people use for evaluating income streams. Starting with salary levels, Table 16.3 reports the mean salary level for 35–44-year-olds with different levels of education, as compiled by the Bureau of the Census in 2002.

The table reveals several patterns. First, education pays. People with graduate degrees earn more than people without; people with college degrees earn more than people without; and people with high school diplomas earn more than people without. Second, a bachelor's degree is very valuable. A person with a bachelor's degree earns over 90 percent more than a person who finished high school but never went to college. Third, even without finishing, there is a huge return to college. People who start college but do not finish make on average about 20 percent more than people who stop with a high school diploma. Fourth, and finally, there is a huge return to completing a high school diploma. People who graduate from high school make almost 25 percent more than those who drop out of high school, and people who complete a bachelor's degree earn 60 percent more than people who start college but do not finish.

The best incentive to finish high school, finish college, and even go on to earn a graduate degree is provided by the market. Each of these degrees comes with a significant increase in average salary. In light of our analysis of the decision of whether to get an education, Table 16.3 suggests that the salary gaps are wide enough to make it

TABLE 16.3 Mean Salary Levels for 35–44-Year-Olds	
Highest Education Level Attained	*Mean 2002 Salary*
No high school	$ 22,803
Some high school but no diploma	28,101
High school grad or GED	34,559
Some college but no degree	41,356
Associate's degree	42,446
Bachelor's degree	66,006
Master's degree	81,553
Professional degree	120,061
Doctoral degree	98,211

Source: U.S. Bureau of the Census

worthwhile for people to continue school and pursue advanced degrees, as long as they do not discount the future too heavily and they have the required aptitude to complete the schooling.

Estimates of discount rates come from an analysis of retirement choices by members of the armed services.[1] In 1991 the Department of Defense was authorized to reduce active duty strength by 25 percent, with the reduction to come from every experience level. This was a difficult task because ordinarily in the military retirement benefits can be collected only after 20 years of service. For obvious reasons the military did not want to fire soldiers, so they created incentives for soldiers to leave. Military personnel who voluntarily departed were offered their choice of two pay packages, both based on the number of years of service and annual salary. One package offered a lump sum payment, and the other offered a set of annual payments.

For example, an O-3 officer (e.g., an army captain) with nine years of service could get a $46,219 lump sum or an annual payment of $7,703 for 18 years. An E-6 enlisted man (e.g., an army staff sergeant) with 12 years of service could get a $35,549 lump sum or an annual payment of $5,925 for 24 years. In both cases the discounted value of the stream of annual payments is the same as the lump sum if the discount rate is 19 percent. So, personnel with discount rates higher than 19 percent should take the lump sum because they are too impatient to wait for the annual payments, and personnel with discount rates below 19 percent should take the annual payments.

More than half of the officers and over 90 percent of the enlisted men who chose to leave the military took the lump sum. This suggests that more than half of the officers, virtually all of whom are college graduates, and almost all of the enlisted men have discount rates higher than 19 percent. These are very high discount rates, and they are high enough to keep people from getting an education. For comparison purposes, the interest rate at the time was about 7 percent, and by taking the lump sum the military personnel actually saved the U.S. government quite a bit of money.

We can use the numbers from Table 16.3 along with the discount rate deduced from the decisions of military personnel to work out a real-world example of an education choice. Let us consider a 40-year-old worker with a bachelor's degree who is thinking about going back to school for two years to get a master's degree. She plans to retire at age 65. She is a resident of Texas, and tuition and fees at the University of Texas total $3,000 per year. To go back to school she must give up her $66,000 per year job, but after college she will earn $81,500. Her discount rate is 20 percent, which is consistent with the discount rate

---

[1]Warner, John T. and Saul Pleeter, "The Personal Discount Rate: Evidence from Military Downsizing Programs," *American Economic Review* 91 (March 2001), 33–53.

TABLE 16.4   Should a 40-Year-Old Get a Master's Degree?

Year	Net Benefit	Discounted Net Benefit	Cumulative Discounted Net Benefit
1	–69,000	–69,000	–69,000
2	–69,000	–57,500	–126,500
3	15,500	10,764	–115,736
4	15,500	8,970	–106,766
5	15,500	7,475	–99,291
6	15,500	6,229	–93,062
7	15,500	5,191	–87,871
8	15,500	4,326	–83,545
9	15,500	3,605	–79,941
10	15,500	3,004	–76,937
11	15,500	2,503	–74,433
12	15,500	2,086	–72,347
13	15,500	1,738	–70,609
14	15,500	1,449	–69,160
15	15,500	1,207	–67,953
16	15,500	1,006	–66,947
17	15,500	838	–66,108
18	15,500	699	–65,410
19	15,500	582	–64,828
20	15,500	485	–64,342
21	15,500	404	–63,938
22	15,500	337	–63,601
23	15,500	281	–63,321
24	15,500	234	–63,087
25	15,500	195	–62,892

for officers. Should she go back to school? The answer from a purely financial perspective is no, as shown by Table 16.4. Even though the tuition cost is negligible, the foregone income while she goes back to school is so high that she is never able to make up for it when the future is discounted so heavily.

EDUCATION AS A SIGNAL OF QUALITY

Let us return to a situation with adverse selection. There are two types of workers, high-productivity and low-productivity, and the employer cannot tell apart the two types. The workers have an option to get a college degree. Is there any way that the two types can self-select by using the college degree? In particular, are there situations in which one type of worker gets a college degree and the other does not?

In this section we construct an example in which exactly this type of self-selection occurs. In the example, both workers have 40 years until retirement. There are two types of jobs. One pays $4,000 per month, but it requires a college degree. The other pays $3,200, and it requires only a high school diploma. College tuition and fees cost $40,000 per year. To ease calculations, assume that the future is not discounted.

If both types require the same amount of time to complete college, then both types will decide to do exactly the same thing. But suppose that whatever characteristic makes high-productivity type workers have high productivity also allows them to finish college in four years, whereas whatever characteristic makes low-productivity type workers have low productivity also makes them take five years to finish college. Now there is a reason why high-productivity workers might choose to go to college but low-productivity workers will not.

Consider the choice facing high-productivity workers. If they choose not to go to college, they can work for a full 40 years at $3,200 per month. Their total income from not going to college is $(40)(12)(\$3,200) = \$1,536,000$. If they choose to go to college for four years, they must pay $40,000 per year for each of those four years, but then they earn $4,000 per month for the remaining 36 years. Their total income is therefore $(4)(-\$40,000) + (36)(12)(\$4000) = \$1,568,000$. If they go to college, their lifetime income is higher by $32,000.

Now look at the choice faced by low-productivity workers. Their total income from not going to college is the same as for high-productivity workers, $1,536,000. If they choose to go to college, however, they must go for five years, paying $40,000 per year in tuition. Afterward they work for the remaining 35 years and earn $4,000 per month. Their total lifetime income when they go to college is $(5)(-\$40,000) + (35)(12)(\$4,000) = \$1,480,000$. If they go to college, their lifetime income is lower by $56,000.

In this example, high-productivity workers choose to go to college but low-productivity workers do not. Consequently, the firm can tell apart the two types of workers; the high-productivity workers have college degrees, but the low-productivity workers do not. By choosing to go to college, the high-productivity workers are able to distinguish themselves from their low-productivity counterparts and benefit from having high productivity.

In this example a college education is a **signal**, a costly activity that has no effect on the individuals' type but whose cost is related to their type. Let us make sure that both parts of the definition work here. First, does getting an education make workers have high productivity? The answer is no. If high-productivity workers get a college degree, they remain high-productivity workers, and if low-productivity workers get a degree they remain low-productivity workers. In the example, college does not change low-productivity workers into high-productivity workers; it only labels people who get college degrees as high-productivity workers. That takes care of the first part of the definition of a signal, that the activity has no effect on productivity. What about the second part, that the cost of the activity is related to productivity? In the example, low-productivity workers need one more year to complete college than high-productivity workers, and that extra year costs $40,000 in tuition and (12)($3,200) = $38,400 in foregone wages for a total of $78,400.

This example gives a rather cynical view of the value of a college education. If education is really just a signal, then students learn nothing of value that makes them more productive in the first place. Instead, education just labels students as high-productivity workers, allowing them to get better jobs and higher pay in the future. If this is true, then education is socially wasteful because it does nothing to increase the productivity of workers in society. Instead, it uses up resources in the labeling of workers.

Is education really just a signal, or do students get something from it that makes them more productive? This is a valid issue, and one to which we return later.

SIGNALING AND EQUILIBRIUM

We can think of signaling as the outcome of a game between the two types of workers and the employer. In all of the games we have considered so far, an equilibrium is a situation in which all players best-respond to the equilibrium strategies of their opponents. Here, however, something different is happening, and it is worth seeing what that difference is.

The game has a new ingredient: the employer's beliefs. In the example just completed, the firm offering $4,000 per month believes that a worker with a college degree has high productivity and one without a degree has low productivity. The firm's best response to these beliefs is to hire only workers with college degrees. A high-productivity worker's best response to the firm's strategy is to get a college degree, and a low-productivity worker's best response is to forego college and get a job with the alternative employer.

All of the strategy choices come from the firm's beliefs. But are these beliefs reasonable? Put another way, are these beliefs consistent with the strategies chosen by the two types of workers? It turns out that they are. Because high-productivity workers go to college and low-productivity workers do not, the firm is correct in its beliefs that all college graduates have high productivity and all nongraduates have low productivity.

For a general signaling game, let us call the player who sends the signal the Sender and the player who receives it the Receiver. The

Sender can be of two types, high or low, and the Receiver forms beliefs about the Sender's type. An equilibrium has three requirements (in this type of game, it is customary to refer to the Sender as "he" and the Receiver as "she"):

1. The Receiver's strategy is a best response to her beliefs.
2. The Sender's strategy is a best response to his type and to the Receiver's strategy.
3. The Receiver's beliefs are consistent with the behavior generated by the Sender's strategy.

An equilibrium in which the different types of Senders use different strategies is called a **separating equilibrium**. In contrast, an equilibrium in which all Senders use the same action is called a **pooling equilibrium**. Because we are looking for a situation in which high types take actions that distinguish themselves from low types, we are necessarily looking for a separating equilibrium.

We close this section by showing that a different set of beliefs cannot generate a separating equilibrium. Using the example from the preceding section, suppose that the firm believes that workers with college degrees have low productivity and those without degrees have high productivity. These beliefs are the exact opposite of those in the preceding section. The firm's best response to these beliefs is to hire workers without degrees because they are believed to have high productivity and not to hire workers with degrees because they are believed to have low productivity. Clearly, a high-productivity worker's best response is to not get a degree. But a low-productivity worker's best response is also to not get a degree because getting a degree is costly and has no benefits. So neither type of worker gets a degree, and the firm ends up hiring both types. Because neither type gets a degree, the firm's belief that low productivity workers get degrees is inconsistent with behavior. Our third criterion for an equilibrium fails, and we cannot get a separating equilibrium with these strange beliefs.

IS EDUCATION REALLY JUST A SIGNAL?

A signal is a costly action that has no effect on the sender's type, but its cost does depend on the sender's type. If education is a signal, it has no effect on the productivity of the students who complete the education. All it does is indicate to employers that the students had high productivity before they started school. But if education is not just a signal, then it does have an impact on the productivity of students, and it is not socially wasteful. So, is education really just a signal?

One can see why this is an important question. If education's only purpose is to allow high-productivity workers to distinguish themselves from low-productivity workers, the state has no valid reason to support education. Because education does nothing to improve worker productivity, there can be no spillovers that help the state as a whole, and the only benefits go to the workers and their employers. Therefore, workers should pay the entire cost of education themselves. Conversely, if education is not just a signal, a system of free or subsidized education makes the state's citizens more productive and can improve the incomes of everyone in the state.

This is a tricky question to sort out, however. If education is not just a signal, then it increases the productivity of workers who should then be paid more. As Table 16.3 shows, workers with more education are paid more on average than workers with less education. On the other hand, if education is just a signal, higher-productivity workers get more education to distinguish themselves from lower-productivity workers. Because higher-productivity workers are worth more to the firm than lower-productivity workers, firms can afford to pay them more. Also, to make it worthwhile for higher-productivity workers to get more education, they must be paid more. Thus, the signaling model also predicts that workers with more education are paid more, consistent with the data in Table 16.3 but for completely different reasons. Because the traditional rationale for education, that it makes workers more productive, and the signaling rationale are both consistent with the data in Table 16.3, we need to look deeper into the issue of which explanation drives the data.

The idea behind the signaling explanation is that because employers cannot distinguish between high- and low-productivity workers, high-productivity workers have an incentive to pursue further education in order to distinguish themselves from their low-productivity counterparts. This reasoning does not apply to self-employed workers, however, because they presumably know their own productivity levels and do not need an education to distinguish themselves from anyone else. If education is only a signal and does not make workers more productive, self-employed people should not go to school as long as other workers. A study found that self-employed workers obtained almost the same amount of education on average as salaried workers, suggesting that education does more than just signal a worker's type.[2]

Another study found that individuals who dropped out of high school in eleventh grade were roughly twice as likely to quit their jobs as individuals who completed high school, and in general, more highly educated workers are less likely to quit than less highly educated workers.[3] This suggests that a high school degree is a signal, in this case revealing the worker's reliability and willingness to stay with a job, both qualities that employers value.

[2]Wolpin, Kenneth I., "Education and Screening," *American Economic Review* 67 (December 1977), 949–958.
[3]Weiss, Andrew, "Determinants of Quit Behavior," *Journal of Labor Economics* 2 (July 1984), 371–387.

A third study is based on GED test scores.[4] GED exams are national, but different states have different thresholds for passing. So, for example, someone who barely failed in state A could have barely passed in state B. If education is a signal, then a person who barely passed in state B should be paid more than a person who barely failed with the same score in state A. Conversely, if there is no signaling effect, workers with the same score should get the same pay in both states. The study found that workers who passed the exam got paid more than workers with the same score who did not pass, suggesting that the GED also has value as a signal.

Taken as a whole, the evidence suggests that education serves both purposes: It raises productivity and it acts as a signal.

OTHER EXAMPLES OF SIGNALING

Signaling exists in other settings beside the one in which a firm must distinguish between high- and low-productivity workers. This section provides some examples.

Dressing for Success

Everyone knows that when they interview for a job they are supposed to dress up in business attire. But why? Wearing business attire to an interview does not make people more productive than they would have been if they had not worn a suit. Besides, wearing business attire is costly. Because wearing business attire is a costly activity that has no effect on productivity, it can serve as a signal. To see what it signals, imagine yourself on the other side of the interview table. You see two candidates who seem to be equally qualified, but one wears business attire and the other wears jeans and a sweatshirt. Which one would you hire? The one who did not wear business attire could not be bothered to dress up for the interview. There are probably other things that applicant cannot be bothered with, like paying attention to deadlines, showing up on time, and filing reports regularly. You would hire the one who wore the business attire, because the effort involved in putting it on provides a signal about certain qualities that are valuable to the firm.

Licensing

States issue licenses for many things, from driving to practicing medicine or other professions. These licenses serve as a signal. To take a simple case, consider a license to practice medicine. Someone who is

---

[4]Tyler, John H., Richard J. Murnane, and John B. Willett, "Estimating the Labor Market Signaling Value of the GED," *Quarterly Journal of Economics* 115 (May 2000), 431–468.

qualified to practice medicine already has all of the knowledge needed to pass the licensing exam, but someone who is unqualified will find it very difficult to meet the licensing requirements. It is much more costly for an unqualified individual to obtain a license, so unqualified individuals choose not to become doctors. Because only qualified doctors take and pass the exam, the license is a signal of the doctor's qualifications.

Celebrity Endorsements of Charities

Many charities rely on contributions for their funding. It is difficult for an individual to look at the long list of charities and tell which are honest and use the contributions for charitable works and which are less honest and use a large part of the contributions on overhead or on frivolous expenses. This is where celebrity endorsements come in. A celebrity endorsement does not make the charitable works more worthwhile. However, the fact that celebrities are willing to attach their names to a charity means that they (or their agents) were satisfied with the functioning of the charity. A celebrity endorsement is a signal of the honesty of a charity.

Deductibles in Insurance

As discussed in Chapter 15, insurance companies have a hard time telling how risky potential customers are, and in many cases, the customers have better information about their own riskiness than the insurer does. Consider the case of car insurance for drivers who have no citations on their records. Some of them drive safely and carefully, while others speed regularly and engage in reckless behavior but have not yet been caught. The safe drivers can distinguish themselves from the risky ones by purchasing insurance policies with high deductibles. If they get in an accident, they must pay the deductible before receiving any claim. A policy with a high deductible is less costly for a safe driver than for a risky driver because a safe driver is much less likely to have to pay the deductible. Willingness to have a high deductible signals to the insurer that the driver is safe.

Warranties

When the Hyundai Motor Company wanted to enter the U.S. market, it had some hurdles to overcome. One of the biggest was that it had no reputation for quality, and consumers were unable to tell whether the cars were well built and would last. To counter this, Hyundai offered longer warranties than its competitors, with a 5-year, 50,000-mile bumper-to-bumper warranty and a 10-year, 100,000-mile warranty on the power train. In part because of the warranty, Hyundai's U.S. sales rose 41 percent during a period when the overall automobile market contracted.

A product warranty is a signal of the product's quality. The warranty itself does not make a good product more reliable, although it does insure the consumer against defects. However, the promise to repair any defects during a set period of time is more costly for the producer of a poor product than it is for a high-quality product, so a warranty serves as a signal that the product is of high quality.

Signals in Nature

Strong, healthy males of some species of elk grow huge antlers. These antlers are a burden because they require energy to grow and carry and they put a strain on the elk's neck muscles. It is clearly more costly for an elk to grow large antlers than small ones. However, because only the strongest, healthiest elk can grow and carry these large racks, the antlers provide a signal to potential mates about the male's health and strength, and females can discern the quality of the male for mating purposes.

Homework Problems

1. What is a signal?
2. Suppose that an individual must pay $10,000 this year and then receives $20,000 next year. What is his cumulative discounted net benefit if his discount rate is 20 percent?
3. An individual must decide whether to go to school for an extra year. If she does not go to school, her wage will be $18,000 per year every year. If she does go to school, her wage will be $36,000 per year every year. She cannot work while she goes to school. The year of school costs $25,000. The individual discounts the future at a rate of 20 percent per year.

   a. How long would she have to work after going to school to make going to school worthwhile?

   b. Compute the discounted net present value of schooling if she works for 2 years after going to school.

4. Workers come in two types, high-productivity and low-productivity. High-productivity workers generate net revenue of $100,000 per year to their employers, and low-productivity workers generate net revenue of $50,000 a year. Individuals work for 4 years. Before they start working, workers have the opportunity to take a licensing exam. To pass the exam, a high-productivity worker would have to study nights, and the implicit cost would be $20,000. A low-productivity worker would have to study nights and weekends and take a special test-taking course, for a total cost of $40,000. Assuming that low-productivity workers are paid $50,000 per year in an alternative industry, what range of salaries can a firm offer to licensed workers to guarantee that only high-productivity workers seek licenses? Assume that the future is not discounted.

CHAPTER

17 SEARCH

W hen employers look for new employees or when workers look for new jobs they must go through a search process. The purpose of the employer's search is to identify a better worker to hire, and the purpose of the worker's search is to find a better job to take. This has the potential to be a really major task. Taking the employer's perspective, the set of potential hires can be huge, and it would be extremely costly to look at all of them. How does the firm decide how to go about searching among all of the potential workers? That is the topic of this chapter.

BENEFITS AND COSTS OF SEARCH

The fundamental question addressed in this chapter is, "How much should an individual search?" Because this is a how much question, the answer involves marginal analysis and, in particular, involves a comparison of marginal benefits and marginal costs. Before we can do this comparison, however, we must first identify the benefits and costs of search.

Costs

The cost side of the problem is the easier of the two. When a firm looks for a new worker, it must evaluate the applications and then interview some candidates. Evaluating the applications takes time away from other activities, so evaluating applications is costly. Interviewing a candidate can be even more costly. To conduct the interview, the firm must bring the candidate to the firm, which could involve significant travel expenses. The firm must then house and feed the candidate, entailing additional expenses. Finally, during the interview the candidate meets with a number of different employees of the firm, and those interviews take time away from other productive issues. All told, these costs can be significant.

It is easiest to think about the firm's search as involving interviews. Specifically, more searching means interviewing more applicants. Because each interview entails additional travel, hotel, food, and time costs, the cost-of-search function is increasing. The marginal cost of search is the cost that arises from interviewing one more applicant.

Benefits

Benefits are a little more complex than costs. The benefit a firm receives from hiring a worker is the net revenue that worker produces minus the amount the firm pays the worker. This difference is the profit generated by the employment relationship. Different workers generate different amounts of profit, and searching allows the firm to find workers who generate more profit.

Although it is true that higher-productivity workers generate more net revenue for the firm than lower-productivity workers, it is not necessarily true that they generate more profit than lower-productivity workers. If higher-productivity workers have better outside options, the firm must pay them more to attract them, and this extra pay cuts into profit. Another way to think about this is that the difference in the amount of net revenue generated by the workers might be smaller than the difference in the amount they must be paid, and if so, the lower-productivity workers are more profitable than the higher-productivity workers.

This said, what is the benefit of search? Search can potentially allow the firm to find a worker who generates a large amount of profit. Because of the uncertainty inherent in search, however, the firm cannot tell which workers will generate a large amount of profit and which will not before it interviews them. So when the firm interviews job candidates, it might find out that they will generate a large amount of profit, or it might find out that they will generate no profit at all. This means that before the search takes place, the benefits of search are *expected* benefits because the firm cannot know whether the search yields a high level of profit or a low level until after the search is over.

The marginal expected benefit of search is the expected benefit from searching one more time, that is, from interviewing one more candidate. After the first search, one candidate is the most profitable so far, and further search is only beneficial when it leads to someone who is even more profitable. Put another way, searching one more time will not lead the firm to hire someone less profitable than its best candidate so far, so the marginal expected benefit of search is the expected *gain* in profitability, beyond that of the best candidate so far, from searching one more time.

An example can help clarify the issues. Suppose that there are five types of workers. Type-1 workers generate no profit at all; type-2s generate $2,000 profit; type-3s generate $4,000 profit; type-4s generate $6,000 profit; and type-5s generate $8,000 profit, as shown in Table 17.1. Each of these types is equally likely because they make up equal fractions of the candidate pool, and the probability of drawing any specified

TABLE 17.1 Computing the Marginal Benefit of Search, Marginal Cost = $650

Type	*Profit*	*Probability*	*Marginal Expected Benefit of Search*
1	$ 0	0.2	$(0.2)(\$8{,}000 - 0) + (0.2)(\$6{,}000 - 0) +$ $(0.2)(\$4{,}000 - 0) + (0.2)(\$2{,}000 - 0)$ $= \mathbf{\$4{,}000}$
2	2,000	0.2	$(0.2)(\$8{,}000 - 2{,}000) + (0.2)(\$6{,}000 -$ $2{,}000)) + (0.2)(\$4{,}000 - 2{,}000)$ $= \mathbf{\$2{,}400}$
3	4,000	0.2	$(0.2)(\$8{,}000 - 4{,}000) + (0.2)(\$6{,}000 -$ $4{,}000) = \mathbf{\$1{,}200}$
4	6,000	0.2	$(0.2)(\$8{,}000 - 6{,}000) = \mathbf{\$400}$
5	8,000	0.2	**$0**

type of worker is 0.2. Further suppose that the firm has already searched and has identified a type-4 candidate. What is the marginal expected benefit of search? The only way the firm can benefit is from finding a type-5 worker because with any other type the firm is at least as happy with the type-4 worker it has already found. The probability of finding a type-5 employee is 0.2, and the gain from finding a type-5 worker is $8,000 – 6,000 = $2,000. The expected gain is therefore (0.2)($2,000) = $400, and this is the marginal expected benefit of search.

What if the best candidate so far is a type-3 worker who can generate $4,000 in profit? Then the firm benefits from finding either a type-4 or a type-5. The expected gain from finding a type-4 worker is (0.2)($6,000 – 4,000) = $400. The expected gain from finding a type-5 worker is (0.2)($8,000 – 4,000) = $800. The marginal expected benefit is the sum of these two, or $1,200.

The last column of Table 17.1 shows the marginal expected benefit of search for situations in which the best worker so far is of each different type. When the best candidate so far is a type-5 worker, there is no possible way to benefit from further search, so the marginal expected benefit of search is zero. As the best candidate so far becomes less profitable, the marginal expected benefit of search increases, and it is as high as possible when the best candidate so far is the worst type, a type-1 worker.

OPTIMAL SEARCH

This section addresses the question, how much should the firm search in order to maximize its expected profit? As mentioned in the preceding section, the answer involves marginal benefits and marginal costs. Let us look at the same problem as in the preceding section, where a firm is looking for one new worker and the candidates' profitability levels are given in Table 17.1. When the firm picks a worker randomly, it has an equal chance of getting a worker who will generate $8,000 in profit, one who will generate $6,000 in profit, one who will generate $4,000, one who will generate $2,000, and one who will generate no profit at all. To determine which type of worker the candidate is, the firm must conduct an interview at a cost of $650.

Marginal analysis tells us that if the marginal benefit of an activity exceeds the marginal cost the individual should engage in more of the activity, and if the marginal benefit is less than the marginal cost the individual should either stop or engage in less of the activity. Because the benefits generated by search are random, depending on the profitability of the worker drawn from the applicant pool, the benefits are expected benefits.

Suppose that the firm searches and finds a worker whose profitability is $2,000. Should it hire that worker or should it keep looking? Table 17.1 shows that the marginal expected benefit of search is $2,400 when the best candidate so far has profitability of $2,000. The marginal cost of search is the cost of interviewing one more candidate, or $650. Because the marginal expected benefit of search exceeds the marginal cost, the firm should continue looking.

This example poses the question in the following way. If the best candidate the firm has found so far has profitability x, should the firm hire that worker or should it keep looking? It should keep looking if the marginal expected benefit of search is greater than the marginal cost, and it should hire the worker if the marginal benefit of search is less than the marginal cost. Looking at Table 17.1, we can see that the marginal expected benefit of search is greater than the $650 marginal cost when the best candidate so far generates zero profit, $2,000 in profit, or $4,000 in profit. When the best candidate so far generates either $6,000 in profit or $8,000 in profit, the firm should stop looking and hire that worker.

Important Features of the Optimal Search Rule

The above example illustrates several important features of optimal search rules.

1. *Optimal search relies on a stopping rule.* A **stopping rule** is a set of conditions under which a process stops. If the conditions are satisfied the individual ends the process, but if the conditions are not satisfied the individual continues the process. Optimal search uses a simple stopping rule: End the search if the marginal expected benefit of search is less than the marginal cost.

2. *Optimal search sometimes means hiring someone who is not the best possible worker.* In the example, the firm does not hold out for the most profitable worker, one who can generate $8,000 for the firm. Instead it takes any worker who can generate at least $6,000 profit. When it finds someone who can generate $6,000

profit, the expected benefit from searching one more time is only $400, while the cost of interviewing one more worker is $650. It is not worth searching for the best possible type, and one useful interpretation of the stopping rule is that the firm continues searching until it finds a worker who is "good enough."

3. *Because optimal search relies on a stopping rule, the searcher never passes up a candidate and then goes back and hires him.* A second useful interpretation of the stopping rule is that the firm sets a standard and hires the first candidate who meets or exceeds the standard. Consequently, any worker who was passed over was deemed not good enough and, barring any change in the distribution of workers or in the cost of search, he will never be good enough.

There is another good reason for the firm to avoid waiting to hire a candidate it judges good enough. If the firm continues to interview after finding a good candidate, there is a chance that some other firm will come along and find that same good candidate. If the other firm acts first, the candidate who met the standard might not be available when the firm finally gets around to offering a job. The use of a stopping rule means that the firm does not have to worry about this consideration because it immediately offers a job to the first candidate it deems to be good enough.

DO PEOPLE USE THE OPTIMAL SEARCH STRATEGY?

The optimal search strategy states that individuals search until they find something that meets or exceeds some standard, and then they stop searching. If the search costs are sufficiently high, they stop searching before they find the very best alternative. Do people really do this?

Barry Schwarz, of Swarthmore College, and his colleagues performed a study on just this question. They found that some people are apt to exhibit the "satisficing" behavior consistent with the optimal search rule, but not everybody is. They labeled a large fraction of their subjects "maximizers," and these people tend to keep searching until they either find the best possible alternative or they run out of time, whichever comes first. Schwarz and his colleagues' most striking finding, however, is that the maximizers tend to be less happy than the satisficers.

This finding is consistent with our model. Satisficing, or taking the first alternative that meets or exceeds some standard, is optimal, which means that it is

(continued)

the rule that maximizes the searcher's utility. Doing anything else, like maximizing, lowers utility and makes people less happy.

The Internet has vastly expanded people's choices. It has given people more places to search, and at the same time has lowered search costs because they can now search without ever leaving their desks. The optimal response to this change is to search more. But this generates a real problem for maximizers because they feel a need to look at every possible option to find the best one. As the choices have expanded, they have become even less happy.

SOURCE: Schwartz, Barry, "The Tyranny of Choice," *Scientific American* (April 2004), 70–75.

DETERMINANTS OF THE AMOUNT OF SEARCH

What does it mean for a firm to search more or less when trying to hire a worker? After all, when the firm uses a stopping rule, the number of candidates it must interview is random. In the example we have been using, the firm stops when it finds a worker who will generate at least $6,000 in profit. The probability that it hires the first worker it interviews is 40 percent because the probability of finding a worker worth $6,000 is 20 percent and the probability of finding one worth $8,000 is 20 percent. The probability that the firm must interview another worker is 60 percent, and the probability that the second worker is hired, given that the first worker was not, is again 40 percent. The firm could take a long time before it gets a worker who fits the criterion of being good enough. So how can we talk about searching more?

The short answer is that we cannot. What we can talk about, however, is the standard the firm sets for whom it will hire. If the firm sets a stricter standard, in a sense it searches more because it holds out for a more profitable worker. Similarly, if it loosens the standard, it is willing to settle for a less profitable worker, which is one way of thinking about searching less.

The standard a firm sets is determined in part by the distribution of workers in the pool. In Table 17.1 the five types of workers are equally likely, and the firm sets the standard at $6,000 profitability; that is, it hires the first worker it finds who can generate at least $6,000 profit. Now look at Table 17.2, where the five types are no longer equally likely. This time the firm is most likely to find someone who is entirely unsuited for the job and generates zero profit. We can compute the marginal expected benefit of search in exactly the same way as in Table 17.1. Because the marginal search cost is $650, the firm stops when it finds someone who generates $4,000 in profit. The

TABLE 17.2   Search when the Worst Outcome Is More Likely, Marginal Cost = $650

Type	Profit	Probability	Marginal Expected Benefit of Search
1	$ 0	0.6	$(0.1)(\$8,000 - 0) + (0.1)(\$6,000 - 0) +$ $(0.1)(\$4,000 - 0) + (0.1)(\$2,000 - 0)$ $= \mathbf{\$2,000}$
2	2,000	0.1	$(0.1)(\$8,000 - 2,000) + (0.1)(\$6,000 -$ $2,000) + (0.1)(\$4,000 - 2,000)$ $= \mathbf{\$1,200}$
3	4,000	0.1	$(0.1)(\$8,000 - 4,000) + (0.1)(\$6,000 -$ $4,000) = \mathbf{\$600}$
4	6,000	0.1	$(0.1)(\$8,000 - 6,000) = \mathbf{\$200}$
5	8,000	0.1	$\mathbf{\$0}$

marginal expected benefit from searching after finding someone worth $4,000 is only $600, which is less than the cost of interviewing one more candidate.

Table 17.3 shows a third distribution of workers. This time the firm is most likely to find the best possible worker. Now the firm holds out for the best possible worker. When it finds someone who generates $6,000 in profit, the expected benefit from interviewing one more candidate is $1,200, but the cost of the interview is only $650. The firm should keep interviewing until it finds someone who can generate $8,000 in profit.

The final example for this section is found in Table 17.4. Table 17.2 made the worst outcome more likely, and the firm lowered its hiring standard. Table 17.3 made the best outcome more likely, and the firm raised its hiring standard. The new table makes both the best and worst outcomes more likely compared to Table 17.1. The intuition

TABLE 17.3   Search when the Best Outcome Is More Likely, Marginal Cost = $650

Type	Profit	Probability	Marginal Expected Benefit of Search
1	$ 0	0.1	$(0.6)(\$8,000 - 0) + (0.1)(\$6,000 - 0) +$ $(0.1)(\$4,000 - 0) + (0.1)(\$2,000 - 0)$ $= \mathbf{\$6,000}$
2	2,000	0.1	$(0.6)(\$8,000 - 2,000) + (0.1)(\$6,000 -$ $2,000)) + (0.1)(\$4,000 - 2,000)$ $= \mathbf{\$4,200}$
3	4,000	0.1	$(0.6)(\$8,000 - 4,000) + (0.1)(\$6,000 -$ $4,000) = \mathbf{\$2,600}$
4	6,000	0.1	$(0.6)(\$8,000 - 6,000) = \mathbf{\$1,200}$
5	8,000	0.6	$\mathbf{\$0}$

TABLE 17.4 Search with a Riskier Distribution,
Marginal Cost = $650

Type	Profit	Probability	Marginal Expected Benefit of Search
1	$ 0	0.35	$(0.35)(\$8,000 - 0) + (0.1)(\$6,000 - 0) +$ $(0.1)(\$4,000 - 0) + (0.1)(\$2,000 - 0)$ $= \mathbf{\$4,000}$
2	2,000	0.1	$(0.35)(\$8,000 - 2,000) + (0.1)(\$6,000 -$ $2,000)) + (0.1)(\$4,000 - 2,000)$ $= \mathbf{\$2,700}$
3	4,000	0.1	$(0.35)(\$8,000 - 4,000) + (0.1)(\$6,000 -$ $4,000) = \mathbf{\$1,600}$
4	6,000	0.1	$(0.35)(\$8,000 - 6,000) = \mathbf{\$700}$
5	8,000	0.35	$\mathbf{\$0}$

from Table 17.2 suggests that the firm should lower its standard, while the intuition from Table 17.3 suggests that it should raise the standard. Which effect dominates?

Table 17.4 shows that the firm searches until it finds someone who can generate the maximal profit, $8,000. When it finds someone worth $6,000, the expected benefit from one more interview is $700 but the cost of that interview is only $650. The firm keeps interviewing until it finds the best possible worker.

The distribution of workers in Table 17.2 is worse than the distribution in Table 17.1, and we found that the worse distribution leads to a lower standard. The distribution in Table 17.3 is better than the distribution in Table 17.1, and we found that the better distribution leads to a higher standard. The distribution in Table 17.4 is neither better nor worse than the one in Table 17.1. Instead, it is *riskier* because it increases the chances of getting an extreme outcome and reduces the chances of getting an intermediate outcome. The firm responds to the riskier distribution by raising its standard.

All three of these patterns really show the same effect. Table 17.2 reduces the chance of finding the best worker, but Tables 17.3 and 17.4 both increase the chance of finding the best worker. When finding the best worker becomes more likely, the firm raises its standard. It does not really matter what happens to the chance of the worst outcome because the firm does not stop there anyway. The key to determining how much a firm will search is the probability of the best outcome, not the probability of the worst.

JOB SEARCH

The problem of a worker searching for a job is very similar to that of a firm searching for a worker. To see the similarities, suppose that different

TABLE 17.5   Job Search

Type	Net Benefit	Probability	Marginal Expected Benefit of Search
No job	$ 0	0.5	$(0.1)(\$50,000 - 0)$ $+ (0.2)(\$40,000 - 0)$ $+ (0.2)(\$30,000 - 0)$ $= \mathbf{\$19,000}$
Satisfactory	30,000	0.2	$(0.1)(\$50,000 - 30,000)$ $+ (0.2)(\$40,000 - 30,000))$ $= \mathbf{\$4,000}$
Good	40,000	0.2	$(0.1)(\$50,000 - 40,000)$ $= \mathbf{\$1,000}$
Great	50,000	0.1	$\mathbf{\$0}$

jobs yield different levels of net benefit for workers. If they get a job at a great firm, their net benefit is high and equal to $50,000. If they get a job at a good firm, their net benefit is lower, equal to $40,000. If they get a job at a satisfactory firm, their net benefit is equal to $30,000. Finally, sometimes they interview for a job and do not get it, which yields net benefit of zero.

Table 17.5 shows the probability of the different outcomes from applying for a job. The most likely outcome is no job offer, and the least likely outcome is a great job. Satisfactory jobs and bad jobs are equally likely. The table also calculates the marginal expected benefit of search for each type of job offer.

How much will the workers search for a job? That depends on their marginal cost of search. If the marginal cost of search is less than $1,000, they hold out for a great job, but if it is more than $4,000, they settle for the first job they find. Which of these is more likely depends on the worker's circumstances.

Searching for a First Job

When workers search for their first job, many of the costs of search are fixed. They must prepare a resume, but that is a fixed cost and does not depend on how many jobs they apply for. They must purchase an outfit suitable for interviews, but again that is a fixed cost because they can wear the same outfit to every interview. Because fixed costs do not change with the number of jobs workers apply for, they do not contribute to marginal costs.

Variable costs include the costs of contacting the firm to apply for the job and traveling to the interview. They would also include wages lost while interviewing, but because this is the workers' first job, they have no wages to forego. Also, many firms pay any travel costs associated with an interview, so these costs are small, too. It would seem, then, that the only component of the marginal cost of search is the cost of contacting one more firm to apply, which should be much less than $1,000. This suggests that the worker should hold out for the best job.

This is not the whole story, however. Job offers do not always come rapidly, and months may pass between offers. If workers turn down a satisfactory job, they forego the wages they would have earned at that job while waiting for the next offer. These foregone wages can be substantial. Think about the problem this way. Suppose that the worker is offered a satisfactory job, which will generate $30,000 in net benefits. By turning it down, the worker expects to forego $5,000 in net benefits before the next offer comes in. Should the worker take the job? The answer is yes. The expected cost of searching one more time is $5,000, while the expected benefit of searching one more time is $4,000. The worker should take the satisfactory job.

Even though we know that any worker willing to take a satisfactory job is also willing to take a good job, let us look anyway at what happens if a good job is offered. Now the marginal search cost is higher for two reasons. First, the worker is foregoing the benefits of working at a good job instead of at a satisfactory one. Second, the worker now waits for an offer of a great job, which could take longer than waiting for an offer of a good job or a great job. For both of these reasons, the worker's marginal expected search cost rises to, say, $10,000. The marginal expected benefit of search is only $1,000, so the worker should accept a good job when it is offered.

The key to this analysis is recognizing that, when workers are searching for their first job, part of their search cost is the foregone benefit from working at the jobs they turn down. Because this foregone benefit can be large, workers searching for their first job seldom hold out for their dream jobs.

Searching for a Job when Already Employed

When job searchers are already employed, their search costs change in two ways. First, having a job decreases the value of the wages foregone when a job is turned down because workers can continue at their old job while waiting for the next offer. This reduces the marginal cost of search. The other change is that workers may have to take time off from work to go to an interview. This requires either giving up paid hours or using vacation time, and either way it requires giving up something valuable. Thus, missing work for an interview increases the marginal cost of search.

Two effects govern the comparison of marginal search costs between a worker who already has a job and one who does not. One effect pushes the marginal search cost downward, and the other pushes it upward. Which effect is likely to dominate? If workers do not have a job yet, turning down a job entails foregoing the benefits of working for several months. If workers have a job, these foregone benefits are reduced. If workers do not yet have a job, they do not miss any work while interviewing. Workers with a job may have to miss a few days of work. One effect is the reduction in the foregone benefits over several months, and the other is the foregone benefits from working for a few days. The first effect is likely to dominate, and the marginal search cost for workers who already have a job is probably lower than the marginal search cost for workers looking for their first job.

This may seem counterintuitive, but look at the implications. Suppose workers with a job have marginal search costs of $800, compared to workers without a job, who have marginal search costs of $5,000. According to Table 17.5, the workers who already have a job will turn down an offer of a bad job and will also turn down an offer of a good job. They hold out for a great job. They can afford to do so because they are still paid when they turn down a job.

Searching for a Job while Collecting Unemployment Benefits

One case lies between the two already discussed. Some workers who are laid off from their previous jobs collect unemployment benefits. The benefits pay them a fraction of the wages they earned before. Because they are still being paid, the costs associated with turning down a job are reduced from the first-job case, but they are not reduced as much as they would be if the workers still had their original job. Consequently, unemployment compensation reduces the marginal cost of search compared to the case where workers never had a job, but it increases the marginal cost of search compared to the case where workers have a job.

Suppose that a worker with unemployment compensation has a marginal search cost of $2,500, which is between that of a worker looking for a first job ($5,000) and that of a worker who already has a job ($800). According to Table 17.5, those workers turn down a satisfactory job but will accept a good job.

Unemployment compensation leads people to hold out for a better job, which means that they tend to search longer. While they are searching they stay unemployed, and they continue to collect unemployment compensation. This leads to an often-discussed policy conundrum: The same policy that helps out workers who are laid off by providing unemployment compensation also increases the level of unemployment in the country. Whenever politicians discuss reducing the duration of unemployment compensation, this is the reason.

Homework Problems

1. List the components of search costs for a firm.
2. List the components of search costs for a worker. How does the list depend on whether the worker has a job?

3. A firm is searching for a worker. There are two types of workers, high-productivity and low-productivity. High-productivity workers generate $12,000 profit for the firm. Low-productivity workers generate only $9,000 profit. Two-thirds of all workers are low-productivity workers. It costs the firm $2,000 to fly a worker out for an interview and do all of the associated paperwork. The worker's type is revealed during the interview. Should the firm hire the first candidate it interviews or should it hold out for a high-productivity worker?

4. A firm is searching for a worker. There are three types of workers. High-productivity workers generate $9,000 in profit for the firm; medium-productivity workers generate $8,000 profit; and low-productivity workers generate $7,000 profit. Twenty percent of all workers have high productivity, 30 percent have medium productivity, and the rest have low productivity. It costs the firm $600 to interview an applicant. If the first applicant interviewed turns out to have low productivity, should the firm hire that applicant or interview someone else?

CHAPTER

18 BARGAINING

S earch is the first phase of the hiring process, and negotiation is the second. After a firm identifies a worker it would like to hire, it then negotiates with the worker over the compensation package. Economics has several things to say about the negotiation process, and these are the subject of this chapter. Everything in this chapter holds for all types of negotiations and both sides of the bargaining table. Everything holds for firms trying to hire workers, workers trying to get the best possible compensation package from firms, people trying to buy houses or cars, and salespeople trying to sell houses or cars.

THE GOAL OF BARGAINING

Whenever two parties enter into a voluntary relationship, it must be because they both benefit from the relationship. After all, if the relationship makes one of them worse off, that individual would elect not to participate in the relationship. When a firm decides to hire a worker, the firm must expect to benefit from the employment relationship. Similarly, when a worker decides to accept a job with a firm, the worker must expect to benefit from the relationship. In general, any voluntary exchange relationship benefits all parties involved.

In Chapter 4 we referred to the expected total net benefit to both parties in an employment relation as the **surplus** from the relationship. Because both parties in a voluntary relationship expect to enjoy positive net benefits from the relationship, the sum of the expected net benefits must be positive. So, all voluntary relationships generate surplus to be shared by the participants.

Each participant's goal in bargaining is to get as much of the surplus as possible. This can happen in two ways. First, the parties can reach an agreement that makes the surplus as large as possible, so that they have as much as possible to share. Second, each individual can try to get as large a share of the surplus as possible. To achieve the first alternative, the parties work together to find agreements that maximize the shared surplus. The second alternative, however, is contentious because when one party gets a larger share of the surplus, the other party has to get a smaller share. Most of the attention in this chapter is devoted to the contentious type of bargaining, that is, the splitting of the surplus.

Because positive surpluses result from all voluntary exchanges, the analysis of bargaining presented here applies to a wide variety of settings. The chapter is based on the employment relationship and tends to take the perspective of a firm negotiating with a worker, with the firm trying to get as large a share of the surplus as possible. The analysis also works for negotiations between the buyer and seller of a house or a car and for negotiations between a union and management at a large corporation.

SEQUENTIAL BARGAINING

In this chapter we will take two separate approaches to the analysis of bargaining. The first relies on game theory. The idea here is to construct a realistic game that captures what happens in a negotiation setting and then to analyze the game to determine what factors enable an individual to get a larger share of the surplus.

The Simplest Possible Bargaining Game

We begin with the simplest possible bargaining game, in which one player makes a take-it-or-leave-it offer to the other player. To make this concrete, suppose that the total surplus to be shared is S. Player 1 (she) offers to give an amount x to player 2, and then player 2 (he) has the option of either accepting or rejecting the offer. If he accepts the offer, he gets x and player 1 gets $S - x$, but if he rejects, he and player 1 each get zero.

What are the equilibrium strategies in this game? To find them we use backward induction, starting with the last move of the game and working our way back to the beginning. The last move is the decision by player 2 to either accept or reject the offer of x. Accepting gives him a payoff of x, and rejecting gives him a payoff of zero. If player 2 prefers more money to less, he should accept any offer in which $x > 0$.

Given player 2's strategy, what is player 1's best response? She should offer the smallest amount that player 2 will accept, which is the smallest positive offer she can possibly make. Suppose that offers must be in increments of a dollar and that S is much larger than a dollar. Then player 1 should offer \$1 to player 2, who will accept the offer.

Many people think that a strong negotiating ploy when buying a car, for example, is to let the car dealer make one offer and they will either take it or leave it. They reason that the dealer will offer to sell the car for a low price in order to ensure that it gets to sell a car and that, therefore, the customer will get a good deal. The above analysis shows, however, that if you must participate in take-it-or-leave-it bargaining, you should make sure that you are the one making the offer. The player making the take-it-or-leave-it offer gets almost all of the surplus, and the player deciding to take it or leave it gets almost none of the surplus. Thus, people who let car dealers make take-it-or-leave-it offers get a bad deal, while those who make a take-it-or-leave-it offer to a car dealer would probably do better.

A Two-Round Bargaining Game

Now let us make the bargaining game a little more complex. As above, suppose that the surplus to be shared is S and that offers must be in one-dollar increments. In the first period, player 1 offers x to player 2, who can either accept or reject. If player 2 accepts, he gets x and player 1 gets $S - x$. If player 2 rejects, he gets to make a counteroffer of y in round 2, which player 1 can either accept or reject. If she accepts, she gets y and player 2 gets $S - y$, and if she rejects, both players get zero.

Using backward induction to solve the game, we begin with player 1's decision of whether to accept or reject player 2's offer of y. If player 1 prefers more money to less, she accepts any offer with $y > 0$. Knowing this, player 2's best response is to offer as little as possible above zero, which is $1. Thus, in round 2, player 2's equilibrium strategy is to offer $y = \$1$ to player 1, and player 1's equilibrium strategy is to accept any offer of $1 or more. If the game makes it to round 2, then, player 1 gets a payoff of $1 and player 2 gets a payoff of $S - 1$.

Now move to the last decision in round 1, which is player 2's decision to either accept or reject player 1's offer of x. If he accepts the offer, he gets x, but if he rejects the offer the game moves into round 2, where he gets a payoff of $S - 1$. He will therefore reject any offer that pays him less than $S - 1$, so his equilibrium strategy is to accept any offer of $x \geq S - 1$. Player 1's best response is to offer $x = S - 1$. The outcome of the game is player 1 gets $1, and player 2 gets $S - 1$. Player 2 gets almost all of the surplus.

A Three-Round Bargaining Game

In the one-round, take-it-or-leave-it game, the first-mover gets almost all of the surplus, but in the two-round game, the second-mover gets almost all of the surplus. The common feature in both games is that the player who makes the last offer gets most of the surplus. To make sure this is true, let us see what happens when the game has three rounds.

In the first round, player 1 offers x to player 2, who can either accept or reject. If he rejects, the game moves to the second round, where player 2 offers y to player 1, who either accepts or rejects. If she rejects, the game moves to the third and final round, where player 1 offers z to player 2 who either accepts or rejects. If he rejects the offer, both players get zero.

As before, in the last round the player making the accept/reject decision accepts any offer that is better than rejecting, so player 2 accepts any offer with $z \geq \$1$. Player 1's best response in round 3 is to offer $1. In round 2 player 1 knows that she can get $S - 1$ if she holds out to round 3, so she rejects any offer with $y < S - 1$. Player 2's best response is to offer $y = S - 1$. Moving to round 1, player 2 knows that he can do no better than $1 if he rejects the offer, so he is willing to accept any offer with $x \geq \$1$. Player 1's best response is to offer $x = \$1$. Player 1, who makes the last offer in the three-round game, gets $S - 1$, and player 2 gets $1. Once again, the player who makes the last offer gets most of the surplus.

IMPATIENCE, UNCERTAINTY, AND RISK AVERSION

So far the only aspect of the game that impacts a negotiator's bargaining power is the order of play, specifically who makes the last offer. In this section we explore two additional factors that affect bargaining power — impatience and risk aversion.

Impatience

Consider the two-round game in which the surplus to be shared is S, and player 1 offers x to player 2, who either accepts or rejects; if he rejects, he makes a counteroffer of y to player 1. If player 1 rejects the offer in the second round they both get zero. Otherwise they get their agreed-upon payoffs. Offers must be made in increments of a dollar.

To account for impatience, suppose that player 1 has a discount factor of r_1 and that player 2 has a discount factor of r_2. (Discount factors were reviewed in the first section of Chapter 16). This means that $1 in round 2 is worth $\$1/(1 + r_2)$ to player 2 in round 1. The larger r_2 is, the smaller $\$1/(1 + r_2)$ is, and the less player 2 values the future payment. Higher values of r_2 make player 2 more impatient, and higher values of r_1 make player 1 more impatient.

In the previous section we analyzed a game in which $r_1 = r_2 = 0$, so that both players were perfectly patient, and we found that player 2 gets a payoff of $S - 1$ while player 1 only gets $1. Let us reanalyze the game with r_1 and r_2 greater than zero so that both players are impatient. As usual we start with the last decision and work our way back to the beginning of the game. The last decision is player 1's decision of whether to accept or reject the offer of y in round 2. Assuming she prefers more money to less, she accepts any offer with $y > 0$. Player 2's best response is to offer the smallest possible positive amount, which we assume is $1. If the game gets to period 2, player 2 gets a payoff of $S - 1$ and player 1 gets $1. This is the same as before.

The analysis changes when we start analyzing round 1. Look at player 2's decision to accept or reject an offer of x. He knows that if he rejects the offer his payoff will be $S - 1$, but that payoff is in the future, so it is discounted. He is indifferent between receiving $S - 1$ in round 2 and receiving $(S - 1)/(1 + r_2)$ in round 1. Consequently, he is willing to accept any offer with $x \geq (S - 1)/(1 + r_2)$. Player 1's best response is to offer $x = (S - 1)/(1 + r_2)$.

In this game player 2 has all the bargaining power, because he makes the last offer, but that power is diminished when he is impatient. This is most easily seen with some numerical examples. Suppose that $S = \$21$. When he is completely patient with $r_2 = 0$, his payoff from bargaining is $S - 1 = \$20$. If he is a little impatient, with $r_2 = 0.05$, his payoff falls to $\$20/1.05 = \$19.05$. If he becomes more impatient, with $r_2 = 0.10$, his payoff falls farther to $\$20/1.10 = \$18.18$. The less patient player 2 is, the worse he does in bargaining.

Car dealers know this and use it to their advantage. When someone tries to buy a car, the salesperson makes the first offer, writing down a price that is very close to the sticker price of the car. The buyer makes a counteroffer, which the salesperson then takes to her manager. The two leave the customer alone with nothing to do in a little cubicle while they do something else, and eventually the salesperson comes back with a slightly better offer than the original one, but not much. An impatient buyer will get fed up at this point and try to speed up the bargaining process by giving away a greater amount of the surplus. The salesperson and her manager, in contrast, are very patient because this is their job. By negotiating slowly, they are able to capture more of the surplus.

Uncertainty

Bargaining processes break down for a variety of reasons. When a firm negotiates with a prospective employee, sometimes the candidate gets a better offer from a different firm, and the negotiation process ends. Sometimes while the negotiations are going on, the firm suffers a negative demand shock and the position disappears. Sometimes circumstances arise for the candidate making it undesirable to move to the city where the firm is located, thereby ending the candidate's interest in the job.

To add randomness, consider once again the two-round bargaining problem, assuming that the two participants are perfectly patient. Without any randomness, player 2's payoff is $S - 1$ and player 1 gets $\$1$. To introduce uncertainty, suppose that something happens between round 1 and round 2. If player 2 accepts player 1's offer in the first round they both get their agreed-upon payoffs. If player 2 rejects, however, a random event occurs, and with probability p the game ends and both players get nothing. With probability $1 - p$ the game moves on to the second round, and player 2 makes an offer to player 1, which she can either accept or reject, as usual. If she accepts they get their agreed-upon payoffs, and if she rejects they both get nothing.

The presence of uncertainty changes the outcome of the bargaining game even if the players are not risk averse. To see why, suppose that player 2 is risk neutral, caring only about the expected value of the payoff and not caring whether it is random. Start at the end of the game. If the game makes it to round 2, player 1 accepts any offer greater than zero, and player 2 offers her $1, which she accepts. Thus, if the game makes it to round 2, player 2 gets $S - 1$ and player 1 gets $1. Now look at player 2's decision to accept or reject the offer in round 1. If he rejects the offer there is a probability p that he gets nothing and a probability $1 - p$ that he gets $S - 1$ because the game continues to round 2. His expected payoff is $p \cdot \$0 + (1 - p) \cdot (S - 1)$ which is less than $S - 1$, so he is willing to accept less in round 1 because of the chance that round 2 will never happen.

If the probability of breakdown is sufficiently high, bargaining power can switch from the party making the last offer to the one making the first offer. Suppose that the surplus is $21 and that the probability of breakdown is $p = 0.6$. Then player 2 is willing to accept any offer $x \geq (1 - p)(S - 1) = (1 - 0.6)(\$21 - 1) = \$8$, and player 1's best response is to offer $8. Player 1's surplus is $21 - 8 = \$13$, and player 2's is $8. Compare this with what happens when the probability of breakdown is zero. Because player 2 makes the last offer, his share of the surplus is $20, and player 1 only gets $1.

Risk Aversion

The above analysis looked at a sequential alternating-offers bargaining problem in which the process breaks down with some probability. We saw that the existence of uncertainty alone had an impact on the players' bargaining power, even in the absence of risk aversion. People tend to be risk averse, however, and risk aversion has a further effect on the bargaining outcome.

When people are risk averse, they are willing to pay a positive risk premium to remove the randomness and receive the expected payoff for sure, and the more risk averse they are, the higher the risk premium they are willing to pay. Look at player 2's decision in round 1. He knows that if he rejects the offer he can get $S - 1$ in round 2 with probability $1 - p$, and he gets 0 otherwise. The expected value of this gamble is $(1 - p)(S - 1)$, and he is willing to pay a risk premium of RP_2 (where the subscript is for the player, not the period) to avoid the risk. Consequently, the gamble is worth $(1 - p)(S - 1) - RP_2$, and he is willing to accept any offer in round 1 of $x \geq (1 - p)(S - 1) - RP_2$. Player 1's best response is to offer exactly $x = (1 - p)(S - 1) - RP_2$, which player 2 accepts. Player 1's payoff is $S - x$, which can be rearranged to get

$$
\begin{aligned}
S - x &= S - [(1 - p)(S - 1) - RP_2] \\
&= S - [S - 1 - pS + p - RP_2] \\
&= p(S - 1) + 1 + RP_2
\end{aligned}
$$

Player 2's risk aversion hurts player 2 but helps player 1. The more risk averse player 2 is, the higher the risk premium he is willing to pay to avoid the randomness. Consequently, being more risk averse worsens player 2's bargaining position.

Being risk averse herself does not hurt player 1 in the two-round game. It would in the three-round game. At the end of round 2, player 1 would have to decide whether to accept player 2's offer. If she does, she gets that payment for sure, but if she rejects it, she has a $1 - p$ chance of getting $S - 1$ and a p chance of getting zero. If she is risk averse she is willing to pay a premium to avoid this gamble, and the more risk averse she is the higher the premium she is willing to pay. Let us work the three-round game through to find the payoffs of the two players. We already know that if the game gets to round 3 player 1 receives $S - 1$ and player 2 receives 1. Letting player 1's risk premium be RP_1, she is willing to accept any offer $y \geq (1 - p)(S - 1) - RP_1$ in round 2. Player 2's best response is to offer exactly $y \geq (1 - p)(S - 1) - RP_1$, which player 1 would accept. Player 2's payoff if the game reaches round 2, then, is $p(S - 1) + 1 + RP_1$. Moving back to round 1, if player 2 rejects player 1's offer he then faces a gamble that pays $p(S - 1) + 1 + RP_1$ with probability $1 - p$ and pays zero with probability p. The expected value of this gamble is $(1 - p)[p(S - 1) + 1 + RP_1]$, and he is willing to pay a risk premium RP_2 to avoid the randomness. Consequently, he is willing to accept any offer

$$x \geq (1 - p)[p(S - 1) + 1 + RP_1] - RP_2$$

and player 1 offers exactly this amount, which player 2 then accepts.

The right-hand side of the above expression is player 2's payoff in the three-round bargaining game with risk. Player 2's payoff rises when player 1 becomes more risk averse but falls when player 2 becomes more risk averse. Because player 1 gets S minus player 2's payoff, player 1's payoff increases when player 2 becomes more risk averse but decreases when player 1 becomes more risk averse. This leads to a simple summary: Being risk averse reduces a player's bargaining power.

THE NASH APPROACH TO BARGAINING

Besides giving us our notion of equilibrium in games, John Nash analyzed bargaining problems in a non-game-theoretic way. Instead of looking at the give and take of a protracted negotiation *process*, he decided to look at the characteristics that a bargaining *outcome* should have, ignoring the process by which the outcome is reached. The resulting outcome is known as the **Nash bargaining solution**.

Nash identified four properties he thought a "nice" bargaining solution should have. Before discussing those four properties, however, we must set up some notation. There are two individuals bargaining over a surplus of size S, and we will call them 1 and 2. If they reach an agreement, player 1 gets x_1 and player 2 gets x_2. If they fail to reach an agreement player 1 gets a payoff of d_1 and player 2 gets d_2. These are their **disagreement payoffs**. The Nash bargaining solution allocates x_1^* to player 1 and x_2^* to player 2.

We can now list Nash's four properties of a nice bargaining solution.

1. *Pareto efficiency:* The allocation of x_1^* to individual 1 and x_2^* to individual 2 should be a Pareto efficient allocation, which means that there is no other allocation that makes one individual better off without making the other worse off. To see what this means in a bargaining setting, it is useful to look at an allocation that is *not* Pareto efficient. The allocation that gives each player $S/3$ is such an allocation. The total allocation to the two players is then $2S/3$, with $S/3$ left on the table and claimed by nobody. It is possible, for example, to give player 1 more without taking away from player 2 because of the money left on the table. In our setting the Pareto efficiency requirement is simply a requirement that the two parties leave no money on the table, that is, they split the entire surplus.

2. *Invariance to equivalent representations:* The allocation should not depend on how the payoffs are measured. For example, it should not matter whether the payoffs are measured in dollars or euros. The same split of the surplus should result no matter which way the payoffs are counted.

3. *Symmetry:* If the two parties are identical, they should get the same shares of the surplus. Given the setting, the only way that the two parties could differ is by having different disagreement points. The symmetry requirement states that if the two parties have the same disagreement payoffs then they must split the surplus equally.

4. *Independence of irrelevant alternatives:* This requirement is the trickiest to explain, so let us begin with an example. Suppose that when the surplus to be shared is $S = 20$ and the disagreement payoffs are $d_1 = 3$ and $d_2 = 2$, the two players reach an agreement that gives 12 to player 1 and 8 to player 2. Now suppose that the bargaining is restricted so that the players are not allowed to reach an agreement that gives either player a payoff less than 6. Because both players were already getting more than 6 anyway, restricting the bargaining in this way does not impede them from reaching the same agreement they would have reached before the restriction. So the restriction is irrelevant, and it should not have any impact on the agreement.

In the preceding example, we restricted the bargaining process in a way that ruled out **irrelevant alternatives**, that is, alternatives that would not have been reached by the bargaining process anyway. The requirement is that ruling out irrelevant alternatives does not change the bargaining outcome.

Ruling out *relevant* alternatives can impact the bargaining solution. Suppose that in the above example bargaining is restricted so that players are not allowed to reach an agreement that gives either player a payoff less than 9. This would rule out the previous bargaining outcome that gave player 1 a payoff of 12 and player 2 a payoff of 8. The new restriction rules out this alternative, and it is a relevant alternative. The players would have to reach a different agreement.

Nash found that a unique bargaining outcome satisfies these four requirements of Pareto efficiency, invariance to equivalent representations, symmetry, and independence of irrelevant alternatives. Moreover, the unique solution to the bargaining problem is

$$x_1^* = \frac{S + d_1 - d_2}{2}$$

and

$$x_2^* = \frac{S + d_2 - d_1}{2}$$

This is a slick piece of mathematics, showing that a set of seemingly innocuous requirements yields a single formula for the bargaining solution. We cannot prove that these formulas are the *only* ones that satisfy the four requirements, but we can verify that the four requirements are satisfied.

As already discussed, Pareto efficiency holds if there is no money left on the table; that is, if the two shares add up to S, the total surplus available. Adding the two yields

$$x_1^* + x_2^* = \frac{S + d_1 - d_2}{2} + \frac{S + d_2 - d_1}{2} = S$$

The two shares add up to S, the total surplus, so it is impossible to give one player more of the surplus without taking some away from the other.

Invariance to equivalent representations states that if we count the benefits differently, we still end up with the same shares. To see how this works, suppose that x_1^* and x_2^* are the amounts of surplus the two players get when the surplus and disagreement payoffs are measured in dollars. Player 1's share of the surplus is x_1^*/S and player 2's share is x_2^*/S. Now suppose that the surplus and disagreement payoffs are measured some alternative way, with the exchange rate given by e, so that the amount y in dollars is worth $z = ey$ in the alternative measurement system. The Nash bargaining solution for the new measurement system is

$$z_1^* = \frac{eS + ed_1 - ed_2}{2} = e \cdot \frac{S + d_1 - d_2}{2} = ex_1^*$$

and

$$z_2^* = \frac{eS + ed_2 - ed_1}{2} = e \cdot \frac{S + d_2 - d_1}{2} = ex_2^*$$

Because the total surplus under the new measurement system is eS, player 1's share is $ex_1^*/eS = x_1^*/S$ and player 2's share is $ex_2^*/eS = x_2^*/S$. These are the same shares as under the original measurement system.

Symmetry states that if the two bargainers have the same disagreement payoffs then they get the same amounts of surplus. Let d be the common disagreement payoff, so that $d_1 = d_2 = d$. Then player 1's share is

$$x_1^* = \frac{S + d - d}{2} = \frac{S}{2}$$

and player 2's share is

$$x_2^* = \frac{S + d - d}{2} = \frac{S}{2}$$

Both players get half of the surplus when their disagreement payoffs are the same, which is consistent with the symmetry requirement.

Finally, independence of irrelevant alternatives states that if we remove outcomes that are not the solution from consideration, we do not change the solution. This follows from the fact that x_1^* and x_2^* depend only on the total surplus available, S, and the two disagreement payoffs, d_1 and d_2. Because they do not depend on anything else, they cannot depend on which outcomes are allowed and which are not.

What Can We Learn from the Nash Bargaining Solution?

From our perspective, the major difference between the Nash approach to bargaining and the game theory approach is that the Nash bargaining outcome is driven primarily by the disagreement payoffs, whereas the game-theoretic outcome is driven mostly by the order of play, specifically who makes the last offer. Because the Nash bargaining solution has variables not considered in the game theory approach, we can learn something new about what strengthens an individual's bargaining power.

Look at player 1's payoff from the Nash bargaining solution, rewritten as

$$x_1^* = \frac{S}{2} + \frac{d_1}{2} - \frac{d_2}{2}$$

Written this way, it becomes clear that there are three ways to make x_1^* larger. First, if the surplus S grows, player 1's payoff increases. According to the Nash bargaining solution, an increase in the size of the surplus makes both players better off. This is in contrast to the game theoretic solution, in which the player making the last offer gets $S - 1$ and the other player gets $1. In the game theoretic solution, only one player gains when the surplus grows.

Player 1's payoff in the Nash bargaining solution also grows when her disagreement payoff, d_1, gets larger. The disagreement payoff is the amount player 1 gets if the two players fail to reach an agreement. An increase in the disagreement payoff makes player 1 better off if they disagree, allowing her to be more discriminating about the agreements she makes. To entice player 1 to reach an agreement, player 2 must give up more, so player 1 gets a higher payoff when her disagreement payoff rises. For the same reasons, player 1 gets a higher payoff when player 2's disagreement payoff falls. When 2's disagreement payoff falls, player 1 need not give up as much in order to get 2 to agree, so 2's bargaining position is weakened.

GENERAL LESSONS

By using the two approaches to bargaining, we have learned five lessons about what improves individuals' bargaining power and allows them to increase their share of the surplus.

1. *The order of play matters, and it is advantageous to be able to make the last offer.* In the game-theoretic model in this chapter's second section, the player who makes the last offer gets almost all of the surplus, and the other player gets almost none.
2. *The disagreement payoffs matter, and it is advantageous to have a higher disagreement payoff than your opponent.* The disagreement payoff is the payoff a player gets if the negotiation process fails to result in an agreement. In the Nash bargaining model a higher disagreement payoff leads to a larger share of the surplus.
3. *Impatience hurts.* Being impatient makes future payoffs less valuable, and if the negotiation process takes time, an impatient bargainer is willing to settle for a smaller share of the surplus in order to reach an agreement sooner.
4. *The existence of uncertainty helps the individual making the first offer.* When there is some chance that the negotiation process will end before an agreement is reached, both parties are willing to settle for less to avoid the risk. In particular, the party making the accept/reject decision in the first round is willing to settle for less because there might not be a second round after a rejection.
5. *Risk aversion hurts.* Risk averse negotiators are willing to pay a premium to avoid risk, which means they are willing to pay a premium to avoid the possibility that negotiations break down. This translates into being willing to accept lower offers, and the more risk averse negotiators are the worse offers they are willing to accept.

Homework Problems

1. What are the players' objectives in a bargaining game?
2. What are the differences between the alternating-offers approach and the Nash approach to bargaining?
3. Suppose that two players play an alternating-offers bargaining game with a surplus of $100. Offers must be in increments of $5. The game is played for four rounds, with player 1 making the first offer. Both players have discount rates of zero, and the probability that the game ends between rounds is zero.

   a. Describe the strategies for both players.
   b. What agreement is reached, and when is it reached?

4. Suppose that two players play a two-period alternating offers bargaining game with a surplus of $100. Offers must be in increments of $1. Both players have a discount rate of 50 percent. Find the equilibrium of this game.
5. Suppose that two players play a two-period alternating offers bargaining game with a surplus of $100. Offers must be in increments of $1. The future is not discounted, but if no agreement is reached in the first period, there is a 90 percent chance that the game ends and both players get payoffs of $0. Neither player is risk averse. Find the equilibrium of this game.
6. For the situation in problem 5, find the highest probability of breakdown that guarantees that player 1 gets at least half of the surplus.
7. In the Nash bargaining game, the surplus is $10,000, player 1's disagreement payoff is $500, and player 2's disagreement payoff is $2,000.

   a. Find the Nash bargaining solution.
   b. What happens to the Nash bargaining solution when player 1's disagreement payoff doubles to $1,000?

19 TRAINING

W hen workers begin their first jobs, they often come unequipped with the skills needed to perform well. Because of this, companies commonly send new employees through training programs. These programs may cover such topics as the company's product line, general sales skills, or internal accounting procedures and can last any-where from a few days to months or even years. The employees are paid while they are trained and often get a raise when the training session ends.

Perhaps the most visible example of training is that of new restaurant servers. Usually when a server is being trained, he is followed by an experienced server. The trainee does all of the work under the trainer's supervision. The trainer gets all of the tips, so that she gets her usual pay. The trainee is typically paid minimum wage during the training period. After the training period ends, he moves to the standard restaurant server com-pensation plan, which is typically a small hourly wage plus tips.

Training raises an interesting issue for the employment relationship, and this chapter examines that issue.

TRAINING IN PROFESSIONAL SPORTS

When a player starts out in professional baseball, almost invariably he begins his career in a team's minor league system. Before making it to the major leagues, he must work his way through three tiers of minor league teams. The minor leagues allow players to hone their talents and, at the same time, they allow teams to identify that talent. Players are paid for playing in the minor leagues, averaging about $1,500 per month. Meanwhile the average salary for major league players is about $2.4 million per year.

What makes this interesting from our perspective is that the major league teams pay minor league players and, at the same time, provide them with skills that enable some of them to have extremely lucrative careers in the majors. Once a player works his way through the minor leagues, he is valuable not only to the team that paid for his training, but to all of the teams in the major leagues. Those other teams could offer him a higher salary and entice him away from the team that trained him and could thereby get all the benefits of a training program without having to incur the expense of running training programs themselves. Nevertheless, all of the teams have minor league systems.

Why does a team not simply dispense with its minor league system and steal talented rookies from other major league teams? The answer is that although a team is free to dispense with its minor league system, baseball rules prohibit them from outbidding other teams for their newest players. Players cannot become free agents and sell their services to the highest bidder until they have completed six seasons in the majors.

The minor league training program and the free agency rule go hand in hand. Without the free agency rule, teams would never receive the benefit from their training programs because all of the players they trained successfully would be bid away by other teams. This would allow players to enjoy all the benefits of the training program because the result of the training would be extremely high salaries. The free agency rule, however, makes players wait six years before getting these extremely high salaries. Teams can pay them less than they are worth (but still a lot of money) for their first six years in the majors. In essence, when a player enters the minor leagues, he promises to allow the team to capture some of the benefits of the training for his first six years in the majors.

Other sports operate differently. Football, for example, does not have a traditional minor league system, using college football as a training system instead. Because NFL teams do not pay for the college training, they have less to lose when a player is bid away early in his professional career. This has led to a less restrictive free agency rule. In the NFL, a player is tied to his original team for his first two seasons. In his third year he is a restricted free agent, which means that he can negotiate with other teams, but his original team has a right to match the competing offer. Beginning in his fourth year he is an unrestricted free agent and can sign with any team he wants. The NFL's free agency rule restricts a player's choices for about half as long as baseball's.

TRAINING AND HUMAN CAPITAL

Training is just like education except for who pays for it. Students (or their families) pay for their own education. Firms pay for their workers' training. The firm's training costs include not only the costs of instruction and materials but also the amount they pay the trainees during the training period. Because the trainees produce very little during training, they generate very little or no revenue to offset these costs.

The reason that firms train their workers is to make them more productive. Training is not the only way to achieve this goal, however. Instead, the firm could provide the worker with more or better equipment that would allow the worker to produce more output per hour of work. In economic terminology, equipment is a form of capital, and capital makes labor more productive. Because training also makes workers more productive, training can also be thought of as an investment in capital. This time, however, it is **human capital**, the skills, knowledge, and experience that make workers more productive. Training is an investment in human capital.

It is useful to distinguish between two components of human capital — general skills and specific skills. **General skills** are skills that make workers more productive and are useful at other firms beside the one where they currently work. **Specific skills** are skills that make workers more productive at their current employer but do not make them more productive anywhere else.

Most skills you can think of are general skills. Being able to type, fly an airplane, drive a forklift, write a will, or make a sale are all general skills because they are useful at more than one employer. If one firm trains its workers to provide them with one of these skills, that worker could use the same skill at another employer. For example, if a firm trains a worker to fly an airplane, the new pilot could also fly airplanes at different airline companies.

Specific skills are a little harder to think of because almost all skills can be used at more than one firm. But examples do exist. Some firms use unique accounting or inventory software, and knowledge of these systems makes workers more productive as long as they stay at their current employers, but they do not make the workers any more productive anywhere else. Being able to connect a missile to the underside of a fighter jet is a useful skill in the air force, but it is not so useful in other lines of work. There are also more mundane examples. If the firm has a long-standing but difficult client with very peculiar tastes, being able to work with that client is a valuable skill as long as the worker is at the current firm, but it is not a valuable skill once the worker leaves.

It is also useful to look at some skills that are not specific. Being able to hit a curve ball is a useful skill to a baseball player but not to anyone else. However, being able to hit a curve ball makes the player valuable to every baseball team, and because there are over 30 major league teams, the skill makes the player productive at more than one employer. Being able to hit a curve ball is a general, although highly specialized, skill.

Just because individuals acquire specific skills does not mean that they cannot acquire general skills, too. For example, learning the tastes of a difficult client is a specific skill, but learning to be more tolerant of difficult people is a general skill. Nevertheless, we will look at the two types of skills as if they are separate because they have different implications for how the firm behaves, as will be seen in the next two sections.

BARGAINING AND THE VALUE OF TRAINING

After workers acquire skills through company-sponsored training, they are more valuable to the firm than they were before. If they acquire general skills, they are also more valuable to other firms, but if the skills are specific skills, they are only more valuable to their original firm.

For the training to be potentially valuable to the firm, it must generate a surplus; that is, the benefit from the acquired skill must outweigh the cost of the training. Denote the potential benefit to the firm from training by X, and it measures the increase in net revenue generated by the worker's new skills. The cost of training is C, and it is the sum of the expense of running the training program and the amount paid to the worker during the training period. Because training generates a surplus, it must be the case that $X > C$. Finally, to provide a framework that covers both general and specific skills, suppose that if workers leave the firm after completing training, their next best alternative pays them an amount Y more than they make at the current firm.

Bargaining

After they complete the training program, employees find themselves more valuable to the firm than they were before. After all, the training program makes them more productive, able to produce more net revenue than before. The firm earns higher profit, and it is natural for the employees to want a share of the surplus. So they bargain with the firm for higher pay and threaten to leave the firm if an agreement is not reached.

To find the outcome of the bargaining process, we must choose one of the bargaining solutions from Chapter 18. There we had two basic approaches. One was the sequential approach, in which the party that makes the last offer gets almost all of the surplus; the other was the Nash bargaining approach, in which the two parties share the surplus. Bargaining power in the sequential approach is determined by the rule determining who makes the last offer, however, and there is no clear reason why either the worker or the firm would always be the one to make the last offer. Because the Nash approach does not rely on the order of the offers, it makes sense to use the Nash approach here.

To use the Nash approach, we must first find three figures: the surplus, the worker's disagreement payoff, and the firm's disagreement payoff. This is trickier than one might think, however. After the training is complete, the firm's training cost C is sunk, so it no longer matters for the analysis. The surplus is the additional net revenue the firm can potentially receive from workers applying their new skills, X. If the firm and workers fail to reach an agreement, the workers leave for a new job. The firm's disagreement payoff is zero and, as already discussed, the workers go to the alternative firm where their pay increases by the amount Y.

According to the Nash bargaining solution, when the surplus is S, player 1's disagreement payoff is d_1, and player 2's disagreement payoff is d_2, player 1's payoff from bargaining is

$$x_1^* = \frac{S + d_1 - d_2}{2}$$

and player 2's payoff is

$$x_2^* = \frac{S + d_2 - d_1}{2}$$

Letting the worker be player 1 and the firm be player 2, we determine that the surplus is $S = X$; the worker's disagreement payoff is $d_1 = Y$; and the firm's disagreement payoff is $d_2 = 0$. When the negotiation concludes, the worker's payoff is

$$W = \frac{X + Y}{2}$$

and the firm's payoff is

$$F = \frac{X - Y}{2}$$

To see how the two parties fare, let us try some numbers. Suppose that $X = \$20,000$, $C = \$10,000$, and $Y = \$4,000$. The firm pays a training expense of $\$10,000$ to get a potential gain in net revenue of $\$20,000$. By leaving the firm, a worker can receive a pay increase of $\$4,000$ from the other firm. According to the Nash bargaining solution, after completing the training program and renegotiating salary, the worker gets a raise of $W = (\$20,000 + 4,000)/2 = \$12,000$. The firm's payoff is $F = (\$20,000 - 4,000)/2 = \$8,000$.

This suggests a problem. The firm spends $\$10,000$ training the worker but is only left $\$8,000$ after renegotiating the worker's salary. Training is not worthwhile for the firm. The worker gets too much of the benefit of the training, and the firm gets too little. Because the firm can foresee the outcome of the renegotiation process, it never bothers training the worker in the first place.

Conditions for Training to Occur

We have found that if the firm trains a worker at an expense of C, its benefit from the training is $F = (X - Y)/2$, where X is the firm's gain in net revenue if an agreement is reached and Y is the increase in pay the worker gets by going to the next best alternative employer. Several conditions must occur for the firm to find training worthwhile.

1. *For training to occur, the worker must be better off staying at the current firm.* The only way for the firm to get a positive benefit

from training the worker is if $X > Y$, so that $F > 0$. Thought about in a different way, the most the firm can offer to the worker is X, and that would give away all of the benefit from training to the worker. A worker who can get more than X by going to the other firm will do so.

2. *For training to occur the firm must recover the costs of training.* The firm knows before it trains the worker that its benefit from training will be $F = (X - Y)/2$. Because the training program costs the firm C, it only undertakes the training program if $F > C$. Because $F = X/2$, the training cost cannot exceed half of the potential benefits if the program is going to be worthwhile for the firm. In addition, the more valuable the skills are to other firms, the less the firm is willing to spend on training.

3. *The worker benefits from both general and specific skills, but benefits more from general skills.* The worker's payoff after being trained and renegotiating salary is $W = (X + Y)/2$, where X is the additional net revenue the skills generate from the firm and Y is the additional pay the worker could get from the next best alternative firm. Because it must be the case that $X > 2C$ for the firm to even consider having a training program, the worker makes at least C.

The difference between general and specific skills is found in the value of Y. General skills are valuable to the alternative employer, while specific skills are not. Consequently, $Y > 0$ for general skills, and $Y = 0$ for specific skills. In general Y reflects the **portability** of the skills; that is, how much of the value of the skills goes with the worker who moves to another firm. Specific skills are not portable at all. At the other extreme the general skills are completely portable in the sense that they are just as valuable at another firm as they are at the original firm, which implies that $Y = X$.

Completely portable skills are a problem for the firm. If $Y = X$, then the firm's benefit from training is $F = (X - Y)/2 = 0$. The firm gets no benefit from providing completely portable general skills.

4. *In this model the worker benefits more than the firm.* The worker's benefit is $W = (X + Y)/2$, and the firm's is $F = (X - Y)/2$. The difference is $W - F = Y$. The additional benefit is the amount the worker would receive from the other firm after failing to reach an agreement with the original firm.

When one considers the training cost, the worker does even better. The worker receives Y more in benefits than the firm, and the firm pays C more in costs; the gap between the worker's net benefit and the firm's net benefit is $Y + C$.

MAKING TRAINING WORTHWHILE FOR THE FIRM

The preceding section painted a bleak picture for the firm. The firm benefits from training only when the costs involved are small and the skills imparted to the worker are either specific or not very portable. Even so, the worker benefits more than the firm. The firm's net benefit from training is $F - C = (X - Y)/2 - C$. The firm can do two things to increase its net benefit from training. It can reduce the training costs C or it can reduce the portability of the skills so that Y falls.

Sharing the Training Costs

The only way for the firm to reduce the training costs is to share them with the worker. The way to do this is to negotiate the worker's pay *before* the training begins. When bargaining occurs before the training begins, the training costs are no longer sunk and, therefore, matter to the firm. The surplus being negotiated over is $X - C$, the additional net revenue generated by the new skills minus the cost of providing them.

This is not the only change, however. If the worker and the firm fail to reach an agreement, the outcome is that the worker does not receive any training and does not acquire any new skills. This does not make the worker any more valuable to outside firms, so the worker's disagreement payoff is zero. The firm's disagreement payoff is also zero, because it incurs no training expense and gets no benefit.

Because the worker and the firm have the same disagreement payoffs, the Nash bargaining solution splits the surplus between them so that

$$W = F = \frac{X - C}{2}$$

The worker and the firm share the benefits and the costs equally.

A problem remains, however. After completing training, a worker is more valuable to the firm and, depending on the skills, may also be more valuable to outside employers. The worker could threaten to leave unless salary is renegotiated. Recognizing this in advance, the firm will have to agree to pay the same salary after training that it would have if it negotiated the deal after the training ended. Thus, the worker's share of the training costs have to be paid up front, before the training ends. This is, in fact, the way most firms handle their training. They make workers accept low salaries during the training period and then provide raises after the training ends. Minor league baseball salaries provide a good example of this pattern.

Reducing the Portability of Skills

Portability refers to the value of the skills to other firms. One way to reduce portability would be to provide training only in skills that are not very portable. This does happen, and the best evidence is college education. Most students (or their families) pay their own way through college, and only rarely do firms send their workers to college. A college education provides very portable general skills, and it would not make any sense for an employer to provide these skills.

Sometimes, however, a firm finds it desirable to train a worker in general skills, but it still wants to reduce portability. It can do this by having the worker sign a contract agreeing not to leave the firm for a certain period after the training ends. This does two things. First, it makes the worker less valuable to other firms because they will not get the worker for as long. Second, it provides a period in which the firm does not have to pay the worker as much because it does not have to match salary offers by outside firms. Professional baseball uses this sort of contract to make minor league teams profitable. Because players cannot negotiate with other teams during their first six seasons in the majors, teams can pay the players less during this time.

A PUZZLE: WHY DO SOME FIRMS REIMBURSE EMPLOYEES FOR COLLEGE TUITION?

Corporations in America spent an estimated $10 billion on tuition reimbursement in 2003. These payments were made to reimburse employees who spent their own money on college tuition, and most corporations capped their reimbursement levels at $5,250 per employee per year. At the same time, they paid little attention to which courses their employees took. Furthermore, about half of the corporate respondents in a survey were unsure that tuition reimbursement adds value to the company.

The analysis in the preceding section argues that by reimbursing tuition firms provide their workers with general skills, and that it is difficult for firms to benefit from providing such skills. Why, then, do so many firms do it? The explanation may well be that they are a leftover from pre-Internet days. Tuition reimbursement programs were introduced in the 1970s and 1980s, when workers would have to scrape together degrees from the few nighttime courses offered by local two- and four-year colleges. In the 1990s, however, on-line, for-profit universities became more common, offering relevant courses that are available after business hours. Today about 60 percent of their attendees receive at least some financial support from their employers.

SOURCE: Meisler, Andy, "A Matter of Degrees," *Workforce Management* 83 (May 2004), 32–38.

TRAINING AND THE INCENTIVES TO REMAIN WITH A FIRM

From the above discussion, it would seem that training gives workers an incentive to leave the firm, especially because it is the threat of leaving that allows them to benefit from the training. Specific skills, however, give workers an incentive to stay with the firm as long as possible.

Specific skills are skills that are valuable to the current firm but not to any other firm. As we saw earlier, workers benefit from acquiring specific skills because the firm is willing to pay them more to keep them from leaving and taking their specific skills with them. Because of this, the workers are worth more at their current firm than at any alternative firm, and they are paid more at their current firm than they could get an any alternative firm. Specific skills provide workers with an incentive to stay with the firm longer.

The same sort of incentives occur in other places. One is college. If a student transfers from one college to another, some of the credits from courses at the first college will transfer and count toward a degree at the new college and some will not. The more credits that will not transfer, the less incentive the student has to change schools.

An interesting application of this reasoning is to marriage. The longer people are married to each other, the more they learn about their spouse's likes and dislikes and the more skills they have at keeping each other happy. These are highly specific skills, because they will probably not work with different partners. The logic of specific skills says that the longer a couple is married, the more likely they are to stay married. Children can also be considered a form of specific capital, worth more in the current marriage than in any future marriage. The prediction is that couples with children are more likely to stay together than couples without children. Both of these predictions, that divorce rates are lower for couples who have been married longer or who have children, turn out to be verified by the evidence.

Homework Problems

1. Define human capital.
2. List two general skills and two specific skills.
3. Suppose that a firm has trained a worker and provided $10,000 worth of completely portable general skills. Because the skills are completely portable, the worker's disagreement point is $10,000. The firm's training cost is $2,000. What are the payoffs for the worker and the firm? Should the firm have trained the worker?
4. Suppose that a firm has trained a worker and provided $10,000 worth of nonportable specific skills. Because the skills are completely nonportable, the worker's disagreement point is $0. The firm's training cost is $2,000. What are the payoffs for the worker and the firm? Should the firm have trained the worker?
5. Suppose that a firm has trained a worker and provided $10,000 worth of semiportable skills. Because the skills are semiportable, the worker's disagreement point is Y. The firm's training cost is $2,000. What is the smallest value Y can take for the firm to regret having trained the worker?

20 BENEFITS

Companies provide their employees with a wide variety of benefits, which are nonmonetary components of the compensation package. Some common examples of benefits are health insurance, paid sick leave, and paid vacation leave. But benefit packages can include more unusual items, too. Many large companies are building fitness centers and outdoor walking and jogging trails for their employees, and some companies are providing their employees with monthly chair massages. One of the newer areas in which companies are focusing their attention is the quality of the coffee and snacks to which employees have access.

Large companies spend about $2.50 per hour on employee benefits such as these, so benefits are a significant component of the compensation package. Benefit packages raise many issues that are relevant for economic analysis, and this chapter explores several of those issues.

THE ISSUE OF CHILD CARE

A current topic of some contention in firms, especially large ones, is whether they should provide child care for their workers. Most of the issues that arise about benefits in general appear in arguments for or against child care facilities in firms, so we begin the chapter with an overview of this debate.

Let us start with some facts.[1] According to the U.S. Census, 60 percent of mothers return to work within a year of having a baby. About half of those families rely on day care centers to look after their children. A study by the Children's Defense Fund found that fees at day care centers were higher than tuition at a state university. In 2003, only 5 percent of companies overall and 10 percent of large companies provided on-site or near-site day care.

---

[1]This section is based on Kiger, Patrick J., "A Case for Child Care," *Workforce Management* (April 2004), 34–40.

In spite of its rarity, there is evidence that company-sponsored day care facilities can be attractive to both workers and firms. One study found that at companies with day care facilities, 42 percent of their employees said that day care was the reason that they joined the company, and 20 percent said that they had passed up better opportunities because they wanted the child care. A second study found that worker absenteeism falls significantly when the company provides day care, presumably because workers do not have trouble with babysitters who are sick or fail to show up. A third study showed that the availability of child care for emergencies actually saves the company $176 in lost productivity every time a worker uses it. Evidence also suggests that workers who place their children in company-sponsored day care facilities perform better and stay with the firm longer. Finally, the federal government and many states offer tax advantages to companies that operate day care centers for their employees.

Given that on-site day care centers have so many advantages, why do so few companies have them? There seem to be two main reasons. The first is that they are expensive. One study estimates that providing on-site day care costs companies somewhere between $4 and $8 per employee per hour, which is a substantial amount to spend on benefits for employees. In fact, companies typically spend only about $2.50 per hour on benefits, including health care, vacation time, and so on, and so the day care expense represents a significant increase. Many of the employees would rather just have the extra money. The second reason is that subsidized child care helps workers with young children but does nothing for workers without young children. This raises fairness issues: Why should the firm pay an extra $10,000 per year benefit to some workers but not others? Essentially, workers without young children subsidize those with young children because without the day care center their pay could be higher.

Many analysts think that large companies will soon have to build on-site day care centers in order to remain competitive. The reasoning goes like this. Younger workers will be attracted to companies with day care centers because they are the ones who benefit most from the existence of the centers. Older workers will be attracted to companies without day care centers. In many industries younger workers are more productive than older workers, and in many other industries a firm with a mix of younger and older workers will outperform firms with only older workers. In order to achieve the right mix and meet the performance goals, large companies will have to have day care centers.

This discussion has raised several issues that will receive attention later in the chapter. Why is it that firms offer benefit packages that are better for some workers than for others, raising fairness issues? Why do firms not just pay workers more and let them buy their own benefits? And why are large firms different from small firms?

PREFERENCES OVER BENEFITS AND PAY

One of the issues raised in the preceding section on child care was the possibility that workers would be better off if they were given enough extra pay to purchase their own benefit packages. This section explores that issue in more detail.

Workers earn income because it can be used to buy the things they care about, the goods and services that generate utility. Benefits are also goods and services that generate utility. However, income is used to buy hundreds of different goods and services, and benefits packages contain still more types of goods and services. Rather than talk about workers choosing amounts of hundreds of different goods and services, it is easier to divide the goods and services into two types, those provided in the benefits package and those bought with income.

Figure 20.1 shows the consumer choice problem for a worker deciding how to divide his total compensation between the goods and services provided in benefits packages and those purchased with income. The horizontal axis is labeled benefits, and it measures the amount of goods and services contained in benefits packages that the worker consumes. The vertical axis is labeled consumption, and it measures the amount of goods and services consumed that are not contained in benefits packages.

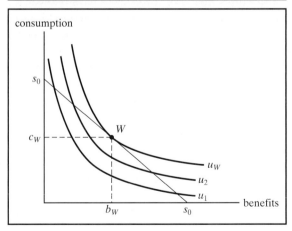

FIGURE 20.1   Finding the Worker's Optimal Mix of Benefits and Pay

The budget line shows all of the combinations of consumption and benefits that add up to the same total compensation, s_0. The worker's most preferred point is the one on the highest indifference curve, W. At this point the worker chooses a benefit package of size b_W and consumes the rest, c_W.

Let us begin with the following question. Suppose that the workers' total compensation package is worth s_0 and that they can use this money to buy either consumption goods or benefits. How much would they spend on benefits? This is a standard consumer choice problem, and we answer it using the tools of consumer theory. Figure 20.1 shows the budget line the workers face. If they spend nothing on benefits, they can spend a total of s_0 on consumption. For every dollar they want to spend on benefits, they must give up a dollar of consumption on other goods and services, so the slope of the budget line is –1.

The workers' problem is to find their most-preferred point on the budget line. We can show this using indifference curves. An indifference curve is the set of all points that generate the same amount of utility. In other words, movements along the indifference curve leave the workers indifferent, neither increasing nor decreasing their utility. Movements to the northeast in the graph represent movements to points that have more consumption *and* more benefits, and because the workers like more of both of these, movements to the northeast cannot leave them indifferent. For the same reason, movements to the southwest give workers less of both consumption and benefits, making them worse off, not leaving them indifferent. Indifference curves can only move from northwest to southeast, making them downward-sloping, as in the figure. Because movements to the northeast give the workers more of both types of goods, movements to higher indifference curves make them better off.

The most-preferred point on the budget line is the one on the highest indifference curve. This indifference curve must be tangent to the budget line, because it intersects the budget line at only one point. The most-preferred point is labeled W (for worker) in Figure 20.1, and at that point the workers spend b_W on benefits and c_W on consumption. The workers' most-preferred benefit package is b_W.

The Most-Preferred Package Versus the One Offered by the Firm

Figure 20.2 is very similar to Figure 20.1, except now there is another point, labeled F (for firm). The workers' most-preferred point is again W, but the firm does not let them choose. Instead the firm chooses for them and offers the point F with a benefit package of size b_F. The total compensation is the same and equal to s_0 at both points, but the firm's benefit package is larger than the worker's most-preferred benefit package, b_W.

In this case the workers are worse off than they would be if they could choose their own benefit package anywhere along the budget line. We can tell this because the point F is on a lower indifference curve than the point W. In fact, F has to be on a lower indifference curve than W because W is the point on the budget line that is on

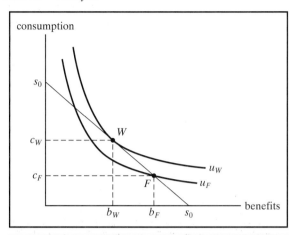

FIGURE 20.2   The Firm Offers Too Many Benefits

The worker's most-preferred combination is W, where
the benefit package is b_W. The firm, however, offers
the combination F, which has a larger benefit package, b_F.
This makes the worker worse off than if he could choose
himself, since F is on a lower indifference curve than W.

the highest indifference curve. Unless the firm offers the benefit
package b_W, the workers are worse off than they would be if they
could choose their own allocation of benefits and pay. Basically, by
fixing the size of the benefit package the firm places a constraint on
the workers' choice, and constraints on choice can only hurt in this
setting.

We can measure how much the constraint hurts the workers.
The dashed budget line in Figure 20.3 is parallel to the original budget line, but it is tangent to the indifference curve that runs through
F. If the workers had faced this new budget line, they would have
chosen a compensation plan that they would have found indifferent
to the one at point F. But this new budget line intersects the vertical
axis at s_1, which is lower than s_0, so having the firm choose for them
gives the workers the same amount of utility as getting paid s_1 and
choosing their own benefit package. But the workers' initial compensation package was worth s_0, not s_1, so the firm's choosing the
benefit package for them is equivalent to reducing their total compensation by $s_0 - s_1$.

Figures 20.2 and 20.3 show a case in which the firm's benefit
package is larger than the workers' most-preferred benefit package.
It is easy to think of examples that fit this scenario. For child care,
this would be the case of workers without young children. The

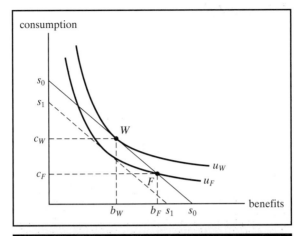

FIGURE 20.3 Finding the Worker's Welfare Loss from Non-Optimal Benefits Packages

When the firm forces the worker to adopt the benefit package b_F instead of the most-preferred one, the worker's utility drops from u_W to u_F. The worker could also get utility u_F if his total compensation fell from s_0 to s_1 and he then chose his own benefit package from the dashed budget line. Because the firm's constraint on the benefit package reduces utility by the same amount as a decrease in total compensation of $s_0 - s_1$, this difference is a monetary measure of the loss caused by the worker not getting to choose his own benefit package.

workers get no utility from an on-site day care center and so would prefer to have less of their total compensation spent on child care. Another example is single workers who get no utility from health insurance coverage for spouses. Because they have no spouse, they would prefer to have less of their total compensation devoted to spousal insurance. A third example is workers who do not drink coffee and would prefer to have the money the firm spends on coffee instead of the coffee itself.

Figure 20.4 shows a case in which the worker would prefer more benefits than the firm provides. Once again the worker's most-preferred point is W, but the point offered by the firm, F, has a smaller benefit package than the worker would like because $b_W > b_F$. Examples of this scenario would be a worker with young children at a firm that does not provide on-site day care, or a worker with a family at a firm that does not provide family health coverage.

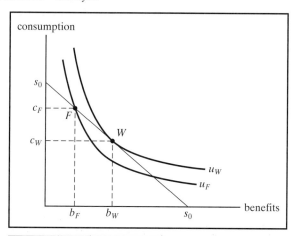

FIGURE 20.4   The Firm Offers Too Few Benefits

This figure shows the case in which the firm forces
the worker to accept a smaller benefit package than
the most-preferred package. As in the previous figures, the
constraint on choice reduces utility.

COST ADVANTAGES FOR THE FIRM

The previous section established that if workers could purchase benefits at the same price the firm pays for them, the workers would be
better off being paid more and choosing their own benefit package.
But this is not what happens in the real world. Many firms allow workers to purchase extra benefits, such as additional life insurance or
additional health insurance for family members, but they do not allow
workers to purchase fewer benefits. Why is this?

One reason is cost advantages. Firms can purchase the goods and
services in the benefits package more cheaply than individual workers
can. Before we explore why firms have this cost advantage, let us see
how it impacts the workers' utility. Figure 20.5 shows what happens. If
the workers' entire compensation package comes in the form of pay
and not benefits, their income is s_0 as before. If the firm provides a dollar's worth of benefits, it does so by reducing pay by a dollar, so the
slope of the budget line when the firm pays for the benefits is -1. When
the workers buy benefits, however, they must pay more for them than
the firm would because of the firm's cost advantage. The budget line
faced by the workers is steeper than the one on which the firm operates.

Suppose the firm offers the compensation package F with benefit
package b_F. If the workers chose their most-preferred compensation
package on the steep budget line, they would choose point W, which is
where their indifference curve is tangent to the steep budget line. As
shown in the figure, however, W is on a lower indifference curve than F.
Because of the cost advantage, the workers are better off with the firm's

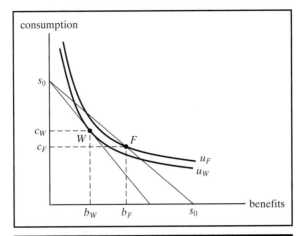

FIGURE 20.5   Exploiting the Firm's Cost
Advantage

Because of the firm's cost advantage, when the firm chooses
a compensation package it chooses a point on the higher
budget line, but when the worker chooses a compensation
package she must choose a point on the lower budget line.
The firm offers point F. If the worker took all of her
compensation in cash and then purchased her own benefits,
the best she could do would be point W, which is on a lower
indifference curve than point F. The worker is better off
with the compensation package offered by the firm.

benefit package than they would be getting more pay and buying their
own benefits.

The Sources of Cost Advantages

There are many reasons why a company can purchase the goods and
services in benefits packages more cheaply than individual workers
can. The most obvious example is volume discounts. Large firms can
often negotiate volume discounts with vendors. For example, a large
firm might be able to negotiate low health club membership fees for
its employees. Without the volume discount, individual workers would
have to pay the same membership fee as everyone else.

Three other reasons are more important than volume discounts.

1. *Spreading fixed costs over workers.* Some companies provide their
    workers with monthly chair massages. Most of these workers would
    not go out and purchase massages on their own. An individual
    worker would have to pay quite a bit for a masseuse to come to his
    place of employment to give him a chair massage because she
    would have to be compensated for her travel time and expenses. A
    company, however, can hire the masseuse for an entire day, or even
    full-time, and spread those travel costs over all of the workers,
    greatly reducing the cost of a massage.

Many benefits entail costs that can be spread over workers. When firms provide their workers with paid vacation and paid sick leave, they must assign someone the task of keeping track of all of the leave time. This cost can be spread over all of the workers, reducing the cost of providing these benefits. Another example is when the firm provides a facility such as a weight room or a cafeteria. The fixed cost of building the facility is spread over all of the workers, making the facility affordable for the firm.

The spreading of fixed costs works better for large firms than for small ones because they have more workers over whom to spread the costs. A five-person firm is unlikely to hire a human resource officer to oversee the benefits package because the cost of that person's salary would have to be spread over the other five workers. They would be unwilling to take the pay cut necessary to hire the human resource officer.

2. *Solving the adverse selection problem.* If individual workers wanted to purchase health insurance, they would face an adverse selection problem, as explained in Chapter 15. The only reasons workers would purchase health insurance are if either they were a high enough risk that the expected benefits outweighed the cost or if they were sufficiently risk averse to be willing to pay the large premium. Workers in the second group would be profitable for the insurance company to cover, but workers in the first group would be unprofitable. Because workers have information about which group they are in, the adverse selection problem makes it difficult and expensive for low-risk but very risk averse workers who would like to buy health insurance.

Firms can solve this adverse selection problem because they hire workers for reasons that have nothing to do with their health status. The workers in a large firm, then, are representative of a cross-section of the working-age population in terms of health status, and insurance companies have enough information to make a profit from a cross-section of the population. The large firm cannot exploit an informational advantage because it is unlikely to have one. Small firms, however, still face an adverse selection problem. Workers at small firms know each others' health status, and can still use this information to take advantage of the health insurer.

3. *Tax advantages.* When a firm provides benefits, those benefits are a cost for the firm and reduce the firm's tax bill. When an individual buys benefits, those are ordinary consumption expenses and cannot be deducted from the tax bill. Thus, when the firm purchases benefits the government pays part of the cost, but when individual workers purchase the same goods and services the government does not share the cost. This makes it cheaper for all firms, both large and small, to purchase the benefits than it is for individual workers to buy the same goods and services.

This is not the only tax advantage, however. When workers receive benefits from their employers, that income is not taxed. If they were to receive the dollar value of the benefits instead, with the intention that they go out and purchase the same goods and services for themselves, that income would be taxed. After paying income taxes on the additional income, the workers would no longer be able to afford the same bundle of consumption goods and benefits that they could afford when the firm provided the benefits.

4. *Externalities.* Workers are not always the only ones who benefit from consuming the goods and services in benefits packages. Often the firm profits when the workers use the benefits the firm provides. The best example is sick leave. When workers do not have sick leave they tend to come into work when they are sick. Not only are they unproductive when they are sick, but they sometimes infect co-workers, exacerbating the problem. Workers with sick leave can stay home when they are sick, which is actually more profitable for the firm.

Health club memberships and vacation leave can also be profitable for the firm. Workers who do not take care of themselves tend to be less productive and also get sick more often. Vacations rejuvenate workers, making them more productive. This is why so many companies allow their workers to take paid vacation.

PHARMACIES AT CAESARS CASINOS

Caesars Entertainment, which operates Caesars Palace and other casinos in Las Vegas and Atlantic City, has 32,000 employees. In 2004 it began setting up pharmacies in its casinos to dispense free generic prescription drugs to its employees.

With this move, the company hopes to save itself money in two ways. First, by making medication cheap and easy to get, it hopes that its workers will both recover from illnesses more quickly and not infect as many co-workers. The second source of savings comes from moving employees from subsidized brand-name drugs to generic drugs. Before the new program, Caesars paid an average of $28 per generic prescription and $100 per brand-name prescription. Under the new program, it is able to reduce the price of the generic medications to an average of $15 for a 30-day supply, and it is able to get more of its workers to switch to generic medications.

SOURCE: Roberts, Sally, "Caesars Betting Onsite Pharmacy Will Yield Savings," *Workforce Management* (May 3, 2004).

THE PROBLEMS FACED BY SMALL FIRMS

As already noted, small firms do not share in all of the cost advantages that large firms enjoy. They cannot solve the adverse selection problem for health insurance; they do not have enough employees over whom to spread fixed costs; and they do not provide enough volume to get any volume discounts. This means that large firms can pay their workers the same amount as small firms but provide better benefits packages, making it difficult for small firms to attract workers. To get workers, then, small firms must provide their workers with larger compensation packages, reducing the profitability of small firms.

Economists expect that in cases like this the market would provide a solution, and it has. Professional employer organizations (PEOs) are firms whose business is providing benefits to employees of other firms. A PEO signs on client firms and takes over the human resource duties of those client firms. By pooling workers from a large number of small firms, the PEO has all of the cost advantages of a large firm. Health insurance risks are pooled over a large population, so it can provide affordable health insurance. The administrative costs borne by the PEO are spread over all of the workers at all of the client firms, so the advantages from spreading fixed costs can be realized. Finally, the PEO can negotiate volume discounts with the providers of benefits.

One PEO is Houston-based Administaff, Inc. It has grown from $750,000 in revenue in 1986 to $892 million in revenue in 2003, and it currently serves 4,500 companies and 75,000 workers. Administaff is not unusual. The National Association of Professional Employer Organizations has more than 700 members. The industry has grown by 20 percent per year for the past six years, and generates $43 billion in revenue.

Homework Problems

1. How do the fixed benefit costs per worker change when the firm grows?
2. Why is it that large firms can solve the adverse selection problem for health insurance but small firms cannot?
3. Draw a graph with salary on the vertical axis and benefits on the horizontal axis that shows the case in which the firm makes workers consume more benefits than they would if they could choose the benefit package themselves.
4. Draw a graph similar to that in Figure 20.5 in which workers must pay a higher price for benefits than the firm would on their behalf but the workers would still prefer to take all of their compensation in salary.

Glossary

Adverse selection—a situation in which the bad types behave like the good types in order to be selected for a transaction.

Backward induction—a technique for solving sequential games in which one starts by finding best responses at the end of the game and works back toward the beginning of the game.

Best-response curve—a graphical representation of the best-response function. It shows one player's best response to each of the other player's actions.

Best-response function—a mathematical function identifying one player's best response to each of the other player's possible actions.

Call option—an option that gives the owner the right to buy a share of stock for a prespecified price during a designated time period.

Collusion—when workers get together to reduce their output in order to manipulate the compensation scheme offered by the firm.

Complementarity—a situation in which the members of a team can produce more when they work together than they can when they work individually.

Contest—a situation in which two or more players compete for a prize.

Cooperation—when workers work together to increase the firm's output.

Disagreement payoff—the payoff a participant in a bargaining problem receives if no agreement is reached.

Discount rate—the rate, like an interest rate, used to value future payoffs. Higher discount rates make future payoffs less valuable, and reflect greater impatience.

Duopoly—a market with exactly two firms.

Efficiency wage scheme—a situation in which the firm pays the worker an above-normal wage and the worker exerts extra effort.

Efficient effort level—the effort level that leads to Pareto efficient allocation.

Equal Compensation Principle—if the firm's profit is maximized when the employee undertakes more than one costly activity, all of the valuable activities must be compensated equally at the margin; otherwise the employee undertakes only those activities that are rewarded most highly.

Equilibrium—a situation in which there is no pressure for anything to change.

Exercise price—the prespecified price at which an option-owner can purchase a share of stock.

Externalities—situations in which the actions of one individual or firm affect the net benefit of another individual or firm.

Favoritism—the tendency for the supervisor to select one worker over the other even though all evidence suggests that the other worker should have been selected.

Forced rating system—a situation in which supervisors must place a certain percentage of their employees in each rating category.

Free-riding—the tendency of individuals not to contribute their efforts to a public good but instead to rely on the contributions of others to provide the public good.

Gain-sharing—a compensation scheme similar to profit-sharing except the firm shares increases in some variable other than profit, such as revenue or cost-savings. The firm sets a target level for the variable and pays the employees a fraction of any increase in the variable above the target level.

Game—a situation in which two or more parties interact to jointly determine their payoffs.

Game tree—a representation of a sequential game.

General skills—skills that make workers more productive and are useful at firms other than the one where they currently work.

Global optimum—the activity level that maximizes net benefit.

Human capital—the skills, knowledge, and experience that make a worker more productive.

Incentive compatibility constraint—a condition that states that a high-productivity type worker cannot be better off mimicking a low-productivity type worker.

Incentive Intensity Principle—the optimal piece rate (or the optimal sales commission rate) is higher when: (1) the firm's marginal net revenue is higher; (2) employees are less risk averse; (3) the employer can measure effort more accurately; and (4) employees are less concerned with fairness.

Income risk—random fluctuations in income.

Influence activities—activities that improve a worker's probability of promotion without adding to the profitability of the firm.

Information rent—the additional net benefit workers receive to induce them to reveal that they have high productivity. Information rents are paid to avoid moral hazard.

Local optimum—an activity level for which there is no other nearby activity level that generates strictly higher net benefit.

Marginal analysis—the identification of local optima through a comparison of marginal benefit and marginal cost.

Marginal benefit—the additional benefit from engaging in one more (small) unit of an activity.

Marginal condition—a mathematical expression in which marginal benefit is set equal to marginal cost.

Marginal cost—the additional cost involved in engaging in one more (small) unit of an activity.

Marginal net revenue—the additional net revenue generated by producing and selling one more unit of output.

Marginal probability—in a tournament, the additional probability of winning generated when a worker exerts one more unit of effort.

Marginal revenue—the additional revenue generated by selling one more unit of output.

Marginal revenue product of labor—the additional revenue resulting from the employment of one more unit of labor.

Moral hazard—a situation in which the high types mimic the low types.

Mutual best responses—a pair of strategies, one for each player, with the property that each player's strategy is a best response to the other player's strategy.

Nash bargaining solution—a particular solution to the bargaining problem that satisfies the properties of Pareto efficiency, invariance to equivalent representations, symmetry, and independence of irrelevant alternatives.

Nash equilibrium—in a game, a combination of strategies that are mutual best responses.

Net benefit—benefit minus cost.

Net revenue—revenue minus all nonlabor costs.

Node—in a game tree, a point at which a player makes a decision.

Noise variable—a random variable with an expected value of zero.

Nonexclusionary—a good is nonexclusionary if it is impossible for the producer to prohibit anyone from consuming it.

Nonrival in consumption—a good is nonrival in consumption if one individual consuming it does not preclude another individual from consuming it, too.

Option value—in a tournament, the value of the right to compete in higher levels of the tournament.

Pareto efficient allocation—an allocation is Pareto efficient if there is no other allocation that makes someone better off and no one worse off.

Pareto efficient effort level—the effort level that generates a Pareto efficient allocation.

Participation constraint—for workers, a condition that states that they must receive at least as much net benefit working at the job in question as in the next-best alternative use of their time. For the firm, a condition that states that its profit from employing the worker in question must be at least zero.

Payoff matrix—a tabular representation of the payoffs to the players in a simultaneous game.

Peter Principle—in every hierarchy, each employee tends to rise to his own level of incompetence.

Piece rate—a payment to a worker for every unit of output produced.

Piece rate compensation scheme—a compensation scheme consisting of a (possibly negative) salary and a piece rate.

Player—a participant in a game.

Pooling equilibrium—an equilibrium in which different types use the same strategy.

Portability (of a skill)—how much of the value of the skill goes with workers when they move to another firm.

Probationary contract—a contract requiring new workers to go through a probationary period in which they receive low pay and at the end of which the firm can fire the workers.

Professional employer organization (PEO)—a firm whose business is providing benefits to employees of other firms.

Profit-sharing—a compensation scheme in which the firm pays to employees a share of profits above some target level, provided that target level of profit is met.

Public good—a good that is nonexclusionary and nonrival in consumption.

Put option—the right to sell a share of stock for a prespecified price during a designated time period.

Rating inflation—a situation in which all employees receive higher ratings than they deserve.

Residual demand curve—in a duopoly, the demand left over for one firm after the other firm has sold all of its output.

Revenue—the amount a firm receives from the sales of its output.

Risk—random fluctuations in income or payoffs.

Risk averse —individuals are risk averse if they are willing to pay to avoid risk.

Risk premium—the amount a risk averse individual is willing to pay in order to avoid randomness and receive the expected value of the gamble for sure.

Sales commission—a payment to a worker for every dollar of revenue generated by that worker.

Self-selection—a situation in which one type chooses to enter a market and the other type does not.

Separating equilibrium—an equilibrium in which different types use different strategies.

Sequential game—a game in which time passes and players can observe their opponents' past actions.

Signal—a costly activity that has no effect on an individual's type but whose cost is related to his type.

Simultaneous game—a game in which the players make their choices at the same time.

Socially efficient —Pareto efficient.

Solution (of a game)—a prediction of what strategies the players of the game will choose.

Specific skills—skills that make workers more productive at their current employer but do not make them more productive anywhere else.

Stock option—the right to buy a share of stock for a prespecified price during a designated time period.

Stopping rule—a set of conditions under which a process stops.

Strategy—a choice made by a player in a game. In a sequential game a strategy is a complete contingent plan.

Total surplus—the combined net benefit of all parties in a transaction or economic relationship.

Tournament—a sequence of contests in which the winners of the first round compete in the second round, the winners of the second round compete in the third round, and so on.

Training—education provided or paid for by the employer.

Index